ASPECTS OF INDIAN ECONOMIC DEVELOPMENT

a companion volume to

READINGS IN INDIAN AGRICULTURAL DEVELOPMENT
edited by Pramit Chaudhuri

Contents

A. Rudra: Relative Rates of Growth: Agriculture and Industry

S. Mehra: Surplus Labour in Indian Agriculture

B.S. Minhas and P. Vaidyanathan: Growth of Crop Output in India, 1951–5 to 1958–61

R. Thamarajakshi: Intersectoral Terms of Trade and Marketed Surplus of Agricultural Produce, 1951–2 to 1965–6

T.N. Krishnan: The Marketed Surplus in Foodgrains

Raj Krishna: Government Operations in Foodgrains

B.S. Minhas and T.S. Srinivasan: New Agricultural Production Strategy: Some Policy Issues

D.K. Desai: Intensive Agricultural District Programme: Analysis of Results

K.N. Raj: Price Behaviour in India; An Explanatory Hypothesis

W. Ladejinsky: Extracts from Study of Tenurial Conditions in Package Districts

ASPECTS OF INDIAN ECONOMIC DEVELOPMENT

A Book of Readings

With an Introduction by
Pramit Chaudhuri
University of Sussex

London · George Allen & Unwin Ltd
RUSKIN HOUSE MUSEUM STREET

First published in 1971

ISBN 0 04 330187 8 *cased*
ISBN 0 04 330188 6 *paper*

Printed in Great Britain
in 10 on 11 point Times Roman
by Billing & Sons Limited
Guildford and London

Preface

This book, together with its sister volume, *Readings in Indian Agricultural Development*, is designed to bring a small selection of writings on Indian economic development to a wider body of readers. In spite of the current mood of disenchantment and impatience about India, hers remains one of the most important examples of the effort to deal with the immense, intractable problem of development. It is, moreover, a *relatively* well-documented case. In spite of major gaps in our knowledge about India, for example in the field of employment or the impact of foreign aid on the economy and society of the country, much more is known and can be found out with tolerable accuracy about India than about many other developing areas. However, much of the writing on India has appeared in journals and official documents which do not enjoy a very wide circulation. These two volumes are designed to overcome the problem of accessibility in a small way.

When one begins to look at the available material, one is very soon surprised by the very substantial volume of material that exists. Although some of the articles and books have dated and some are of poor quality, the volume of material that can lay a serious claim to inclusion is indeed very large. For practical reasons, only a small number of articles can be selected. It would be foolish to deny that, in such a situation, a certain degree of arbitrariness in selection might creep in. It is, therefore, worth saying a few words about the criteria, if that is not too strong a word, that I have tried to use.

My first impulse, which I subsequently carried through, was to concentrate on articles representing an empirical treatment of problems. I deliberately left out articles dealing with pure theory and with mathematical planning models. I also decided to omit articles that are available in the pages of the major journals, such as the *Economic Journal* or the *Oxford Economic Papers*. They are readily accessible. I also deliberately concentrated on one or two major areas, such as agriculture, human resources, aid, rather than aiming at including all the 'best' articles on all aspects of Indian development. To my chapter, 'India: Objectives, Achievements and Constraints', I have attached a fairly long bibliography as a partial amendment to the limited coverage of these volumes. To all the serious scholars who have contributed so much to our understanding of the problems of Indian economic development, and whose names do not appear in the books, I can only tender a very sincere apology, in the name of exiguity of space.

In practically all cases, I have tried to reproduce the articles whole. Where, for one reason or another, I have had to excise parts, this is indicated in the editor's note to the title. I would wish to add that the articles that appear do so, not because they purport to say the last word on the topic under discussion but because they direct our attention to important problem areas that merit serious study. They attempt a careful and systematic study of the empirical evidence rather than dwelling on preconceptions and in turn raise dissension and further discussion. In the case of India, as of many other developing countries, we have, from the best of motives, been too eager to supply the right answers before we were aware of what were the right questions to ask.

Although for practical reasons, the two volumes *Aspects of Indian Economic Development* and *Readings in Indian Agricultural Development* appear separately, they were conceived as an organic whole. They are complementary and designed to be read together. If they are taken together, as they are meant to be, they can lay a small but honest claim to introducing the reader to a serious empirical study of some of the major problems of Indian economic development.

What merit these books of readings have owe a great deal to many friends who have been so generous with their help and so restrained with their criticisms. Professor Amiya Bagchi, of the Presidency College, Calcutta, first mooted the idea of such a book of readings. He has throughout been the most encouraging and constructive of critics. Dr Ashok Desai supplied both physical and intellectual sustenance during my stay in Delhi during the summer of 1969. At this end, Mr David Berk, Mr Martin Brown, Mr Robert Porter and Professor Paul Streeten helped with comments on a provisional list of selected articles and by drawing my attention to material I would otherwise have overlooked. In India, I have had much help from Professor Bagchi, Dr Desai, Professor B.S. Minhas, Dr I.G. Patel, Dr H.K. Raina, Professor K.N. Raj, Professor A.K. Sen and Mr C.S. Swaminathan. Professor Sen, Mr Clive Bell and Mr Michael Lipton of the Institute of Development Studies at Sussex, and Professor Walter Elkan, read a preliminary draft of the introductory article and provided detailed comments. If they have not always been successful in saving me from my errors, they have at least succeeded in making me see my prejudices with a greater clarity. To anybody who is at all familiar with the works of all those whose names appear above, it should hardly be necessary to add that the many shortcomings of these books are solely my responsibility.

Professor Austin Robinson and the Oxford University Press are to be thanked for letting me look at part of the proceedings of the 1969 Kandy Conference and the book by Professor Bhagwati and Dr Desai mentioned in the list of articles cited, before publication. I have also had very generous help from the Librarian and staff of the following libraries: National Council of Applied Economic Research Library, New Delhi; India House Library, London; the University of Sussex Library and the Institute of Development Studies Library at Sussex. Miss Renée Auckland and Mrs Anne Harland typed various versions of the introduction with great efficiency and forbearance. I am grateful to them for their patience. I am also grateful to the University of Sussex for financial support to enable me to undertake a trip to India during the summer of 1969. My publishers, too, have shown remarkable understanding with an editor totally ignorant of publishing procedures. Finally, and most sincerely, I must thank all those who have permitted me to reproduce their writings in this book. The source is given, after the author's name, as a footnote at the opening of each article.

University of Sussex,
Brighton

P.C.

Contents

1. Pramit Chaudhuri — 17
India: Objectives, Achievements and Constraints

2. E.A.G. Robinson — 92
Economic Progress in India
(*Three Banks Review*, March 1970)

3. I.G. Patel — 116
Strategy of Indian Planning
(C.R. Roe, ed., *Essays in Econometrics and Planning*)

4. R. Cassen — 125
Population Control: Aims & Policies
(P. Streeten and M. Lipton, *Crisis of Indian Planning*)

5. A.K. Sen — 144
Crisis in Indian Education
(Lal Bahadur Shastri Memorial Lecture, delivered in 1970)

6. P. Streeten and R. Hill — 160
Aid to India
(P. Streeten and M. Lipton, *Crisis of Indian Planning*)

7. Government of India, Ministry of Finance — 180
Utilization of External Assistance
(Report of the Committee on Utilization of External Assistance, 1964)

8. Dharam Narain — 196
Aid Through Trade: Case Study of India
(UNCTAD Papers TD/BC/C, 3/57, 1968)

9. Reserve Bank of India — 213
Foreign Investment through Subsidiaries
(Foreign Collaboration in Indian Industry, 1969)

10. J. Bhagwati and P. Desai — 237
Industrial Licensing
(J. Bhagwati and P. Desai, *India: Industrialization and Trade Policies since 1951*)

11. Government of India, Ministry of Steel — 259
Extracts from the Report of the Committee on Steel Control, 1964

Index — 286

Note

1 crore = 10,000,000
Before June 6, 1966, 1 $ (U.S.) = Rs. 4·76
After June 6, 1966, 1 $ (U.S.) = Rs. 7·5

Editor's Note

Although the total volume of writings relating to the study of economic development in India during the Planning period is very large, they are of uneven quality and coverage. In a work of this scale, the first is no problem, because one could fill several volumes with matter which ought to be essential reading for the serious student. The second, however, does pose a problem. Firstly, Professor Austin Robinson's very balanced exposition apart, there are very few up-to-date reviews of the contours of Indian economic development. Even the facts of the macro-economic life of the economy, so to speak, are not easy to establish. W. Malenbaum's *Prospects for Indian Development* or John Lewis's *Quiet Crisis in India* are now seriously out of date. The various Plan documents that set out to offer a resumé of progress under the previous Plans are of limited use. It is by no means easy to establish from those accounts what has happened to certain basic magnitudes, such as the domestic savings ratio or the rate of investment over time. It is still more difficult to relate performance to the Planners' promises. Secondly, there are very important problem areas about which very little or nothing is known. As one begins to hunt through the journals and official reports, one is drawn to the conclusion that, paradoxically, the more important the problem and the more vigorous the controversy, the more tenuous the factual bases on which the controversy is waged. Take, for example, the population problem or the problem of employment or the problem of what impact foreign aid and foreign resources have actually had on the economy.

It will be clear that any selection of such material will fail to give a complete picture of the situation. I have confined my choice to those problem areas which are both important and have available suitable published material for inclusion. Apart from the first two articles, the areas covered are, broadly speaking, those of human resources, foreign resources and experience with direct control. (Articles dealing with agriculture appear in the separate volume, *Readings in Indian Agricultural Development*, published by George Allen & Unwin Ltd, 1971.) In a fairly long article, I have attempted to fill in some of the lacunae left by the material available. I have tried to give a short account of the main features of the development in the Indian economy. I have also tried to sketch out in the barest outline the operation of the three critical constraints, agricultural production, foreign resources and industrial capacity, upon the economy. Needless to say, what is contained there is not final wisdom. It will, I hope, shake our faith a little in capsule judgments and make us take a fresh look at the problems.

I have already referred to Austin Robinson's over-view of progress in the Indian economy. I.G. Patel's article contains a lucid non-mathematical exposition of the logic of the so-called 'heavy industry' strategy. He also draws attention to the important question of the optimal allocation of resources in an 'open economy'. Given the importance of the problem, studies of the economic, as opposed to the demographic aspects of the population problem in India are surprisingly few. Robert Cassen's article fills an important gap. The technical solution has not been as easy to derive as was once thought. However, effective population control remains very much a matter of the provision of adequate resources and organizational inputs in the widest sense of the term.

Amartya Sen's essay on the economics of Indian education should be read together with A.C. Harberger's 'Investment in Men *vs.* Investment in Machines'[1] and M. Blaug, R. Layard and M. Woodhall, *Causes of Graduate Unemployment in India*. That rate of return analysis should be used with caution in under-developed countries still requires a reminder. Moreover, Sen raises the question of the allocation of a given amount of educational expenditures amongst different beneficiaries.

The next four articles deal with the problem of foreign resources. Streeten and Hill is a very useful summary of the basic magnitudes of the aid flow. That aid prospects have since turned darker and the debt servicing burden has mounted hardly need stressing. The Reserve Bank of India study performs a similar function for direct private foreign investment. In this field, Michael Kidron's *Foreign Investments in India* remains the best study. On the issue of the large country facing the corporations, one should read M. Tanzer's *The Political Economy of International Oil and the Under-developed Countries*, Part II. The Report of the Rao Committee on Utilization of External Resources points out some of the practical problems of foreign aid from the recipient's point of view, an aspect that is too often ignored by academic economists and donor countries. That point of view ought to be put, although some may suspect that some part of the resulting inefficiency can be avoided by improvements in aid management and project preparation.

Dharam Narain's is a careful study of the effects of bilateral barter agreements. He finds that, for the period under review, the agreements added to India's net export earnings. There was no large-scale switching by the centrally-planned economies of Indian exports to third countries. Nor is there evidence that barter agreements resulted in more unfavourable terms of trade for India, relative to her terms of trade with the so-called free currency areas.

One aspect of the problem that we have not covered and which is very important is that of trade. In particular, of the behaviour of Indian exports during the Plan period and of the Indian Government's policy towards exports. In this field, suitable material is not easy to find. S.J. Patel and B. Cohen's articles[2] suffer partly from having dated and partly from relying too heavily on the establishment of a simple unicausal relationship. Manmohan Singh's *India's Export Trends and Prospects for Self-sustained Growth* is a very careful piece of work and is essential reading. However, it ends in the early 'sixties and its lessons cannot easily be drawn out into the later part of the decade.

An aspect of Indian economic development which has until recently been curiously neglected by economists is her experience with various kinds of direct control. These have played a very substantial part in the management of the economy and have been used by the Government as instruments for allocating scarce resources. Their study is essential to an understanding of the operation of the Indian economy. The last two studies in this book examine two different aspects of the system of direct controls, one dealing with allocation of current output, the other with capacity.

[1] This is included in Anderson and Bowman, *Education and Economic Development* (Cass, 1966).

[2] S.J. Patel, 'Export Prospects & Economic Growth: India', *Economic Journal*, September 1959.

B.I. Cohen, 'The Stagnation of Indian Exports, 1951–1961', *Quarterly Journal of Economics, 1964*.

1

INDIA: OBJECTIVES, ACHIEVEMENTS AND CONSTRAINTS

by Pramit Chaudhuri

Economic growth in India since 1950 has taken an uneven course. The pattern that has evolved over time is a complex one. It is not possible, within the short space of an introduction, to give a satisfactory account of how the economy has behaved over the last twenty years. Still less is it possible give a satisfactory *explanation* of such behaviour. For much of the work that has been carried out by economists is vitiated by attempts to oversimplify the pattern and to explain it in terms of a kind of 'one factor analysis'.[1] This does less than justice to the complex reality of the growth process and, more seriously, leads to misleading policy conclusions. In what follows, we do not lay any claim to originality or to a comprehensive analysis of the problem. Our object is to discuss in a very selective manner certain aspects of economic development in India during the last twenty years. We believe that an understanding of these aspects of the problem is essential for a satisfactory discussion of the lessons of planned economic development in India.

In this Introduction, Section I points out certain basic features of the Indian economy that should serve as a background to any discussion of its performance. This is followed by an outline of the basic contours of economic growth in India during 1950–67. Sec-

[1] See G. Myrdal (1968), Vol. III, Appendix 3 (by Professor Paul Streeten), p. 1949. The two commonest explanations provided by economists run in terms of misallocation of resources and neglect of institutional reforms, see Ladejinsky (1965), Lipton (1968), Mason (1966). Political economists which in the current state of development economics means either Marxists or free marketeers, explain the phenomena in ways they would wish to see it explained; see, e.g., Bettelheim (1968), Bauer (1961). Social anthropologists rightly stress caste alignments, kinship, etc. as critical factors in studies at the micro-level but largely ignore the problems of formulating policies for economic and social change for the country as a whole; see Betteille (1965), Gough (1955), Pocock (1968).

tions III, IV and V deal with Agriculture, use of foreign resources and the role played by the Government, including the Planning Commission, in the formulation and implementation of economic policy.[2]

During the first half of the twentieth century, the Indian economy experienced very little growth in terms of *per capita* real income. Estimates of national income and population are highly tentative for the period but broadly speaking a low rate of increase in total output was counter-balanced by a population growth rate of at first a little under and then a little over 1 per cent per annum. Various estimates of agricultural production show that agricultural output, which formed the bulk of total output, failed to keep pace with the growth of population. An encouraging feature was the establishment and development of a small capitalistic industrial sector, based largely on textiles and basic metals.[3] In assessing the current performance of the Indian economy, it is worth bearing in mind that 'the rate of economic growth that has been achieved in India since 1950–1 is two to three times as high as the rate recorded earlier under British administration'.[4] It is indeed paradoxical that many of those critics who chide the Indians for being in too much of a hurry should forget that the economy has patiently been getting nowhere under a market economy for half a century or longer. India's attempts at planned economic development has to be seen against this background of secular stagnation and the institutional and behavioural patterns that emerge in such a society.

Because she was the first under-developed country to make a serious attempt at planning at a fairly sophisticated level, and to attempt to implement it within a democratic political system, a great

[2] For a useful account containing a great deal of information up to 1961, see Malenbaum (1962). One of the most perceptive pieces of work is J.P. Lewis (1962) which carries one up to the beginning of the Third Five-Year Plan. Most useful also are Mason (1966), Millikan (1968), Rao (1965), and Robinson (1970). On the planning process, see the classic by Hanson (1966), essential reading for anyone who wishes to understand how the Planning process works. The introductory chapters to the *Third Five-Year Plan*, Planning Commission (1961) and the *Fourth Five-Year Plan*, Planning Commission (1966) are also useful. For an excellent section on Planning models, see Bhagwati and Chackravarty (1969).

[3] This paragraph is based on the following sources: Malenbaum (1962), Ch. V, Mukherji (1965). On industrial development see Buchanan (1966), Gadgil (1942); on population, see Davis (1951), Coale and Hoover (1958). According to Professor V.K.R.V. Rao, *per capita* income was roughly the same between 1931-2 and 1951–2 (quoted in Malenbaum, *op. cit.*, p. 109). The level of agricultural production at 1924–9 prices was not more than 10 per cent higher, comparing the average level for 1940–50 to 1900–10. The average decennial growth rates of population are as follows: 1891–1921: 1·7 per cent; 1921–51: 12·9 per cent.

[4] Raj (1965), p. 2.

deal of emphasis has been attached by economists to the Planners and the Plans[5] in evaluating Indian economic performance. This is, of course, quite legitimate. The Planners have had an important part to play in the formulation of economic policy and in initiating discussion in particular of long-term economic policy within an empirical context.[6] Equally, the Plan documents are important sources of information about the aspirations and achievements of economic policy. However, it is very important to distinguish between what the Planners have said or recommended and the policies that the Government have actually pursued. Failure to draw and maintain this distinction in analysing the workings of economic policy in India is liable in no small measure to lead us astray, to make us lay undue emphasis on some aspects and unduly neglect others equally important. And from an incomplete or incorrect appreciation of the problems, hasten on to unhelpful policy prescriptions. Instances are not difficult to find. For example, great stress is laid in the Plan documents on 'establishing a socialist pattern of society'.[7] Some observers have concluded from this that part of India's problems arise from a pursuit of welfare, as opposed to efficiency objectives. Even a cursory analysis of the pattern of government expenditure, or its policy towards the private sector or towards tenurial reforms would show that there is little substance in this charge.[8] Again, many economists have argued at length

[5] By 'the Plans' in this context we mean the official Plan documents published by the Planning Commission, together with ancillary documents such as working papers, and companion volumes such as the *Notes on the Perspective of Development* and the *Material and Financial Balances 1964–5, 1970–1 and 1975–6*. The distinction we wish to draw is between these sets of documents and the very voluminous publications by the various Ministries and Parliamentary Committees, which are a mine of information that has been worked all too little. It is not so easy to say who one should designate as 'the Planners'. Certainly, the economists in the Planning Commission and various experts who have worked in or with the Commission, politicians, such as Pandit Nehru, who had a great deal to do with making planning respectable in India. But are the senior civil servants, whose job it really is to carry out and implement the Plans, to be called 'Planners'? Although it is a fair generalization to say that most of them will share the same views about the basic objectives of economic policy, there are quite distinct and quite legitimate differences about priorities of short-term economic policy.

[6] The work done by official and semi-official bodies and individual research workers in collecting empirical information about the economy is one of the most encouraging developments in India, although a great deal of work remains to be done, particularly in the fields of analysis of the impact of policy measures on the economy.

[7] India Planning Commission (1956), pp. 21 f.; India Planning Commission (1961), pp. 9 f.

[8] Minhas (1969), pp. 10 f.; J.P. Lewis (1962), pp. 204–5. See also pp. 38-42 below.

about the allocation of resources within the economy on the basis of aggregate figures for sectoral outlays contained in the Plan documents, chiefly one suspects because of their easy accessibility. Yet, as we argue later on in this introduction, such figures can at best serve as rough approximations. There are three main reasons why this is so. The ultilization of resources by a sector may vary within a given period from resources authorized for use by that sector, the sector that benefits from the end-use of resources may be different from the sector to which such resources are initially allocated, and resources may be diverted from users to whom they are officially allocated to other non-authorized users. Lastly, in certain critical spheres of control, such as the allocation of scarce foreign exchange and licensing of industrial capacity, the Plan documents either do not lay down any guide-lines or lay down only very impressionistic ones. The actual taking of decisions in these spheres occurs within a set of rules of administrative conduct which may or may not accord closely with Plan priorities but which in any case are not contained in the Plan documents.[9] For these reasons, a great deal more stress has to be laid on the operations of the various ministries as opposed to those of the planning body.

India is a mixed economy, one in which the private sector is easily the dominant sector in terms of size. Agriculture, which in 1965–6 provided about 46 per cent of net Domestic Product at current prices and about 40 per cent in real terms is wholly in the private sector.[10] The share of the public sector in net Domestic Product in 1965–6 was no higher than 13·3 per cent. Although the public sector has been growing very rapidly both in size and importance since the beginning of the Second Five-Year Plan, it still does not dominate the economy. After a very substantial increase in investment, the

[9] Bhagnati and Desai (1970), Medhora (1968) give useful accounts of the Industrial Licensing procedures in India; for a detailed factual account including historical background, see India Estates Committee, *9th Report* (1967); see also p. 74 f. below.

[10] The figures quoted in this paragraph are taken from the following sources: India Ministry of Finance, *Pocketbook* (1968), pp. 30, 32; India Ministry of Finance, *Survey* (1968–9, p. A.6). Investment outlay in the Second, Third and Fourth Plans was as follows: Plan Investment (Rs. crores, current prices)

Plan	*Public*	*Private*	*Total*
Second (actual)	3,650	3,100	6,750
Third (actual)	6,300	4,100	10,400
Fourth (planned)	12,252	10,000	22,252

Source: India Planning Commission, *Material Balances* (1966), p. 116; India Planning Commission (1966), p. 49. It is interesting to note that although the realized investment in the Third Plan is shown to have fallen below the planned figure by Rs. 880 crores, no similar adjustment has been made for the private sector.

sphere of the public sector in the capital stock of the economy is estimated to be no higher than 33·7 per cent for all sectors in 1965–6 and 58·3 per cent in Mining, Manufacturing and Transport, where growth has been fastest.[11] Given the nature of the information available about capital employed in agriculture and private industry, these figures are probably on the high side. The figures underline the point that, in major spheres of economic life, the Government has to rely on the price mechanism and other forms of incentives and disincentives to implement its policy.[12]

Planning in India is in this sense radically different from planning in the communist countries. The fact that the Government has control over two critical 'resources', foreign exchange and industrial licenses, does give it a considerable leverage over the rest of the economy, albeit in a somewhat negative direction. However, the point remains that in interpreting the experience of economic growth in India under Planning, one has to look beyond the problems of Plan formulation and implementation in the narrow sense of derivation and fulfilment of a specific set of targets. One needs to look more systematically and carefully at Government economic policy in general, to look particularly at fiscal and price policies and methods of direct control than economists by and large have done so far. The need to operate direct controls has to an extent been imposed by the critical balance of payments situation facing the economy since 1956–7, when the foreign exchange crisis first developed. Unquestionably, that is the way the causation runs in the short run. It may be true, of course, that in the long run a dismantling of controls is necessary to get the balance of payments right, but that merely goes to underline the very fundamental conflict that arises between short-run and long-run objectives of economic policy in any economy. Due credit is hardly ever given in the discussion of development problems to the difference made to the management of the economy in having a little bit of give in the balance of payments. In a dynamic economy subject to uncertainty, performance will diverge from targets. Targets themselves have to be reformulated during a Plan period. In such an economy, imbalances will arise from time to time, although poor economic management can make the problem much worse. It is foolish for Planners and their critics to pretend otherwise. In such circumstances, imports act as a safety-valve and by maintaining a balance between aggregate demand and available

[11] Hazari and Oza (1970), p. 92.

[12] We should here note and later briefly discuss the view that the Government has relied too little on the price mechanism and attempted to regulate the economy largely through direct controls, resulting in an inefficient allocation of resources.

resources, enable the economy to maintain levels of output and reasonable price stability.[13] Such avenues of escape have been denied the Government for most of the period under Planning. The problem has been exacerbated by the insistence of donor countries, especially the most important of them, i.e. the United States, on project and commodity-tied aid, the high priority given by the Government to meet its debt servicing obligations[14] and the particular industrial strategy followed by the Government. In any discussion of India's economic problems, it is vitally important to bear this point in mind. This brings us to what is perhaps the most obvious and in some ways the most important characteristic.[15] It is the sheer size of the Indian economy, both in the geographic and the demographic sense.[16]

It is not our object here to discuss at any length the relationship between size and development. We wish merely to point out three instances where an appreciation of the size of the country is essential to a balanced assessment of the situation. Firstly, the States which make up the Indian Union have diverse resource endowment and vary significantly amongst themselves in relation to, say, population density or availability of foodgrains. Their growth performance has also been different in many ways. In such a situation, to discuss the behaviour of the Indian economy without looking at the regional patterns of growth is of limited usefulness. In particular, such an approach may draw our attention away from problems whose re-

[13] The relationship between economic development and the balance of payments has been discussed at great length. The opposite side of the coin, i.e. the effects of an adverse balance of payments on planning for development, has received much less attention, particularly its relevance to day-to-day problems of economic management. This in itself is due to the fashionable pretence that macro-economic problems are of lesser importance in some sense.

It is equally important, of course, to be able to export short-term surpluses that arise from time to time, particularly where a great deal of investment is of the kind where it is more economic to build up capacity ahead of demand, e.g. steel, heavy machinery, etc. This latter point itself begs the question, for it depends ultimately on the Planners' time preference.

[14] See below, p. 60 f.

[15] Breecher (1959), p. 516; Patel (1968).

[16] India is second largest in terms of population size, coming after China. In terms of land area, it ranks seventh. The States of Madhya Pradesh, Rajasthan, Maharashtra, Uttar Pradesh and Andhra are each larger than the countries of Western Europe, other than France. Kerala and West Bengal had population densities of 435 and 399 per square kilometre in 1961, Madhya Pradesh and Rajasthan of 73 and 59 per square kilometre, India Ministry of Finance, *Pocket Book*, 1968. The so-called 'surplus' States, e.g. Madhya Pradesh, Punjab and Orissa, produce more foodgrains than they consume, while the 'deficit' States, e.g. Kerala and West Bengal, rely on imports to balance consumption.

solution might have considerable operational significance.[17] Secondly, because of her size her total demand for certain essential inputs such as steel, fertilizers and other intermediate goods is very large. This makes it necessary for her to attempt to supply substantial parts of her requirements out of domestic resources.[18] Even if India's export performance were substantially better than it has been, it is quite unrealistic to suppose that she could or could have obtained the bulk of her import requirements through trade. Even under the assumption that the imports of goods with low development-content is severely restricted, this will hold true for any socially acceptable range of growth rates.[19] The fact that for a developing country, she is relatively well endowed with mineral resources and a supply of industrial skills, also makes such a policy a feasible one.[20] For India, the problem has never been what to import, in the sense of determining in some mutually exclusive manner the commodity composition of imports on the one hand and the composition of domestic production on the other. It is a choice at the margin, so to speak, of what degree of 'self-sufficiency' to aim for and how to phase her programme of industrialization. This holds true, if we exclude from our consideration those mineral resources that India does not possess and a narrow range of the more sophisticated producers' goods. It is a choice of, say, how much steel to import, what kind of steel to import, of how much domestic capacity to create and at what stage of the Planning process.[21] Lastly, the size of the country raises peculiarly difficult problems of communication and co-ordination of policies between the centre and the periphery. It is essential, for efficient planning, to develop a system of information flows whereby Planners can obtain information about the

[17] Planning Commission, *Regional Variations* (1967–8), contains useful information on the regional pattern of development in India. Most of the work done in India has been on agriculture. See Bagchi (1965), Hanumantha Rao (1965), Rao, *E.P.W.*, (1966).

[18] According to the kind of 'model' one likes to use, one can put the problem in one of two ways:
(i) Attempts to increase her exports to earn enough foreign exchange to pay for her import requirements consistent with a given rate of growth of output, will significantly worsen her terms of trade; or
(ii) Given discontinuities in world demand for Indian exports, she will not be able to find markets for the volume of exports she must sell at world prices to meet her import requirements.

[19] Reddaway (1962), Ch. 3.

[20] Lewis (1962), p. 42; Millikan (1968), p. 533; Robinson (1970).

[21] To our knowledge, Professor Reddaway was the first to discuss the problems of 'phasing' of investment decisions in Indian Plans. It is precisely these specific issues that Planners in India have often ignored or settled after inadequate discussion, Reddaway (1962).

economy, on the basis of which policies can be formulated. Policy decisions, once arrived at, have to be conveyed back to the 'grass roots'; the operation of the policy at the 'grass root' level has to be kept in review, deficiencies noted and corrective actions formulated and relayed back, all at the appropriate time. Even if we confine ourselves to the strategic sectors within the economy, which we clearly should, the problems of Planning and Plan implementation in India must appear to be formidable – as indeed they are.[22] Most of the discussion of the shortcomings of India's planning efforts, and in recent years it is the shortcomings that have been talked about most, concentrates on major errors of strategy. Giving low priority to agriculture is one of these, the reliance on heavy industry another. We shall have something to say later on about some of these errors of strategy. Yet, if one looks at the data, one cannot help feeling that much of the problem arises not so much through major strategic blunders as through the inability of the Government machinery to ensure that their policies effected a large enough part of the economy to have any significant impact.[23]

An illustration from agriculture must suffice. As Professor Raj has shown,[24] the 'new agricultural strategy' is not altogether new in conception. What is new about the strategy lies in the specific area of operation chosen by the Government amongst the relevant policy variables, in the light of a technological breakthrough. Yet, in the last analysis, whether the 'new agricultural strategy succeeds in solving India's food problem or not will depend less on the inherent merits of the strategy than it will on the extent to which the Government can bring its impact to bear over a large part of the country.[25] To argue this point of view is not by any means to absolve the Planners from charges of inefficiency. The feasibility of implementing a Plan is just as important a constraint as any technological one.[26] Neglect of such constraints shows inefficiency in Planning.

[22] One of the great advantages of relying on the price mechanism is precisely this: that these intricate problems do not have to be resolved by means of conscious administrative decisions. That is not to say that the price mechanism always does the job well. For a discussion of these problems in the context of agriculture, see Dandekar (1967).

[23] One should probably exempt from this the case of tenurial reforms, where the performance of the Government appears to have been uniformly bad all over the country, Ladejinsky (1965), Dandekar (1962).

[24] Raj (1969), Lecture II.

[25] (We are assuming for the purposes of the argument that the 'new agricultural strategy' is efficient in the technological sense.) The efficiency of public sector enterprises is another such field, where global criticisms substitute for a careful study of dissimilar performance by the different enterprises. See below pp. 78-80 f.

[26] Sen (1970).

II

In this Section, we shall review very briefly the main features of economic growth in the Indian economy since 1950. In assessing the economic performance of a country one must have an index of comparison in mind. The question, 'How well has an economy performed?' raises in turn the question of the 'norm'. Generally speaking, one has three to choose from. We may, first of all, ask how does performance in period x measure up to what has been achieved by the economy in the past. The answer to this was given briefly in section I.[27] Or we can ask, how does the performance of the economy A measure up against the performance of economy B during period t. The game of international league-tables is the fashionable one to play. Yet it is not very clear what significance should be attached to the bold statement that 'the Japanese economy grew at a rate x times faster than India' or that 'the consumption of fertilizer in Taiwan increased by x times the amount of the increase in India'. Such performances are, of course, wholly admirable but they become important only if we can postulate certain basic similarities in the problems facing the economies that are being compared or in terms of the resources that are available to them to back up their performance. Once this point is taken, one should not lightly make such comparisons in a serious discussion of problems of development. They may indeed be extremely valuable but only when they are backed up by a careful study of the economies involved. Otherwise, they should be treated with no greater concern than one shows to fond parents who wonder why their children do not win scholarships to Balliol.[28] We can, however, try to see to what extent the economy has measured up to what was expected of it. Or in other words, the extent to which the performance of the economy has enabled the various policy objectives that were set up to be realized. We turn, therefore, to a consideration of the objectives of economic planning in India.[29]

The various Plan documents list sets of objectives, but the lists are not uniform as between the different Plans. In addition to the lists, various other 'priorities' are stressed in general discussion on Plan strategy contained in the documents. For example, the Second Plan

[27] See p. 18 above.

[28] Anybody who thinks these comments frivolous should look at the various attempts at comparing the economic performance of India and Pakistan that have been made at different points of time in the last twenty years, and ponder what an economist might write on this field, say, two or three years from now.

[29] The key sources are India Planning Commission (1956), pp. 21–50; India Planning Commission (1961), pp. 1–19; India Planning Commission (1966), pp. 1–28; the Industrial Policy Resolutions of 1948 and 1956.

did not list agriculture as a priority. It did not, however, underrate the importance of that sector to the economy, although the Planners seriously misinterpreted the causes of increase in agricultural output that had taken place during the First Plan period and underestimated the amount of effort that was still required to keep agricultural output growing.[30] However, we can say that the Indian Plans in general have had the following objectives:

1. *To secure an increase in national income.* This is the so-called 'growth objective', which was quantified in the Third Plan as being 5 per cent per annum;[31] although stated in terms of national income, it is quite clear in the context that the Plans expected to bring about a rise in *per capita* incomes;

2. *Achieving a planned rate of investment within a given period, to bring the actual investment/income ratio up to a higher planned level.* This was regarded as necessary for two rather distinct reasons. One was that such an increase in output capacity was deemed to be necessary to bring about the planned increase in output. The other was that it was designed to bring the capital stock of the economy up to a planned level at the end of the Plan period, to ensure growth of future output capacity. A failure to achieve this objective would, therefore, have both short-term and long-term repercussions;

3. *Reducing the inequality in the distribution of income and wealth and reducing the concentration of economic power over resources.* No drastic redistribution of income and wealth was planned for. It was perfectly reasonable to argue, as for example Pandit Nehru did, that redistribution of income would have achieved little.[32] It is not apparent that the same holds true for a redistribution of

[30] 'During the First Five-Year Plan it was of crucial importance that agricultural programmes must succeed, for no other consideration had equal significance for the stability of the economy as a whole. In the Second Five-Year Plan agricultural programmes are intended to provide adequate food to support the increased population and the raw materials needed for a growing industrial economy, and also to make available larger exportable surpluses of agricultural commodities. *The Second Five-Year Plan implies, therefore, even more than the first, a close inter-dependence between agricultural and industrial development,*' India Planning Commission (1956), p. 259 (our italics). Population control falls into the same category, being regarded as a 'priority' but not listed as an objective. This distinction between objectives and priorities is, of course, operationally meaningless and reflects the predisposition of Indian Planners to treat everything as a priority. On this, see below, pp. 28-29.

[31] The *Fourth Five-Year Plan*, 1969–74, does not list a formal set of objectives but discusses the problem in general terms. Once bitten, twice shy. The references to India Planning Commission (1956), Chs. I and II, India Planning Commission (1961), Chs. I and IV, India Planning Commission (1966), Chs. I and II.

[32] Nehru (1962), p. 17.

wealth.[33] It follows that most of the reduction in disparities in income and wealth was expected to be brought about by policies that would channel the incremental benefits derived from the growth of the economy largely to the poor. Concentration of economic power was to be reduced, in a relative sense, by building up the 'countervailing power' of the public sector.[34] Large-scale trust-busting was not envisaged. Policies were supposed to be put in force to channel resources to the weaker sections of the producers, e.g. small peasants, small-scale industries, etc.

4. *Providing additional employment.* The Second Five-Year Plan aimed at providing jobs for new entrants to the labour market, as well as 'under-employment' in the agricultural sector.[35] In the Third Plan it was expected that new jobs created would fall short of the increase in the labour force by about 17 per cent.[36] It is worth noting, however, that even the perspective plan does not envisage the possibility of 'full employment' in India.

5. *Adopting measures to alleviate the three 'bottlenecks' regarded by the Planners as being of critical importance, viz. agricultural production, the manufacturing capacity for producers' goods and the balance of payments.* In the industrial sector, the emphasis was to be on 'heavy industry', with a view to building up basic capacity in machinery and basic metals.[37] In the agricultural sector, the prime objective was self-sufficiency in foodgrains. In the third sector, the Plans were to aim at establishing a 'viable balance of payments'.[38]

[33] Cf. Raj Krishna (1959), on land.

[34] Galbraith (1957).

[35] India Planning Commission (1956), p. 26. Knowledge of the employment situation in India is limited, because there are serious gaps in the available data. Moreover, it is theoretically not at all clear what one means by terms such as 'under-employment', 'increase in the labour force', 'the unemployed' etc., in the Indian context. See Raj (1959), Reddaway (1962).

[36] India Planning Commission (1961), p. 51.

[37] The so-called Mahalanobis Strategy. See Mahalanobis (1963) and Raj and Sen (1961), Patel (1963), as well as p. 81 f. below. The ideological planks of this strategy, which were much sounder than most critics of Indian economic performance think, were (i) the identification by some protagonists of a link between growth performance and index of production of certain key commodities, and (ii) at a more sophisticated level, the desire to maximize the rate of growth of the economy, under conditions of limited foreign exchange availability.

[38] What one should mean by this term is not clear. There are difficulties in defining an 'equilibrium balance of payments' even in a static context, except within the context of a specific choice of policy variables, see Nurkse (1962), Meade (1951). The problem is even more difficult in a dynamic economy. The problem does not disappear even if we choose a rate of growth for the economy and define the equilibrium state as one in which there is no 'induced' inflows of capital. Surely it is inappropriate in the long-run context to assume fixed import-

In simplest terms, this meant reducing the dependence of the economy on unilateral inflows of capital to meet the economy's import requirements consistent with the planned rate of growth of output. This obviously links up with the first two sectoral objectives, in so far as the increase in industrial capacity and self-sufficiency in foodgrains were both expected to reduce the dependence of the economy on imports.

Before we look at the empirical data to see to what extent these objectives were realized, one or two words need to be said about the objectives themselves. Did they together make up a consistent set of objectives? How were they 'weighted'? Strictly speaking, it is impossible to answer this question. We come face to face with two different kinds of problems. One is that very few of the objectives are quantified even in a rough way. There is no point in wasting time discussing whether the growth objective will conflict with the reduction in inequality objective or not, unless we have some idea about the degree of redistribution one is to aim for. The other is that one is not always given enough information about the relationship between some of the objectives to form a reasoned judgment whether a pair of them are consistent or not. The best example is that of the output and the employment objectives. It may be that, during the formulation of the Third Plan, it was reasonable to postulate that a growth rate of 5 per cent per annum in output would lead to the creation of 14 million new jobs during the Plan period. However, it is not possible for an outsider to see how these two magnitudes hang together on the basis of the information that is available to him.[39] As for the second question – the most significant point about the objectives is the very peculiar way in which the Plans deal with the problem of choice between objectives. By and large, the problem is

---

coefficients? Should equilibrium be established at, say, the pre-1966 exchange rate or after one devaluation or two? Do we mean 'viable' subject to prohibition of non-essential imports? These difficulties are not merely theoretical; they involve policy choices for the Planners. The Planners would presumably, say at the time of the Second or Third Plan have ruled out devaluation or a reduction of controls over non-essential goods, mostly luxury consumption goods.

[39] Providing information for the benefit of academic critics of a Plan should receive low priority in the eyes of the professional Planners, whose job is to finish a highly important and expert job within a tight time schedule. The above point will not have been made unless we wished to pursue the view further that the Indian Planners have seriously neglected the employment aspects of the Plan. This omission is all the more significant if we bear in mind that the welfare objectives of the Plans were supposed to be achieved without large-scale reforms in the social and political framework of the nation. See Raj (1969), also pp. 80 f. below.

ignored. As Professor Hanson has said, *apropos* of the First Five-Year Plan, '(the Plan) begins to display the schizophrenia which still to some extent remains characteristic of the Commission's attempts to formulate its tasks in general terms. "On the one hand we must concentrate on this, but on the other hand we must not neglect that" is the familiar formula. . . .'[40] Needless to add, the Plans do not mention such things as 'trade-offs' between different objectives.[41] We may here also note the other omission, particularly interesting in the evidence of serious shortfalls in various strategic sectors of the economy, of any discussion of the effects on the Plan of failure to achieve one or other of the objectives. There is no discussion of contingency plans.[42]

National Income, Per Capita Income and the Level of Investment.

Tables I and II give figures of National Product, *per capita* National Product and net investment at current and constant prices.[43] Starting from a level of Rs. 9970 crores in 1951–2, net National Product at current prices has increased continuously throughout the period, except during the year 1965–6, when the fall in agricultural output was severe enough to offset the effects of inflation. Although the series shows some effects of rising prices from as early on as the middle years of the Second Plan, it is only during the Third Plan that inflation becomes a serious problem for the economy, especially after the year 1964–5.[44]

There are now available two series for real National Income figures, the so-called conventional, and the revised series, with base years 1948–9 and 1960–1 respectively. In what follows we have referred to the latter series as being the more up to date. As is brought

[40] Hanson (1966), p. 92.

[41] Marglin (1967), Ch. I.

[42] The point is not whether alternative Plans should be formulated or not. It is whether a well thought-out strategy exists for coping with emergencies or with shortfalls in critical sectors, due to the operation of exogenous factors. In development planning, it might be more important to know the consequences of not reaching certain targets than to know precisely what those targets are.

[43] The 1948–9 base weight series underestimate the growth rate of the economy, especially for the later years. It is possible that even the revised series (1960–1 base) underestimates the growth that has taken place in the service sector. Some economists, especially Professor Kuznets, have argued strongly that much of the growth in the service sector is in the nature of 'costs' and therefore ought not to be included, Kuznets (1959). The investment figures should be regarded as giving rough orders of magnitude only. The changes in the investment index probably most accurately reflect changes in manufacturing investment, especially in the public sector and by the larger manufacturing units in the private sector.

[44] On the behaviour of prices in the economy, see Dantwala (1967), Raj, *Indian Economic Review*, 1966.

Table I

NET NATIONAL PRODUCT, PER CAPITA INCOMES AND INVESTMENT AT CURRENT AND CONSTANT PRICES, 1950–1 TO 1966–7

	Net National Product (Rs. crores)			*Per capita national income* (Rs.)			*Net investment* (Rs. crores)	
Year	*Current prices*	*At 1948–9 prices*	*At 1960–1 prices*	*Current prices*	*At 1948–9 prices*	*At 1960–1 prices*	*Current prices*	*At 1960–1 prices*
(1)	(2)	(3)	(4)	(5)	(6)	(7)	(8)	(9)
1950–1	9,530	8,850	9,650	266·5	247·5	269	534	764
1951–2	9,970	9,100	9,920	274·2	250·3	272	560	743
1952–3	9,820	9,460	10,300	265·4	255·7	277	555	685
1953–4	10,480	10,030	10,970	278·1	266·2	290	640	791
1954–5	9,610	10,280	11,210	250·3	267·8	291	735	897
1955–6	9,980	10,480	11,410	255·0	267·8	291	870	1,030
1956–7	11,310	11,000	11,970	283·3	275·6	299	1,185	1,333
1957–8	11,390	10,890	11,790	279·6	267·3	289	1,299	1,397
1958–9	12,600	11,650	12,610	303·0	280·1	303	1,292	1,343
1959–60	12,950	11,860	12,820	304·8	279·2	301	1,374	1,402
1960–1	14,140	12,730	13,450	326·0	293·2	309	1,600	1,600
1961–2	14,770	13,060	14,040	332·9	294·0	315	1,703	1,631
1962–3	15,380	13,300	14,330	339·0	293·1	314	1,980	1,838
1963–4	17,200	13,950	15,100	370·7	300·6	323	2,252	2,018
1964–5	20,330	14,980	16,220	429·5	315·6	339	2,633	2,292
1965–6	20,590	14,640	15,440	423·9	301·4	315	2,777	2,232
1966–7	23,600	15,050	15,700	474·8	302·8	313	2,820	2,043
1967–8	27,590	16,520	17,280	541·8	324·4	336	3,135	2,168

Source: Cols. 2, 3, 5, 6 from India Ministry of Finance, *Survey* (1969–70), Table 1.1, p. A.4.
Col. 4 from India Planning Commission, *Indicators* (1968), Table 17.
Col. 7 from India Planning Commission, *Indicators* (1968), Table 11.
Cols. 8 and 9 from India Planning Commission, *Self-Reliant Growth* (1968).

Table II

NET NATIONAL PRODUCT, PER CAPITA INCOMES AND INVESTMENT: INDEX NUMBERS AT 1948–9 AND 1960–1 PRICES, 1950–1 TO 1966–7

Year	*Net National Product at 1948–9 prices* (1948–9 = 100)	*Net National Product at 1960–1 prices* (1960–1 = 100)	*Per capita income at 1948–9 prices* (1948–9 = 100)	*Per capita income at 1960–1 prices* (1960–1 = 100)	*Investment at 1960–1 prices* (1960–1 = 100)
(1)	(2)	(3)	(4)	(5)	(6)
1950–1	102·3	71·7	99·2	87·1	47·8
1951–2	105·2	73·8	100·3	88·0	46·4
1952–3	109·4	76·6	102·4	89·6	42·8
1953–4	116·0	81·6	106·7	93·9	49·4
1954–5	118·8	83·4	107·3	94·2	56·1
1955–6	121·2	84·8	107·3	94·2	64·4
1956–7	127·2	89·0	110·4	96·8	83·3
1957–8	125·9	87·7	107·1	93·5	87·3
1958–9	134·7	93·8	112·2	98·0	84·0
1959–60	137·1	95·4	111·9	97·4	87·6
1960–1	147·2	100·0	117·5	100·0	100·0
1961–2	151·0	104·3	117·9	101·9	102·0
1962–3	153·8	106·5	117·4	101·4	114·9
1963–4	161·3	112·3	120·4	104·3	126·1
1964–5	173·2	120·6	126·4	109·4	143·2
1965–6	169·2	114·8	120·8	101·7	149·5
1966–7	174·0	116·8	121·3	101·0	127·6
1967–8	191·0	128·4	130·0	108·7	135·5

Source: Cols. 2 and 4 same as Table I.
Cols. 3, 5 and 6 calculated from sources given in Table I.

out in Table III, the two series show broadly the same pattern of movement over time. Starting from a level of Rs. 9,650 crores, net National Product rose to a level of Rs. 11,970 crores during 1956–7. It then declined for the first time, although the recovery that time was much quicker than was to be the case after the peak in 1964–5. The latter coincides with the bumper harvest of 1964–5, when net National Product stood at Rs. 16,220 crores. Owing to the drought that followed, this absolute level was not again reached until three years had passed. During these years, the Indian population *increased* by about 36 million.

In terms of *per capita* income the 'average' Indian, that mythical being, earned about Rs. 275 per annum before the Plans began. By the time Planning was taken seriously, this had risen to about Rs. 300 per annum. The all-time high came in 1964–5 when the level rose to about Rs. 340. The drought ate up these modest gains and the 'average' Indian was back where he was at the beginning of the Third Plan.[45]

Table III gives the growth rates in net National Product and *per capita* incomes. The draft outline of the Fourth Plan (1967–8) had this to say about the overall performance of the economy: 'The First Plan achieved considerable success. The performance of the Second Plan was also not unsatisfactory. The record of the Third Plan, however, has not, *prima facie*, been good.'[46] As we have said earlier, whether one finds the record satisfactory or not depends on what standard of comparison one has in mind. Seen against her past history, India has done rather well for herself under Planning. In terms of what other countries, very few of them with either levels of poverty or of population comparable to India's, have managed to achieve,[47] there is less cause for satisfaction. What is quite clear, however, is that in terms of the targets laid down in the Plans, achievement has been well below what was expected or deemed feasible by the Government. For a country that is one of the

[45] See also pp. 38-42 below for changes in standards of living and the distribution of incomes.

[46] India Planning Commission (1966), pp. 2–3; the italics, which are in the original, relate to the question whether the actual figures for 1965–6 should be used in the calculations of Plan achievements or not. It was never quite clear what kind of logic it was that would take the credit for the unusually good monsoons of the early Plan years but not the blame for the unusually bad ones of the Third. The Fourth Plan document, while quite legitimately drawing attention to the adverse external conditions, is less coy about this matter.

[47] The other relevant point is that, in *per capita* terms, India has received relatively low amounts of foreign aid.

Table III

(i) REALIZED GROWTH RATES DURING THE PLANS
(Average annual %)

Plans	*Net National Product*		*Per Capita Income*	*Net Investment*
First Plan	@1948–9 prices	3·5	1·6	
	@ 1960–1 prices	3·7	1·8	(7·7)
Second Plan	@ 1948–9 prices	4·0*	1·8*	
	@ 1960–1 prices	3·5	1·3	(4·0)
Third Plan	@ 1948–9 prices	2·8	0·6	
	@ 1960–1 prices	2·8	0·3	(7·4)†

(ii) TARGET RATES OF GROWTH (Annual average %)

Plans	*Net National Product*
First Plan	2·5
Second Plan	5·0
Third Plan	6·0

Source: Plan Documents.

* The rates work out at 3·8 and 1·7 per cent respectively, if statistical adjustments are made to make them comparable to the First Plan period.

† For the period 1961–5. From 1961 to 1964, the rate works out at 8·6 per cent average.

All investment figures at 1960–1 prices and approximate.

world's poorest, this is a sobering conclusion to reach after twenty years of democratic planning.

Yet, one ought to put the problem in perspective, which is all too seldom the case when one talks about the Indian experience. For a developing country, for any country for that matter, maintaining a rate of growth of about 3 per cent per annum over a twenty-year period is a considerable achievement. It is certainly not prima facie evidence of incompetence or mismanagement. Moreover, although the realized rate of growth has fallen below target, the economic distance measured in terms of real income is not unduly long, *provided the lessons of the past are used to improve the performance level in the future.* To quote the Fourth Plan document, '. . . the aggregate real income in 1968–9 will be less than it should have been in 1965–6 on the basis of the growth rate envisaged in the Third Plan. . . . With the revised perspective of long-term growth, the Third Plan target of real income for 1975–6 will be reached only three to four years later.'[48] Indeed, the basic cause for concern is not that the economy is running four or five years behind time, so to

[48] India Planning Commission (1966), pp. 29–30; see also Das Gupta (1966).

Table IV

COMPOSITION OF NET DOMESTIC PRODUCT BY SECTORS AT 1960–1 PRICES
(percentage)

Sector	*1950–1*	*1955–6*	*1960–1*	*1964–5*	*1965–6*	*1967–8*
1. Agriculture, animal husbandry, fishery, forestry	53·8	52·8	51·4	47·4	43·0	44·4
2. Minining, manufacturing small industries	20·3	20·5	20·0	22·1	23·5	22·4
3. Commerce, transport communication	13·7	13·8	13·9	14·9	16·0	15·6
4. Other services	12·2	12·9	14·7	15·6	17·5	17·6
5. Net Domestic Product	100·0	100·0	100·0	100·0	100·0	100·0

Source: India Planning Commission, *Indicators* (1968), Table II, pp. 1–2.

speak, or that particular Plan targets for steel or cement or fertilizers, even, are x or y per cent under-fulfilled. The concern lies in the doubt that these failures cast on the ability of the economy to maintain its momentum to grow in the future. To say that if we grew as we plan to grow in the next ten years, nothing much will have been lost is small comfort to an economy that in the last ten years has never done as well as was planned.

The doubts deepen if one looks at the figures for *per capita* incomes, for the picture that emerges is that of modest gains substantially eaten up, and during the 'sixties almost annihilated, by a large, rapidly-growing population.[49] In the long-run perspective, whether the future Plans will or will not make a substantial inroad into the problem of poverty in India will surely depend on the future growth of population.[50]

The figures for net investment in the Indian economy during the Plan period are best taken as approximations. They are sufficiently

[49] According to the estimate of the Mahalanobis Committee, 96·8 per cent of the increase in national income was required to maintain the same standard of living for a larger population. Only 3·2 per cent was available to increase *per capita* incomes. India Planning Commission (1964), Table 2.1, p. 59. These figures are for the 1948–9 series.

[50] This point is made forcefully by Professor Austin Robinson, Robinson (1970); during 1951–61, population grew at the rate of 2·0 per cent per annum. During 1962–5, the estimated growth rate was 2·5 per cent per annum. According to the Registrar General's projections, the rate of growth during 1969–74 is expected to be 2·5 per cent, falling thereafter to a rate of 1·7 per cent by 1970–81. The birth rate is expected to fall from thirty-nine per thousand to twenty-six by 1980–1, the death rate from fourteen per thousand to nine.

accurate, however, to provide rough orders of magnitude over the periods covered by the different Plans. There are three characteristics of the behaviour of investment that we need to note:

1. The rate of growth of net investment was significantly different during the various Plans. Measured at 1960–1 prices, net investment increased roughly at 7 per cent per year during the First and Third Plans, whereas it appears to have grown at about 4 per cent per year during the Second Plan. If these figures are taken to be broadly correct, then the relatively satisfactory performance in terms of growth of net National Product during the Second Plan and the poor performance during the Third Plan are seen in a somewhat different light. Bearing in mind the fact that investment adds to future output capacity and the relatively long gestation period of much of the investment carried out during these years, it can reasonably be argued that some of the growth achieved during the Second Plan was at the expense of future output gains. Similarly, bearing in mind the effects of the drought and the recession following upon it, the economy might be ready to reap the benefits of some of the investment undertaken during the Third Plan.[51]

2. During the Second and the Third Plan, the volume of investment realized by the economy in real terms was less than the planned amount. At current prices, investment in the public and the private sector together during the First, Second and the Third Plans amounted to Rs. 3,360 crores, Rs. 6,750 crores and Rs. 11,370 crores respectively. Against which the original amounts aimed for in the Second and Third Plans were Rs. 6,200 and Rs. 10,400 crores, at current prices.[52] As costs of investment during the Second and the Third Plan rose by about 19 and 21 per cent respectively, we can say that in real terms realized investment fell short of the target by about 9 and 11 per cent respectively. As the level of investment has remained depressed in the economy from the end of the Third Plan until the last year or so, we can safely conclude that the terminal capital objective of the Plans has not so far been fulfilled;

3. Similarly, the domestic savings rate realized by the economy has also fallen short of the planned amount and the resulting resource gap has had to be bridged by external resources to an extent larger than envisaged in the Plans. The rate of domestic savings at

[51] Desai (1966).

[52] The realized and planned rates of investment and savings are derived from the following sources: India Planning Commission (1966), India Planning Commission, *Indicators* (1968) and India Planning Commission, *Material Balances* (1966). Some of the figures can also be found in Streeten and Lipton (1968); Robinson (1970); India Ministry of Finance, *Pocket Book* (1968).

the end of the Second and the Third Plan stood at 8·5 per cent and 10·5 per cent respectively, as opposed to the planned rates of 9·7 and 11·5 per cent. The shortfall in domestic savings has meant that even with investment below target, the economy has been saddled with a larger volume of external debt.[53]

A brief word can be added here about structural changes in the economy during the period. The most remarkable feature has no doubt been the growth of a large and diversified manufacturing sector. We shall refer to this again below,[54] but a point that needs to be made is that the qualitative changes in this sector are just as important as the magnitude of the development in terms of output or net value added. Economic development implies a lot more than simply the growth of total output. So far as the industrial sector is concerned, the Indian economy has certainly developed in a significant manner.

In quantitative terms, the structure of the economy has not undergone any radical transformation, as Table IV shows. The agricultural sector has continued to be the dominant sector within the economy, although particularly since the beginning of the Third Plan both the manufacturing and the services sector have been increasing their shares in net National Product. In terms of employment, the plans have made no dent at all and about 70 per cent of the labour force derive their livelihood from agriculture. Another important factor is that in terms of the input–output structure of the economy, the agricultural and the industrial sectors remain self-contained, buying little of each other's inputs for production purposes. In this respect, the spread of the 'new agricultural strategy' is likely, if it is successfully adopted, to increase the dependence of the economy on industrial inputs, such as fertilizer, pesticide and pumps.[55]

The Indian Plans do not contain specific regional objectives. Regional considerations are borne in mind partly in relation to the desire of the Government to improve conditions in 'backward' areas and partly in the applications of regulations such as industrial

[53] This is true, *a fortiori*, for the period after 1965–6, when the food shortage, increased defence expenditure and the acute balance of payments problem together led to a recession and increased reliance on foreign aid.

[54] On this point see Raj (1965), Robinson (1970).

[55] India Planning Commission (1965); Manne and Rudra (1965). The degree of interdependence would vary according to whether one classified the textile sector as an agricultural or an industrial one. Logically, it ought to be classified as an industry and this would increase the linkages. The structural implication of a re-classification would be limited, because textiles are not growing as rapidly as the other industrial sectors. The input–output relationship described above does not, of course, imply that the two sectors can grow independently – food is a vital input to the economy.

licensing and location of key public sector projects. Moreover, national income and other related statistics are not available for us to establish regional patterns of development within the economy. However, enough is known for us to be able to point to one or two features of regional development.

Historically, both agricultural and industrial growth has been uneven in India. Agricultural production in different 'provinces' has grown at different rates over time, creating the distinction between 'surplus' and 'deficit' states. Industrial growth has also been concentrated around Calcutta and Bombay. Growth rates in agriculture for the period 1949–50 to 1964–5 are available on a state basis.[56] They are reproduced below in Table V.

In five out of fifteen States the rate of growth of agricultural production exceeded the average all India rate of 3·01 per cent. In others,

Table V

COMPOUND GROWTH RATES OF AGRICULTURAL PRODUCTION, FOODGRAINS PRODUCTION AND POPULATION BY STATES, 1952–3 TO 1964–5

States	*Agricultural Production*	*Foodgrains Production*	*Population*
*Punjab	4·56	3·66	2·61
†Gujarat*	4·55	2·06	2·61
*Madras	4·17	4·17	1·25
*Mysore	3·54	3·31	2·08
*Himachal Pradesh	3·39	3·63	2·22
Bihar	2·97	3·05	2·12
†Maharastra	2·93	2·20	2·32
†Rajasthan	2·74	2·42	2·68
Andhra Pradesh	2·71	3·21	1·63
†Madhya Pradesh	2·49	2·32	2·51
Orissa	2·48	2·39	2·16
Kerala	2·27	3·68	2·33
†West Bengal	1·94	1·14	2·92
†Uttar Pradesh	1·66	0·85	1·84
†Assam	1·17	0·76	3·15
All India	3·01	2·50	2·19

* States where rate of growth of agricultural production is *higher* than all India average.

† States where rate of foodgrain output is *less* than that for population.

Source: India Ministry of Food and Agriculture (1968), Tables 9 and 14, pp. 31 and 42.

[56] The growth rates will be different according to which years are chosen as base.

the rate of growth varied from almost 3 per cent for Bihar and Maharastra to well under 2 per cent for Uttar Pradesh. In terms of foodgrains output, seven States did better than average, the ranking order being different from that for total agricultural output. For foodgrains, the rates of growth varied from 4·17 per cent for Madras to well below 1 per cent for Uttar Pradesh and Assam. More significant, perhaps, the overall rate of growth of food production barely exceeded the rate of growth of population. All the more so if we bear in mind that during this period the rate of growth of population was increasing while that of food production was not. In no less than seven States, the rate of growth of population exceeded the rate of growth of food production. According to the 1961 Census, together these States accounted for 53·18 per cent of the total population of the Indian Union. The problem of feeding a growing population would have been all the more acute for States such as West Bengal which are traditionally 'deficit' States.

We have, unfortunately, to be satisfied with this rather incomplete picture because we do not have comparable figures for industrial development in different States, or for the development of the service sector. The figures for allocation of Plan outlays by States are also of limited usefulness. They take no account of private sector outlays, which have played a considerable part in promoting regional industrial growth in various states. Moreover, a State's share of plan resources need not bear any close relationship to its contribution in terms of value added. It is quite clear that States such as Punjab have grown rapidly both in industry and agriculture. This is borne out by a comparison of *per capita* incomes. On the other hand, States such as Uttar Pradesh, and Bihar and Orissa have done very badly in terms of *per capita* incomes. West Bengal comes surprisingly well out of the comparison. However, one suspects that the benefits of progress have been very unevenly distributed throughout the population, quite apart from the problems created by Calcutta. Any satisfactory explanation of the problems of economic development of India must account for these wide regional variations in growth performance, which we have only hinted at.[57]

Standards of Living and Inequality

The 'average' Indian is among the poorest of the world. The poverty is all too real and one hardly needs any statistics to show that after

[57] Useful references are India Planning Commission, *Regional Variations* (1967–8), Mitra (1970), Bagchi (1965), Hanumantha Rao (1965), Minhas and Vaidyanathan (1965), Parikh (1966), V.K.R.V. Rao (1962).

twenty years of planning, the Indian poor have little to be thankful about. Indeed, in some ways his lot is worse, because with the growth in population his access to agricultural land, housing, water and transport has in many cases deteriorated.[58] The growing wealth of the country too passes him by. Yet a few words badly need to be said if only because the problem is too important to be by-passed.

Much has been written about the distribution of income in India.[59] The data is deficient in many ways and the conclusions reached by various authors are different, according to various assumptions made by them. In any case, for the immediate future, it seems to be more important to concentrate on the absolute level of poverty in India, rather than on its relative distribution. Practically all Plan documents stress the problem of poverty in India and the overwhelming urgency of improving the lot of 'the common man, the weaker sections and the less privileged'.[60]

The standard of living of the common man depends partly on how long he lives to enjoy it. The first point to note is that the expectation of life in India has gone up from about thirty-three years in 1941–51 to forty-one years in 1951–61.[61] Much of it has come from a fall in the death rate due to the increased control over epidemic diseases and very little has come from better nutrition. The second important set of factors are *per capita* incomes and availability of basic necessities, such as foodgrains, on which most of his income is spent.

Per capita consumption in the Indian economy stood at Rs. 254 on average in 1957–8. For the top 5 per cent the level was Rs. 767 and for the bottom 5 per cent it was Rs. 61. Up to the beginning of the Third Plan, consumption for both fractiles grew at about 2 per cent per annum. From then on until 1967–8 the consumption of the bottom 5 per cent has continued to grow at about 2 per cent until it stood at Rs. 77 in that year. The *consumption* of the top 5 per cent has more or less remained constant.[62] This has to be seen against the background of a Working Group report of the Planning

[58] Any statements like this about India is bound to be disputed. It is certainly true that in the established urban centres, the poor are worse off in terms of housing, water and transport. In the growing middle-sized towns and in rural areas close to cities, they might be better off in terms of employment in service industries or transport. In rural areas, the agricultural labourers' lot has certainly not been much improved.

[59] Bhatt and Ohja (1963); India Planning Commission (1964); Lydall (1960); Ranadive (1968).

[60] India Planning Commission (1966), p. 4.

[61] India Ministry of Finance, *Pocket Book* (1968); in terms of calorie requirements the average Indian probably has barely sufficient, although his food intake is highly deficient in nutrients such as proteins.

[62] Minhas (1969), pp. 52–3.

Commission that, taking Rs. 240 *per capita* as a subsistence minimum for a year, 58 per cent of the population in 1957–8 and 54 per cent in 1960–1 remained below that level. And that level fell to 48 per cent in 1967–8.[63] Even this picture of modest benefits is not borne out by available figures for *per capita* availability of foodgrains and other consumer goods. *Per capita* availability of cereals and pulses fluctuates from year to year, according to the harvests and availability of imports. *Per capita* net availability in 1951 per person was 333·5 grams for cereals and 60·5 grams for pulses. The highest levels were reached for cereals in 1965 when, following the bumper harvest of 67 million tons, the *per capita* figure stood at 412·8 grams per day. However, after a run of bad harvests, the level fell to below 360 grams in 1966 and 1967. The net availability figures for the plan periods are as follows:[64]

Table VI

Period	*Per capita net availability in grams/day* (average) Cereals	Pulses
First Plan	358·4	66·4
Second Plan	379·3	67·7
Third Plan	389·3	56·9

Source: India Ministry of Finance, *Survey, 1968–9*, p. A.10.

There are also other reasons for believing that during the Plan period the situation of the very poor has been somewhat worse than the average figures show. The fair price shops, through which the Government has tried to sell foodgrains at relatively cheap prices, have been confined in operation to mainly urban centres and have to a certain extent been the source of cheap food to the not-so-poor.[65] Unemployment has been growing within the economy, and until the year 1968 the level of economic activity had been low due to the recession. It is often forgotten that in a 'mixed' economy where transfer payments play an insignificant role, the standard of living of the poor depends solely on their employment prospects and the

[63] Minhas (1969), p. 53.

[64] These figures are taken from India Ministry of Finance, *Survey* (1968–9), pp. A.10–12. Net Availability = Net Production + Net Imports + Decline in Government Stocks. Net Production is arrived at after an allowance of 12·5 per cent for feed, seed requirements and wastage. Changes in private stocks, i.e. farmers' and traders' stocks are not accounted for.

[65] Bardhan (1966), Raj, *E.P.W.*, 1966.

real wage rate they can command. The employment problem is, therefore, an integral part of the problem of eradication of poverty.

We do not raise here the question of the rural-urban disparities in standards of living, as this is discussed later in the context of transfer of resources from one sector to the other.[66] One point, however, is relevant in the present context. In the rural sector, although not every one is a farmer or a peasant, one's standard of living depends largely on the ownership or the user of land. The ownership of land in India is highly unequal. According to the National Sample Survey, the bottom 40 per cent of rural households held 1·25 per cent of total cultivated land, defined as operational holdings, in 1954–5. This area was further subdivided into plots of less than 1 acre. Similarly, the top 6 per cent of rural households owned or had occupancy rights over 40 per cent of the total cultivated area, held in holdings of 20 acres or over.[67] Indeed, this, together with the lack of security of tenure and high rents, is what gave impetus to the desire for land reform in Indian Planning.[68] However, as practically all evaluation studies of land reform have shown, no substantial progress has been made in India either in the direction of providing security of tenure or enforcement of rent-ceilings.[69] The emergence of 'capitalist' agriculture in India and that of the 'kulak' is today well documented.[70] It is also well known that the lion's share of the new inputs of the 'green revolution' has been going to the more prosperous tenant farmers. We need not question for the moment whether such developments and such allocations of resources are in the long-run interests of the country or not.[71] We can, however, say fairly categorically that these factors taken together show that the standard of living of the rural poor, the agricultural labourer and the small peasant has not improved substantially. The one exception to this are probably those IADP areas where the 'green revolution' has increased the demand for labour.[72] As for the concentration of economic power in the manufacturing

[66] See p. 52 f. below. [67] Gandhi (1966), p. 152.

[68] The need for land reform is probably the first 'programme' to find acceptance in the minds of those Congress leaders who took notions of socialist planning in India seriously. One of the first economic issues that brought Pandit Nehru into touch with the problems of poverty in India was the problem of rural indebtedness in what was then the United Provinces. Nehru (1962).

[69] Ladejinsky (1965) is the best known of these. The Planning Commission published a number of evaluation studies of land reform. An excellent summary is Dandekar (1962); see also George (1968). A critical discussion of the viability of the programme is provided by Raj Krishna (1963).

[70] Ladejinsky (1969); Thorner (1967).

[71] Wharton (1969). [72] Ladejinsky (1969).

sector, Hazari's detailed work on the Private corporate sector goes to show that there was a significant increase in the concentration of economic power in this sector between 1951 and 1958. The four largest groups, Tata, Birla, Martin Burn and Dalmia Sahu Jain increased their share of share capital from 22 to 25 per cent and their share in the net wealth of companies from 17 to 22 per cent.[73] To quote Hazari, 'Whether this development was for the better or for the worse from the standpoint of the rate of industrial growth, efficiency and utilization of resources etc., cannot be established. It is quite clear, nevertheless, that, by itself, the increase in the concentration was inconsistent with the directive principles of state policy laid down under the Constitution and the objectives of planned development stated in the Second and Third Five-Year Plans.'[74]

In a way, it is not difficult to see why so little has been done in the way of improving the lot of the very poor. The basic cause, no doubt, is the inadequate rate of increase in agricultural production, in the face of a large, rapidly growing population. However, it has also to be remembered that it has never been considered a part of planning strategy to ameliorate the condition of the poor through redistribution of income. As we have pointed out above, this was to be done by channelling the incremental benefits of economic growth in the economy to the poor.[75] In so far as these incremental benefits have been small in terms of *per capita* gains, the pool out of which resources were to be redistributed has also been small. Even so, as we go on to argue later in Section V below, it would be oversimplifying the problem to attribute the continuation of gross poverty in India to the general overall low rate of growth of the economy, in relation to the targets set by the plan. The pattern of industrial development that the Government has allowed to develop is in some ways also responsible for the very widespread existence of acute poverty.[76]

Employment

It is particularly difficult to draw any firm conclusions about the magnitude of the problem of unemployment in India and the impact or lack of an impact made by economic policies during the last twenty years. These difficulties are partly conceptual and arise partly from the lack of knowledge about the existing situation.[77]

[73] Hazari (1966), p. 305; see also Bagchi (1967) for a review article; also the more tentative Mahalanobis Report: India Planning Commission (1964).

[74] Hazari (1966), p. 357. The recent discussion relating to the Bank Nationalization issue points in a similar direction. Six hundred customers of the Scheduled Banks in 1969 held 66 per cent of the credit advanced.

[75] See p. 26 above. [76] See pp. 67-8 below.

[77] For a discussion of these problems see Raj (1959).

To put the conceptual difficulties in a capsule form, the basic problems arise from the existence of the institution of family labour in agriculture, the substantial proportion of agricultural labourers in agriculture and the existence of a large service sector, where 'employment' is not so much a means of earning a livelihood as a sort of service rendered in return for a subsistence level of consumption.[78] They make it difficult to draw any firm distinction between employment, under-employment and unemployment in both the urban and the rural sector because of the problem of defining a 'norm' on the basis of which such distinction can be drawn. Moreover, even if such distinctions could be drawn, the problem would remain that some forms of 'under-employment' might reflect not so much a lack of job opportunity as an extremely low level of productivity consequent on lack of demand.[79]

These problems are considerably added to by the lack of any systematic attempts to collect comparable data on employment and unemployment for the economy. No quantitative figures exist on employment in agriculture outside the processing industries. The data on employment in manufacturing excludes the smaller units of production, which in India employ a considerable number of workers. Moreover, changes in methods of collecting data often make it impossible to compare accurately data derived over different periods of time.[80] What we have to say below should, therefore, be interpreted with these difficulties firmly in our minds.

In so far as the Indian plans have a rationale behind their employment policies, it is probably discussed most lucidly in the Second Plan. Indeed, it can be said without too much unkindness that the amount of space devoted to the discussion of the problem of unemployment and the degree of clarity behind the discussion, have both diminished with the increase in the magnitude and urgency of the problem itself.[81] Broadly speaking, it would be true to say that the Indian Planners have not regarded the reduction of unemployment as a major policy objective in the short run. In the short run they have regarded the employment objective as being in conflict with the growth of output objective, having equated a high employ-

[78] The institution of family labour in agriculture gives rise to work-sharing within the family in return for a share in the family output/consumption. In urban centres, much of the employment in the service sector takes this form, without any of the social benefits that a family structure might provide.

[79] Reddaway (1962), Ch. 2.

[80] This is true, e.g. of agricultural labour statistics, cf. India Planning Commission (1969) Ch. 21, Thorner and Thorner (1962).

[81] India Planning Commission (1956), Ch. V; India Planning Commission (1961), Ch. X; India Planning Commission (1969), Ch. 21.

ment strategy with a high consumption/low investment strategy. The argument has been that because the magnitude of the problem of unemployment and under-employment was very large, it could not be eradicated by the existing productive capacity of the economy, which was clearly inadequate to absorb the total working population. It was, therefore, necessary to build up the productive capacity of the economy through a high rate of investment before the problem of unemployment could be tackled seriously. The paradoxical nature of the 'strategy' is reinforced by the clear recognition by the Planners that in the process of catching up, the unemployment problem will itself become more acute.[82] The main force behind the creation of employment during the planning period, as the Planners saw it, was to be the industrialization programme in the Plans. The problem of reducing rural unemployment or under-employment was to be dealt with by the support given to the handloom industry in the Second Plan and the rural works programme in the Third Plan. These were clearly in the nature of adjuncts to the main programme.[83]

Let us now turn briefly to the record of employment creation since the beginning of the Second Plan. During the formulation of the Second Plan, the existing volume of unemployed was estimated to be about 5·3 million.[84] The addition to the labour force during the Second Plan was estimated to be about 10 million, 9 out of the 15·3 million being in the rural sector.[85] Against this a target of about 10 million new jobs to be created was set, as against the First Plan achievement of 4·5 million new jobs.[86] Of these 10 million new jobs, 8 were to result from an outlay of Rs. 7200 crores in the public and the private sector, an additional 2 being the indirect result of policies aimed at developing the agricultural sector.[87]

In terms of achievement, the number of new jobs created during the Second Plan amounted to some 8 million, being 2 million short of target. In addition, only 1·5 million of this was in agriculture. The backlog of unemployment at the end of the Plan rose to 7 million, i.e. by 32 per cent. In addition, about 15 to 18 million were estimated to be under-employed in the rural sector.[88] *Additions* to the labour force would be of the order of 17 million. Against this, development

[82] India Planning Commission (1956), pp. 109 f.
[83] India Planning Commission (1961), pp. 163 f.
[84] India Planning Commission (1956), p. 112.
[85] India Planning Commission (1956), p. 112.
[86] India Planning Commission (1956), p. 119.
[87] India Planning Commission (1956), p. 114.
[88] India Planning Commission (1956), pp. 109 f.; the Third Plan gives the figure as 9 million.

expenditure in the Plan was estimated to create 14 million new jobs, 10·5 million being outside the agricultural sector. However, rural works programmes were estimated to provide an extra 100 days' work per year for an estimated 2·5 million workers.[89] According to the Fourth Plan (1967–8), the number of jobs created during the Third Plan amounted to 14·5 million, of which 10·5 million were in the non-agricultural sector.[90] It is not unlikely, however, that the above figures are somewhat in the nature of an optimistic assessment. The Fourth Plan draft does not give any figures for achievements during the 'sixties in the field of employment. However, we can bear in mind that during the earlier years, the organized manufacturing sector has been the most dynamic in the field of employment creation. The estimated increase in the public and private sector during the 'sixties are given below, in Table VII. It has been said already that these figures do not give an accurate measure of employment in the non-agricultural sector, because it leaves out small-scale enterprises which have been growing rapidly. It is doubtful, however, if this can account for the whole of the discrepancy, especially if we bear in mind that much of the increased employment in the service sector is in the nature of an apparent rather than a real increase, as long as productivity levels are not significantly improved. In addition, as is well known, the problem of urban unemployment and that of the unemployment of skilled labour in the engineering industries has become increasingly serious in the last few years.[91]

As far as the rural works programme goes, the facts are illuminative of certain aspects of planning. The estimated outlay for creating 2·5

Table VII

ESTIMATED EMPLOYMENT IN THE PUBLIC AND THE PRIVATE SECTORS, AS AT THE END OF MARCH
(thousand persons)

	1961		*1965*		*1967*
Public Sector	7,050		8,957		9,634
		(6·8)		(3·8)	
Private Sector	5,040		6,043		6,684
		(5·0)		(5·3)	

Source: India Ministry of Labour (1968), pp. 5–6; figures in parenthesis are for linear percentage increases between the two dates, on an average annual basis.

[89] India Estimates Committee, *55th Report* (1964).
[90] India Planning Commission (1966), p. 106.
[91] Hone (1968).

million jobs was Rs. 150 crores over the Plan period. No financial provision for this was made in the plan but it was assumed that the outlay would be financed out of normal budgetary sources. Up to the financial year 1963–4, Rs. 6·5 crores had been provided over the first three years of the Plan and an additional 0·1 million jobs had been created up to the middle of 1963. Moreover, much of the employment created turned out to have been in non-priority regions, achieved at a *per capita* cost much higher than the original estimates.[92] It is unlikely that agricultural employment prospects would have improved until the end of the drought. To sum up a rather involved discussion of plan objectives and achievements in a few words, we can say that in terms of the growth of national income, the record of performance of the economy is modest and below target. Overall, the economy appears to have been growing at a rate of about 3 per cent per year. The effect of three years' stagnation had been partly made up by much higher rates of growth achieved during the last two years and the economy can now be said to be running about five years behind time. In terms of *per capita*, this is a little less encouraging than it sounds. Starting from very low levels of living, the rate of improvement has not been much higher than 1 per cent a year. If this were all, there would not appear to be much cause for pessimism and despondency. The fact remains that in terms of improving the levels of living of the poor, very little has been achieved. The record in the field of reducing unemployment and under-employment, both in the urban and the rural sector, is admitted to be unsatisfactory. Taken together, these facts cast serious doubt on the ability of the economy to maintain its momentum of growth in the future, because they threaten the political and social stability that is a basic requirement of what is called democratic planning.

We now turn to a brief review of what has been achieved and what problems have arisen in the two critical sectors of the economy, the agricultural sector and the external sector. As the Government had pegged out for itself a major role in the field of industrial development, the problems of industrialization are discussed last within the general contest of the role played by the Government in development process.

III

By now, an enormous volume of literature exists on the problems of agricultural development in India. It covers institutional and be-

[92] India Estimates Committee, *55th Report* (1964); the cost of creating new jobs in this field was estimated to be Rs. 100 per head for 45–50 man-days of employment created, allowing for overhead costs of 23·3 to 25 per cent.

havioural characteristics of that sector, its performance during the Plan period and attempts at explaining such performance. We have neither the competence nor the space available to offer a review of the vast body of work done in this field. It requires not only the competence of an economist but a complete grasp of the very diverse technical aspects of the agricultural situation in India.[93] In this brief section, we shall confine ourselves to a short summary of the behaviour of agricultural output in India during the last two decades. We shall then consider briefly some of the explanations that have been put forward by scholars and try to point out some of the problems of interpretation that they have overlooked.

One or two words of caution are in order. The conditions governing agricultural production in India vary enormously from one region to another. Not only are climatic and soil conditions different. There are large differences in distribution of land holdings and availability of irrigation water. More important, perhaps, are the differences in the attitudes of the 'average' farmer to economic opportunities. It is, therefore, not surprising that research workers engaged in the study of a particular aspect of the problem, e.g. the relationship of the size of holdings to productivity, or the relationship between the size of holdings and proportion of agricultural output that is marketed, have often reached diametrically opposite conclusions. In studying the problem of Indian agriculture one should always beware of such statements as 'as X has shown', for the very good reason that an equally respectable Y would turn out to have shown just the opposite.[94]

The general features of the development of the agricultural sector are well known. Starting from a level of Rs. 52,000 crores, measured at 1960–1 prices, total agricultural production rose at the rate of about 3 per cent per year until 1964–5. Foodgrains production, which accounts for about two-thirds of total agricultural production, rose from a level of 51 million tons in 1950–1 to a record level of 89 million tons in 1964–5. During this period, foodgrains production increased at the rate of 2·8 per cent as opposed to the rate of increase

[93] See Bhagwati and Chakravarty (1969); there is an admirable collection of articles edited by Khusro (1968). For a serious critique of policy, see Lipton (1968). The articles by the following in the list of works cited merit serious attention: Bagchi (1965), Bardhan (1966), Dandekar (1967), Dantwala (1967), Gadgil (1964), Hopper (1965), Hanumantha Rao (1963, 1965, 1966), Khusro (1964), Krishnan (1965), Rudra (1964, 1968), Lipton (1969), Minhas (1969), Minhas and Srinivasan (1968), Minhas and Vaidyanathan (1965), Raj (1965), *E.P.W.*, 1966, Raj Krishna (1963, 1967), A.K. Sen (1964, 1970).

[94] Part of the problem lies in the interpretation of data as well as differences about methodology. See especially Bhagwati and Chakravarty (1969), pp. 29 f.

Table VIII

INDEXES OF AGRICULTURAL PRODUCTION
(Years July–June; 1949–50 = 100)

Commodity	*1950–1*	*1955–6*	*1960–1*	*1965–6**	*1966–7**	*Weights* (per cent)
Foodgrains	90·5	115·3	137·1	120·9	124·6	66·9
Cereals	90·3	114·9	138·3	124·2	129·9	58·3
Rice	87·9	114·2	137·7	121·8	120·9	35·3
Wheat	101·1	131·3	162·8	154·5	170·8	8·5
Non-Foodgrains	105·9	119·9	152·6	156·4	148·2	33·1
Oilseeds	98·5	108·6	134·0	125·4	127·3	9·9
Fibres	108·6	149·7	176·0	168·8	180·4	4·5
Plantations	104·0	113·2	129·2	151·2	157·3	3·6
Sugarcane	113·7	119·8	183·9	201·3	158·0	8·7
All Commodities	95·6	116·8	142·2	132·7	132·4	100·0

Source: India Ministry of Finance, *Pocket Book* (1968).
* Provisional estimates.
Fibres include cotton, jute, etc.; plantations include tea, coffee, etc.

of non-foodgrains output of 4·8 per cent.[95] As has already been said, these rates of increase, though encouraging in terms of past performance of the economy, were inadequate both with respect to the growth of population in the economy and the targets set in the plans.[96] *Per capita* availability of foodgrains increased from a very low level of 334 grams to a level of 413 grams. In addition, the target of self-sufficiency in foodgrains for the Third Plan, embodied in the target for 1965–6 of 100 million tons, was not achieved. In that year, 6·26 million tons of foodgrains were imported, mostly under the U.S. Public Law—480, for surplus disposal at a subsidized foreign exchange cost. This accounted for about 8 per cent of net availability of foodgrains in the economy and about 7 per cent of total production.[97]

[95] The figures are taken from various official publications, e.g. India Planning Commission (1961), India Planning Commission (1966), India Ministry of Food and Agriculture (1968); the production figures are those given by the Ministry of Food and Agriculture and are lower than the figures given in the Economic Survey published by the Ministry of Finance. Output is measured in metric tons. It should be noted that the growth rates cited above and given in Table IX, are linear rates and therefore different from the rates given in Table V. The latter figures are given for easy comparison with rates of population growth. It should be further noted that the linear rates vary according to the base year chosen, the 1952–4 = 100 base yielding 'middle' estimates.

[96] India Ministry of Food and Agriculture (1968), p. 42.

[97] India Ministry of Finance, *Survey*, *1968–9*, Tables 1.7 and 1.8, pp. A.10–A.11; see also p. 37 above.

Inadequate as the performance of agriculture was in terms of needs, the modest gains were dissipated through the effects of two disastrous years of failing monsoons. During the year 1965–6, foodgrains output fell by 16·7 million tons, a decline of 23 per cent. The output level of 1964–5 was not reached again until 1967–8. The availability of foodgrains per head fell to a level not reached since 1958–9, even though 9 to 10 per cent of net requirements were being met out of a record level of imports.[98] The decline in production also extended to non-foodgrains production, with the exception of the plantation crops such as tea and coffee, and of sugarcane.[99]

Certain characteristics of the behaviour of agricultural production should be noted. First of these is the close link that exists between the level of agricultural output and the net National Product. Over roughly a twenty-year period, the rate of increase of net national product approached or exceeded the 5 per cent level on seven occasions.[100] With the sole exception of 1963–4, each of these years saw a substantial increase in agricultural production. The years during which the rate of growth fell below 2 per cent were years of stagnation or falling output in agriculture. It will be readily agreed that until at least the last two or three years, the basic cause behind the increase in agricultural production in particular years has been the weather and not the increased use of superior techniques or inputs such as fertilizers. This underlines the peculiar paradox of Indian planning that, after fifteen years of economic planning, the levels of output and rates of growth of the economy should depend above all on the exogenous, stochastic influence of an unplannable factor, the weather.

The other factor to note is the unequal role played by the two contributory influences on the level of production, the area sown and the level of productivity in agriculture.[101] For the period 1952–3 to 1964–5, as a whole, the area sown increased at a rate of 1·3 per cent and productivity increased at a rate of 1·9 per cent per year. These figures, however, disguise differences in behaviour of the two series for parts of the period. Thus, for total agricultural output, area sown increased most rapidly until 1955–6 and productivity after 1955–6. Indeed, the bulk of the increase in acreage under crops occurred between 1950 and 1959, and there has been very little addition to it

[98] India Ministry of Finance, *Survey*, *1968–9*, Tables 1.7 and 1.8, pp. A.10–A.11. [99] See Table VIII.

[100] The years are: 1953–4, 1956–7, 1958–9, 1960–1, 1963–4, 1964–5, and 1967–8; see India Planning Commission, *Indicators* (1968).

[101] India Ministry of Food and Agriculture (1968); Hanumantha Rao (1965); changes in crop patterns also account for part of the increase in levels of output.

in the 'sixties. The apparent increase in the weight of the yield factor in explaining the behaviour of agricultural output has to be viewed with caution, except for the last two or three years. Peak years for agricultural output, such as 1956–7, 1958–9, and 1964–5 also show peaks in the productivity index. It cannot, however, be deduced from this that agricultural productivity was high in these years, in the sense that the greater level of output was obtained through improvements in input-utilization or superior management. It was due to more favourable weather conditions.[102]

As is well known, the situation has altered radically with respect to foodgrains production, especially wheat and to a lesser extent rice, since the advent of the 'new agricultural strategy'. Foodgrains production has increased very rapidly, leading to an all-time peak in 1969–70. Most of this gain has been due to genuine increases in yield per acre and marks an important technological breakthrough. To what extent the 'new agricultural strategy' has made the food problem in India a thing of the past remains a matter for conjecture, to put it mildly. There are very serious organizational problems relating to its wider adoption, as well as problems of extending the area of controlled irrigation and water-availability, on which the success of the strategy is critically dependent.

Returning to the pre-1966 situation, the importance of a larger acreage sown to crops, and of increased yields, has varied from crop to crop. Taking the two broad groups, area has been more important than the yield factor for non-foodgrains production, whereas for foodgrains the opposite is true. However, in the latter case, productivity has increased faster than area sown to food crops since 1955–6.

A more detailed breakdown shows up important differences between crops.[103] Amongst foodgrains, production of rice, wheat and maize has increased faster than the production of the inferior grains, such as jowar or bajra. Productivity has increased more rapidly for rice, and some of the inferior grains than it has for wheat or maize, where much of the increase in putput has come from a greater acreage sown. Amongst the commercial crops, increase in production has been most noticeable for groundnuts, jute and sugarcane coming from increased acreage sown to these crops, indicating a shift in particular regions from food crops to cash crops, and coffee has shown remarkable increases in yield.

[102] In a formal sense, more rains means more water, and a good monsoon means that it comes at the right time. As water is an input, the increased yield is due to a greater degree of input-utilization! The point is that, in these cases the increased yields were not due to any fundamental changes in agricultural practices.

[103] India Ministry of Food and Agriculture (1968), Table 6, p. 26.

Table IX

STATE-WISE GROWTH RATES OF PRODUCTION, AREA, AND YIELD, 1952–3 TO 1964–5

(in terms of average 1952–3 to 1954–5 = 100)
AVAILABILITY OF FERTILIZERS, 1964–5

	Foodgrains			*Non-foodgrains*			
State	*Production* %	*Area* %	*Yield* %	*Production* %	*Area* %	*Yield* %	*Fertilizer (Kg./Hectare sown)*
Punjab	4·30	1·63	2·26	9·46	4·90	3·03	5·7
Gujarat	2·09	−2·19	5·34	8·03	5·93	1·64	2·5
Madras	4·89	0·75	3·92	4·96	2·45	2·05	9·9
Mysore	3·71	0·91	2·64	4·91	0·59	4·03	2·4
Himachal Pradesh	4·23	0·63	3·40	1·63	3·27	−1·30	2·3
Bihar	3·28	0·64	2·55	2·61	1·84	0·78	2·0
Maharastra	2·29	0·33	1·94	5·15	0·83	3·65	3·1
Rajasthan	2·68	3·03	−0·23	4·89	5·13	−0·09	0·7
Andhra Pradesh	3·65	0·84	2·63	1·83	−1·59	3·93	8·5
Madhya Pradesh	2·58	1·28	1·16	4·50	1·67	2·44	0·8
Orissa	2·60	0·79	1·75	3·40	1·65	1·54	1·0
Kerala	4·37	0·51	3·74	1·83	2·06	−0·20	4·3
West Bengal	1·16	0·26	0·90	4·23	4·29	0·09	1·8
Uttar Pradesh	0·91	0·40	0·49	4·28	2·19	1·72	3·5
Assam	0·80	1·36	−0·48	1·62	1·21	0·35	0·4
All India	2·75	1·02	1·60	4·79	2·56	1·79	3·4

Source: India Ministry of Food and Agriculture (1968), Tables 12, 13 and 15.
See also Table II in Minhas and Vaidyanathan (1965).

More interesting, perhaps, are the wide differences in the performance of various states in the field of agricultural production. We have on the one hand, the *wirtschaftwunder* of the Punjab; on the other the alarming examples of Assam, Uttar Pradesh and West Bengal, especially in relation to foodgrains production. The causes of these discrepancies are examined at length in the articles by Hanumantha Rao and Minhas and Vaidyanathan.[104] They will not be touched upon here. We may note in passing, however, that such differences cannot be satisfactorily explained in terms of simple hypotheses relating to the inequality of the distribution of landholdings or the rates of fertilizer consumption.[105] These points are touched upon below when we consider some of the policy implications of such analyses.[106]

Most of the criticisms of Indian agricultural policy rest on the charge that planners and policy-makers have given low priority to the agricultural sector, and that the poor performance is a reflection of the low priority. Some would attribute this to inefficiency of the planning mechanism, and some to the so-called 'urban bias' in Indian planning. It is not our object here to try to argue for or against these criticisms. We hope, however, to look at some aspects of these criticisms with a little more care than they have so far received.

There are three basic variants to the low priority argument. One argues that this low priority is reflected in the allocation of resources. This line of criticism points to the pattern of allocation of plan expenditure to establish that the agricultural sector has received a sub-optimal share in total resources. The other variant stresses the problem of incentives and the role of prices in the development process. This argues that agricultural prices have been kept too low, so as to make it unprofitable to expand agricultural output. Evidence of the supreme intellectual inconsistency that economists display in the field of political economy is that this school would contain one or two severe critics of the Singer–Prebisch thesis.[107] The third body

[104] Hanumantha Rao (1965), Minhas and Srinivasan (1968); there is an interesting article by Bagchi (1965), suggesting alternative hypotheses for explaining state-wise differences; see also Rao (1962).

[105] See Table IX.

[106] See below pp. 80 f.

[107] There is a substantial volume of literature that criticizes one or other aspect of Indian agricultural policy. It is impossible to provide an exhaustive list. The most serious criticism from the resource angle is Lipton (1968, 1969), both of which merit serious study. Mason (1966) provides a serious but balanced criticism of policy. On prices see Bardhan (1966), Lipton (1968), Raj, *Indian Economic Review*, 1966, among a host of others. On distribution, see Raj, *Economic and Political Weekly*, 1966, and an excellent article by Raj Krishna

of criticism concentrates on the neglect of institutional factors and point to the lack of progress in land reform and the absence of sociologists from the Planning Commission. These divisions are neither exclusive nor homogeneous. One individual may well belong to two schools of criticism, so to speak. More important are the differences among the critics of government price policy, where one body of critics stress the importance of the private sector and the other the need for the Government to exercise more effective control over that sector, particularly in the field of distribution. It is worth noting that very few critics question the feasibility of planning for food in a poor, inegality-ridden country through the market mechanism. It is, of course, not possible to imply that Indian planners have neglected agriculture, which is what the criticisms boil down to, in the formulation of a planning strategy. The Plan documents are full of references to the importance of the agricultural sector to the economy, as they are full of every other good intention. Even the Second Plan, which is held up as the supreme example of a 'heavy industry' strategy, is explicit on this point.[108] 'Urban-bias', therefore, implies a certain degree of schizophrenia in the minds of planners, and the critics usually start by pointing to the pattern of allocation of plan outlay in the successive Plans. However, there are serious objections to starting from this angle, without a more detailed consideration of what lies behind these figures.

If we look at the relative shares themselves, we shall find that the realized outlays in the First, Second and the Third Plans under the head of Agriculture and Community Development are as follows:

	Current prices	*1960–1 prices*
First Plan	14·8%	15·1%
Second Plan	11·8%	11·6%
Third Plan	12·8%	12·6%

Indeed, the large difference comes from a sharp drop in the share allocated to Major and Minor Irrigation in the Plans and *not* in that allocated to Agriculture itself. It is true that the agricultural sector is supposed to be the major beneficiary of irrigation. However, it is also true that the First Plan incorporated the financing of some of the most capital-intensive major irrigation projects.[109] It is in the nature

(1967). On institutional factors, see Ladejinsky (1965). See also Hanson (1969). A very good article on the political aspects is Nicolson (1968). Hanson (1966) is a mine of information about what goes on behind closed doors.

[108] India Planning Commission (1956), p. 259.

[109] These were the Damodar Valley Project, the Hirakund and the Bakhra–Nangal projects.

of these projects that they require a very large volume of resources in construction but it is equally well known that they have a long economic life. It is, therefore, not surprising to find that the share allocated to irrigation should fall sharply once these projects are completed. This does not mean that in the successive plans, the share of 'irrigation' inputs to the agricultural sector fell proportionately as a consequence. We have to remember, moreover, that although the proportions of total Plan outlay ear-marked for the Agricultural Sector have fallen, the total volume of resources going to that sector has shown considerable increases. For example, although the share of resources going to Agriculture fell from 14·8 to 11·8 per cent in the first two Plans, the total amount spent at current prices rose from Rs. 7,240 crores to 9,790 crores.[110] The actual increase of 1 per cent in the Plan allocation reflects a rise from Rs. 9,790 million to Rs. 17,605 million for the Second and the Third Plan, measured at 1960–1 prices. It is not very clear, therefore, what significance should be attached to the percentage figures in the Plan outlays, especially if we bear in mind that a very large proportion of the total outlay in Agriculture is done in the private sector, so that the Plan outlay going to Agriculture is not a measure of its total command over resources. And on all accounts, the amount of self-financed investment in agriculture is seriously under-estimated and this is one of the arguments used to put the case for increasing the share of Plan outlay going to Agriculture.

There is, moreover, another important objection to the line of argument that we have been criticizing above. It is that it assumes implicitly that the Industrial sector and the Agricultural sector are isolated from each other. Whether a particular amount of industrial investment benefits agriculture or not depends very much on the form the investment takes. Is it to be in fertilizers or in machine tools? If it is in steel or cement, does the steel or cement produced go to the agricultural sector or the industrial sector? Is it structurals or sheet steel or alloy steel? Is the cement used for urban buildings or grain-stores? In this context, it does not do to point to the input–output structure of the economy which shows that agriculture buys very little of the industrial inputs.[111] For the reasons behind this factor have been largely technological.

It is not our contention to argue for or against the view that Indian Planners have or have not neglected agriculture. Indeed, we have every sympathy with the view that in the context of overall economic

[110] There are no published figures for First Plan outlays at constant prices available to us.

[111] India Planning Commission, *Material Balances* (1966), Table N.12, p. 13.

policy-making, the importance of agriculture to the economy and particularly the specific conditions necessary for bringing about a substantial increase in agricultural output had been seriously misunderstood by the Planners until about the middle 'sixties. Our objection is to the rather simple view of the planning process that the above criticisms take and the policy conclusion that an increase in the share of resources going to the agricultural sector is the key priority for planning for agricultural development in India.

We have so far been arguing explicitly that the evidence regarding the share in the end-use of resources going to agriculture needs to be interpreted with greater care and implicitly that until the middle 'sixties at least, resources have not been the critical constraint to the development of Indian agriculture. It is, therefore, all the more important to emphasize that in this respect the situation has altered radically in recent years with the onset of the 'green revolution'. The pivotal innovation in this is the development of new strains of seeds that can benefit from the increased application of fertilizers and other inputs, working out of optimal dosages and combinations of these inputs with reference to particular soil and climatic conditions and most important, ensuring of the spread of these techniques to a large enough area of the country to make a substantial impact on total production. It is today increasingly the case that, with the availability of new techniques, the possibility of expanding agricultural production would come to depend more and more on the building up of the output capacity of the fertilizer and other related industries, ensuring an adequate organizational framework for the proper distribution of these inputs and the working out of 'risk-insurance' schemes that are essential for the successful adoption of these high-yield, high-risk varieties.[112] It is debatable to what extent this technological revolution itself could have been speeded up by more emphasis being given to this problem in earlier years. That depends very much on one's views of the nature of the innovatory process. It is true to say, however, that part of the reasons for the failure in earlier years to discover new strains lies to some extent in the type of research work in this field rather than on the volume of research work that was being done in the country. This brings us on to the issue of the role of price policy in the development of the agricul-

[112] See Brown (1970), Desai (1969), India Ministry of Food and Agriculture (1966), Lipton (1968), Millikan (1968), Minhas (1969), Panse (1966), Robinson (1970). There is evidence that the qualitative importance of the new inventions has led to a very high degree of optimism in official circles as to the amount of effort that is required to make a sufficient impact on the field of agricultural production, and the policies required to control the distributive effects of it. One of the most important pieces of work is Wharton (1969).

tural sector. On the one hand, economists like Mason, Millikan or Lipton have argued that one reason for the failure of agricultural output to expand lies in the deterioration of agricultural terms of trade. On the other, an opposite view has been put forward by Dantwala. At a more specific level, Raj and others have argued that the use by the Government of P.L. 480 imports to keep down the urban price of foodgrains has resulted in a low rate of growth of wheat production.[113] The latest empirical study by Thamarajakshi finds, however, that prices paid by agriculturalists for non-agricultural products have risen less rapidly than the prices paid by non-agriculturalists for agricultural products, and that the net barter terms of trade have moved in favour of agriculture at a slow rate.[114] The general debate as to whether the terms of trade have or have not deteriorated is subject to the familiar problems of agreeing on what is to be taken as the 'optimal' level for the index and also on the type of assumptions that are made about the producers.[115] in particular, whether they are profit maximizers in the strict sense or whether they aim at a given or simply a high rate of profit within a particular field of operation.[116] The conclusion is, however, much clearer – that by and large, the use of the foodgrains available under the U.S.P.L. 480 has led to a serious maldistribution of foodgrains. By concentrating on distribution through fair-price shops in the urban centres, it has tended partially to subsidize the not-so-poor classes at the expense of the urban and rural poor. By its failure to use the P.L. 480 imports to build up buffer-stocks, it has tended to increase the reliance of the economy on food imports in years of poor harvests, thus tightening the balance of payments constraint. The problem becomes more strongly highlighted if we recall that official policy does not stress institutional reforms as the main plank in its egalitarian policy. Employment creation for its own sake has never been regarded as a policy objective by the planners. Yet, no-

[113] See footnote 107 for sources; see also Dantwala (1967).

[114] Thamarajakshi (1969). According to Dr Thamarjakshi, 'The income terms of trade have registered a significant rate of increase thus indicating the improved purchasing power of the agricultural sector for non-agricultural commodities. While the rate of rise in the prices received by agriculture compensated for that in the prices that agriculture has had to pay for non-agricultural inputs, the cost of agricultural inputs for the non-agricultural sector has increased at a faster rate than the prices paid by agriculture for all non-agricultural products', *Ibid*, p. A.99.

[115] Bhagwati and Chakravarty (1969), pp. 48 f.

[116] For example, Mason (1966) and others have pointed out the relatively high level of fertilizer prices in India. while Dantwala (1967) has pointed out that the rate of profit from using fertilizers stands at around 400 per cent for some farmers.

body seems to have bothered to ask how, in a market economy with a growing population, additional purchasing power is to be channelled to the poor except through the creation of employment and rising real wages, which are seriously inhibited for the agricultural labourers, the small peasant who meets his food requirement partly through the market and the urban proletariat by rising food prices.

The fact that the problem of creating employment is an integral part of the problem of distributing the gains from the development process, which is in turn one of the key priorities to be settled in a planned economy, needs constant underlining. On the other hand, the very serious administrative problems of implementing a policy of anything approaching compulsory procurement need not be underestimated. Yet, it needs to be pointed out that it is partly a question of priorities. The Government does intercede very substantially in the field of industrial development and foreign exchange controls. It can be asked to what extent it would yield a higher return in terms of the achievements of Plan objectives to shift some administrative resources tied up in these fields on to the field of food distribution. Moreover, the failure of the current food procurement policies of the Government are due in no mean measure to the antagonism of the States and certain vested interests aligned to the State Governments to such a policy.[117] It is a matter for debate whether the problem of food procurement can be made part of the bargaining process for the distribution of central resources that goes on in the Finance Commission. No doubt there are great difficulties here. Yet surely no one would minimize the dangers for the political and social stability of the nation that has been created over the last twenty years with a mixture of hard talk about political realities and soft performance in dealing with the problems of inequality and poverty. It is worth noting, however, that although critics have disagreed amongst themselves as to the right level of prices for agricultural products or about the right kind or degree of control to be exercised over the market, they have not seriously questioned the feasibility of planning for agricultural development within the private sector. We are not in this context thinking of policies of land nationalization but rather of the limited problem of whether any price policy can work, in the sense of fulfilling the various policy objectives, without serious conflicts arising in the process. For example, foodgrains are an important item in the consumption of rich and poor alike. In an economy where total production is limited and where large inequalities in the distribution of income are tolerated, a

[117] Nicolson (1968); Raj Krishna (1967), for a critical discussion of the Government's procurement policy.

proportionately large amount will be cornered by the relatively well-to-do. A food target that can provide 'enough' for the really poor will, given tastes and other factors, contribute much more than enough to the former class. So that the total amount that has to be produced will be greater than the socially desired optimum on the basis of a more egalitarian pattern of income distribution. Moreover, much of the argument on the price policy issue confuses relative income differences and absolute levels of income. Thus, the argument that the low price of foodgrains is socially undesirable because it acts as a subsidy to the urban sector, ignores the fact that a large proportion of the urban population have extremely low absolute levels of income, which do not allow much room for a squeezing of consumption margins through higher levels of food prices. The structure of the rural and urban sector is also not homogeneous. There are landless labourers in agriculture, making up roughly 25 per cent of agricultural *workers*, who would suffer from higher food prices in so far as they are not paid in kind. Higher food prices will benefit the rich peasants, who are very much wealthier than many sections of the urban labour force. Under these circumstances, it can seriously be questioned whether the problem of distribution of foodgrains can be left to the market, with a Government playing a marginal role in that sphere, or whether a system of comprehensive rationing and compulsory procurement of foodgrains is not essential for the success of a programme of development that makes a serious inroad into the problem of mass poverty.

This brings us to the remaining criticisms that relate to the neglect of institutional and other constraints. We are not competent to assay the work of social anthropologists in this field, except to point to the very serious contribution to the understanding of the political and social processes made in the studies by Bailey, Beteille, Epstein, Gough and others.[118] On the issue of land reform, it is generally agreed that beyond the abolition of the zaminders, which turned absentee landlords into *rentiers*, any progress made in this field falls far short of objectives. This is well illustrated by the works of Dandekar, Ladejinsky, etc., as well as many other pieces of research done in this field. Tenancy rights remain ill-defined and unprotected, rents much higher than the fixed ceilings. What is at issue here is not the intention of the planners but the lack of implementation of the programme at the State-level. The possible economic consequences of such failure depend on what view one holds about the relationship between size of holdings and productivity, the viable size of peasant holdings and the role of incentives in the process.

[118] Bailey (1957), Beteille (1965), Epstein (1962), Gough (1955).

Here, as in so many other fields, the findings of research are in conflict.[119]

In the light of this situation, it is perhaps not unreasonable to assume that returns to scale in relation to the size of land-holdings are constant, which argues for a lack of conflict between the efficiciency and equity objectives of a policy of redistribution. As regards the influence of tenancy conditions on incentives, the Hanumantha Rao–Minhas view would not regard this as a serious impediment to increase in output, whereas the Sen-Varghese view would argue the opposite. In this context, an earlier work by Raj Krishna, which questions the whole basis of the land reform policy and stresses the necessity for co-operative farming, on the grounds that the average size of land-holdings resulting from a radical policy of land redistribution would yield non-viable farms, is worth noting. For it raises the question of the extent to which a growing rural population can be absorbed in agricultural production and stresses an area of policy making, that of the possibility of diversification of the rural economy, where very little systematic thinking has been done by Planners.[120]

IV

Apart from the agricultural 'bottleneck' that shows itself largely in the scarcity of foodgrains and partly in the form of pressure on supplies of certain categories of exportables such as oilseeds and coffee, the other key constraint to the development of the economy has been the foreign exchange constraint. Without doubt, these two are the critical constraints to the growth of the economy. They are not identical in their operations.[121] The agricultural constraint mainly affects the supply of consumer goods, it is quantitatively very large and it shows itself in the generation of inflationary pressure

[119] The main contributions are: Hanumantha Rao (1963, 1966), Majumdar (1963), Rudra (1968) and Sen (1964). On land reform see the review article by Dandekar (1962); see also Ladejinsky (1965), and George (1968). On the importance of tenancy, see Hanumantha Rao (1965), Minhas and Srinivasan (1968), and Sen and Varghese (1966).

[120] Raj Krishna (1959); see also Lewis (1962), India Estimates Committee, *55th Report* (1964).

[121] Although they are not identical in their operations, they are not unrelated. Failure of the supply of wage-goods, which in the Indian context are mainly produced in the agricultural sector to keep pace with demand, tightens the balance of payments constraints. This is brought about partly through inflation resulting from a rise in wage-goods prices and partly through the need to import food. A tighter balance of payments position, in its turn, causes serious dislocation in the industrial sector, where a relatively high level of imports of spares and raw materials are required to maintain productive levels near to existing capacity.

within the economy, jeopardizing the stability of the economy. More than anything else it accounts for the continuing, grinding poverty of the country, the persistence of malnutrition and of an intolerable degree of inequality of incomes. In the short run, it can be partially eased through the import of foodgrains, which tightens up the balance of payments constraint. The foreign exchange constraint is quantitatively small in that the net flow of foreign resources adds only a small proportion to the total availability of resources, it mainly affects investment, jeopardizes the future growth prospects of the economy and is a root cause of internal political strife and unrest. It cannot be by-passed in the short run, although foreign resources may be more dispensable in the long run than domestically produced foodgrains.

Both are major constraints. It is, therefore, surprising that in contrast to the problems of agricultural development, there is as yet no serious study of the foreign resources problem in India. Not that this has stopped economists and politicians from offering solutions to these problems! From the point of view of an expert, it would appear that the less well-understood the problem of foreign resources, the greater is the scarcity value of advice given. On the one hand, there have been very severe criticisms from aid givers of the Government's mismanagement of the foreign exchange problem. On the other, important bodies of intellectual opinion in India have accused the Government of having done too well out of foreign aid, to the detriment of the country's long-term future.

As the matter cannot be set right in a few pages, we confine ourselves to a few preliminary remarks on the Indian experience and the lessons, if any, that can be drawn from it. One aspect of this problem is tied in closely with the development of the industrial sector in India, which is discussed in the following section. Here we confine ourselves to the rough dimensions of the problem and to a consideration of the impact that aid has made on the economy. We also discuss very briefly certain policy aspects of the problem of aid administration.[122]

For our present purpose, the period from 1950–1 to the present day can be divided into three sub-periods: from the beginning to the foreign exchange crisis in 1956–7, from 1956–7 to the devaluation of

[122] We have confined ourselves to a discussion of the role of foreign aid and neglected the question of private foreign investment. Readers should consult Kidron (1965). Various issues of the Reserve Bank's monthly *Bulletins* also contain articles on aspects of private foreign investment in India. See, e.g., the issues of January 1960, May 1961, March 1964, April 1966, July 1967 and March 1968.

the rupee in June 1966, and the subsequent three years. India started the planning process with a trade balance in deficit and her current account balance in surplus. Even during the First Plan, which made modest demands on imports, the trade balance was worsening, but this was adequately covered by accumulated sterling balances held by India.[123] The two years 1956 and 1957, which were the early years of the Second Plan, saw a very substantial rise in imports, partly as a result of direct Plan expenditure but also partly due to substantial increases in imports of consumer goods. Foreign exchange reserves declined in the two years by some $1,000 million, leading to the establishment of very severe controls on imports, and strict regulation of foreign exchange use within the economy. This acute balance of payments position has continued ever since. The devaluation of 1966 marks a watershed not because it has had any substantial impact on exports and imports. Indeed, the I.M.F. apart, it is doubtful if anyone is official circles both in and outside India will hold an opposite view in this respect. Its importance lies in some major changes that were introduced in the field of foreign exchange administration in the country, simultaneously with the devaluation.[124]

This acute foreign exchange position facing the economy has been made tolerable by the very substantial volume of foreign aid India has received during the 'sixties. In terms of foreign exchange, India has received $9,400 million during 1951–66. This is the largest amount received by a single country. However, in *per capita* terms, this has worked out at roughly $2·5 per head, which is one of the lowest figures for aid. To what extent was this position avoidable, to what extent was the foreign resource gap ameliorated by suitable policies? On the export side, it is true to say that until well into the Third Plan period the official view was held that India's export prospects were severely limited by factors outside her control. Very little was done to promote exports, although it is now clear that, for a number of commodities, exports were limited by supply factors, which could have been manipulated by domestic policies, given a sufficiently high degree of priority.[125]

Whether we believe that the matter could have been improved in

[123] The reserves stood at $2,161 million in 1950–1, including I.M.F. drawing rights. The average level in the Third Plan period was around $600 million. Even this gives an optimistic picture, because the import requirements of the economy are now higher, and imports of non-essential goods are very severely controlled.

[124] For a study of the licensing experience, see Bhagwati and Desai (1970); see also India Estimates Committee, *9th Report* (1967).

[125] For the 'orthodox' position, see Patel (1960), and the very detailed study by Manmohan Singh (1964).

terms of reducing the import requirements of the economy or not depends partly on the level at which the question is put. If we take the basic strategy underlying the Indian plans as given, that is if we believe that the basic decision to undertake planning was right, that the stress laid on building up an industrial base to the economy was right and that to attempt to do this by manipulating a mixed economy rather than going over to a command economy was right, then we must ask to what extent was the allocation of foreign exchange carried out efficiently by the Government. The answer that we give below is that in many ways the job could have been better managed, particularly if we look back with the hindsight denied the poor civil servant, except in memoirs. However, the improvements that could have been brought about through the unilateral action of the Government were marginal and they would not have abolished the need for foreign aid to bridge a resource gap. The other set of questions, that call into dispute the basic strategy itself, are more fundamental and are essentially a matter of political rather than economic priorities. They are only briefly touched upon in the following pages.

The following Table gives the basic magnitudes of the problem:

Table X

PLAN OUTLAY: SOURCES OF FINANCE
(Rs. crores, at current prices)

	First Plan	*Second Plan*	*Third Plan*	*1966–8*
1. Domestic Surpluses	754	1,230	2,908	872
2. Domestic Borrowing	1,017	2,393	2,113	1,285
3. Total Domestic Resources	1,771	3,623	5,021	2,157
4. Loans and Grants	189	1,049		
from abroad (net)	—	—	2,423	1,779
including PL480 aid	—	160	1,084	712
5. Total Resources	1,960	4,672	7,444	3,936
6. Total Investment	3,360	6,750	11,370	5,868
a. Public	1,460	3,450	7,180	3,818
b. Private	1,900	3,300	4,190	2,050
7. Item 4 as % item 6	5·6	15·1	21·3	30·3

Source: India Planning Commission, *Indicators* (1968), Tables 12, 13. Investment figures are approximate and net of inter-sector transfers); India Planning Commission (1969), pp. 78, 80.

One point to note is that for the whole period, the bulk of domestic investment has been financed out of domestic resources. Indeed, in so far as the investment figures for the private sectors are likely to be under-estimates, the proportion financed by foreign resources is to an extent overstated. This is counter-balanced by two disquieting factors. One is that the share of domestic borrowing in total domestic resources has been very large, although there has been some improvement since the Second Plan in the balance between the two sources. The other is that the share in total investment of foreign resources has been rising alarmingly. Here the figures, being net of debt repayment, seriously understate the dependence of the economy on foreign aid. As Table X above shows, the total amount of aid authorized to and utilized by India has been very much more substantial. In recent years, approximately 28 per cent of gross aid and 26 per cent of export earnings have been required for debt servicing.[126]

The commodity-pattern of imports financed out of foreign resources has undergone significant shifts. Up to the middle of the Third Plan period, the bulk of the imports were made up of capital goods and industrial inputs. The main components of the former were imports of iron and steel and machinery. Since the downturn in 1965–6, these categories have become less important, steel imports particularly having fallen sharply. Many of the imports in later years have consisted of foodgrains and fertilizer imports, as well as products like fuel oils and non-ferrous metals that are not obtainable in India.[127]

The overall figures do not indicate the range of problems that reliance on foreign resources in the form of aid causes, or the various costs that it imposes on the economy. In all this the crucial point to bear in mind is that resources obtained through foreign aid are not perfect substitutes for free foreign exchange obtained through exports.[128] The real purchasing power of a given volume of aid depends on what conditions are laid down relating to commodity or country-tying, relative prices in the donor country and the world market, etc. The net resource transfer over time depends, moreover,

[126] India Ministry of Finance, *Pocket Book* (1968), India Ministry of Finance (1968–9). The figures are for 1967–8. Since then both debt charges and exports have risen, but gross aid has fallen.

[127] For imports, see India Ministry of Finance, *Survey* (1967–8).

[128] Whereas many textbooks on international economics stress the fact that aid supplements a country's resources, not many stress the point that a $-worth of free foreign exchange earned through trade is not equivalent in purchasing power to $-worth of aid given under the existing rules of the game. This is irrespective of the argument about inter-temporal sacrifices.

on the terms of repayment, including interest rates, length of period of repayment, grace periods, requirements of payments in hard currency and similar factors.

One of the key problems in India has been that of utilization of external assistance or aid authorized.[129] The Table below gives the relevant figures:

Table XI

AID AUTHORIZED BY DONOR COUNTRIES AND UTILIZED BY INDIA

(Rs. crores at pre-devaluation rate of exchange)

	Up to end of First Plan	*During Second Plan*	*During Third Plan*	*During 1966–7*
Aid authorized	381·8	2,540·0	2,938·5	991·1
Aid utilized	201·7	1,430·2	2,868·9	701·9

Source: India Ministry of Finance (1968–9), Table 7.2, 7.3, pp. A.66–A.73.

The problem which was most acute during the Second Plan and the early years of the Third Plan has now somewhat eased. However, the total amount involved being large, even a small percentage of aid unutilized implies a loss of the benefits to be derived from a very scarce resource. It has, therefore, attracted serious attention. On the one hand, the problem lies with the efficiency with which the recipient bodies, i.e. the Ministry of Finance and other Ministries concerned with the allocation of aid, can handle aid. Many critics have argued that the Indian Government's excessive reliance on foreign exchange controls and industrial licensing have caused substantial avoidable delays in aid utilization, so that it is somewhat artificial to talk about scarcity of foreign resources as being a bottleneck. Official opinion in India, on the other hand, has pointed to certain forms in which aid is given as the main cause of non-utilization of aid. There is much to be said on both sides. Without in any way trying to apportion blame, one or two points are worth making.

The crucial distinction that has to be made in this connection is that between project-aid and non-project-aid plus free foreign exchange left over after repayment of debt charges. The bulk of the aid that remains non-utilized at any point of time is project-aid. To that extent, it is true to say that in India, lack of availability of

[129] Useful factual information is contained in India Ministry of Finance (1967–8), India Ministry of Finance (1964), and India Estimates Committee, *30th Report* (1968). India Estimates Committee, *11th Report* (1967) also contains a great deal of interesting material, albeit little systematic analysis.

project-aid has not been a serious 'bottleneck'. The main problem has been the difficulty of drawing up and approving worthwhile projects and keeping them going at a rate sufficient to use up aid that has been authorized as it becomes available. Here, as we shall point out later in the following section, very substantial delays have arisen in some cases, some of which could at least have been avoided.[130] On the other hand, there is much to be said for the view that there is danger in haste, if the urge to utilize aid leads to the sanction of projects which are not adequately vetted, and turn out to have been ill-conceived. Which way one leans in the end depends on two points of fact. To what extent is it possible to maintain a shopping list of viable projects, so that delays in project preparation or rejection of one project do not hold up utilization of aid in the pipe-line? And to what extent are the administrative delays avoidable, in the sense that the decision-taking process can be speeded up without a substantial decline in the net value added by the authorized projects?

In India, the major scarcity has been of foreign resources that can be utilized to finance the flow of current imports, chiefly foodgrains and industrial inputs of various kinds.[131] Here, although the licensing processes are complex and time-consuming, there has not been substantial backlogs in the utilization of available resources.[132] On the contrary, the problem has been that of ensuring an adequate flow of foreign exchange that will enable a supply of imported inputs to be maintained, that in turn will enable the desired rate of utilization of productive capacity in the economy. Much of the responsibility for this scarcity lies with the donors, with their strong preference for project aid.

The exchange control and licensing procedures referred to above have been the result of the acute foreign exchange situation, at least in the short run. It is arguable that the operation of licensing regulations has caused a premium to be placed on creation of new capacity rather than the utilization of existing capacity, thus seriously exacerbating the reliance of the economy on foreign resources for a given volume of output. That is to say, it has put an implicit premium on capital goods, as opposed to current inputs: the net value added per unit of the latter being under existing conditions higher within

[130] In recent years, budgetary difficulties in financing the local cost component of projects have also hindered aid utilization.

[131] MacDougall (1964).

[132] A standard lag in the allocation mechanism does not increase the backlog of aid unutilized, although it might seriously delay allocation of foreign exchange to particular users. Unless, of course, the number of applicants, *who could qualify for foreign exchange allocation under the existing criteria*, is rising.

the period of particular Plans. It is also arguable that the procedure for 'clearance from indigenous angle', which is one of the cornerstones of the whole regulatory system, is cumbersome and takes little account of relative costs of alternative sources of supply and net foreign exchange saving.[133]

We turn now to a consideration of the various costs to the economy of foreign aid. It has been pointed out above that a given amount of gross aid given to India adds much less to total foreign resources available to the country, owing to the need for servicing the volume of existing debt, to which the Government rightly gives high priority. Excepting the Centrally Planned Economies, the debt repayments have to be in the form of hard currency, irrespective of whether the original aid was country- and/or commodity-tied or not. The actual burden of debt repayment is, therefore, often greater than the nominal one. In addition, country-tying of aid has imposed an additional burden on India, where the commodity prices of the relevant category of goods are higher in the donor country, compared to world prices.[134] There is no detailed study of the magnitude of this problem, but in rough terms the cost of tying on the average has been about 10 per cent of total aid received.[135] A study by U.N.C.T.A.D. for the chemical industries in India gives the figure of 14 per cent for aid given by the United States.[136]

The costs imposed by the country- and commodity-tying of aid have become obvious. However, there are other costs which are less so. At least, some of the costs have come to be appreciated only after experience in dealing with aid. The first among these is the case of the commodity imports obtained under the U.S. P.L. 480, consisting mainly of wheat, but also containing some other foodstuff and agricultural raw materials. The benefit derived from these is that it enables the country to increase the supply of basic consumer goods and at times staves off starvation. However, there are costs attached to it. Although they are initially paid for in terms of rupees, which are re-lent to the Government and thus virtually become blocked currencies, they have to be imported on American bottoms. The freight charges have to be defrayed in hard currency and the U.S. freight rates are higher than world rates. Moreover, a certain proportion of the rupee balances that are generated are used to defray the costs of maintaining the United States diplomatic presence in India and in loans to private industry, which would presumably give

[133] On the 'clearance from indigenous angle' see pp. 74-7 below.

[134] Two excellent studies are Bhagwati (1968) and Haq (1965), the latter on Pakistan.

[135] Patel (1968).

[136] Lal (1968).

rise to an equivalent inflow of free foreign exchange in the absence of the counterpart funds.[137]

More important than these have been the effects of P.L. 480 imports on the Government efforts to mobilize domestic resources, and on its agricultural policy. Many critics have argued that the provision of substantial budgetary support given by the existence of the counterpart funds has enabled the Government to 'go soft' in its efforts to raise additional tax revenue.[138] Even more numerous have been the criticisms, which are raised both in India and the United States, that the availability of supplies of foodgrains at subsidized prices has led the Government, both directly and indirectly, to ignore the long-run problem of food production in the country.[139]

Coming to that part of foreign aid which does not consist of commodity aid, we can note some of the difficulties that have arisen in this field also. Firstly, the point made above about the budgetary effects of availability of counterpart funds can also be made about foreign aid in general. It will be seen from Table X above, that a substantial proportion of total investment has been financed out of external resources, most of it in the Public Sector. The same is true of public sector development outlay. On the other hand, the fact that such budgetary support extended by the availability of external resources has enabled the Government to finance a growing burden of defence expenditure must have helped the development process. Defence expenditure, however necessary, is non-developmental outlay and would, in the absence of external resources, have made even larger demands on total available resources.

A fundamental if somewhat abstract criticism of the Government's foreign exchange allocation policy, as well as of its industrial licensing policy, is that it has given scant attention to the distributive effects of particular patterns of allocation. A developing economy that is subject to a severe balance of payments constraint develops substantial pockets of excess demand.[140] If, at the same time, there

[137] The loans to the private sector are the so-called Cooley loans, which have played a more important part in Pakistan than in India. Counterpart funds are the rupee funds that are paid into the United States account as payment for P.L. 480 imports.

[138] See India Planning Commission, *Material Balances* (1966), Table F.R. 2, pp. 117–18 for a detailed breakdown of public sector financing. Figures for individual Plans will be found in the relevant Plan documents.

[139] Raj, *Indian Economic Review*, 1966, Rath and Patvardhan (1967), Bardhan (1966); for a good study of one aspect of the problem, arguing that wheat imports under P.L. 480 could have been purchased and distributed more efficiently, see Sundaram (1967).

[140] For the effects of 'excess demand' on industrial efficiency, see below pp. 72-3.

exist large inequalities in the distribution of income and wealth within the economy, then the division of the incremental benefits of growth is decided to a very large extent by the availability of particular types of commodities and the non-availability of others. Over time this depends in turn on the relative rates of expansion of output capacity in various branches of production. In the Indian economy this in turn has depended very largely on the allocation of foreign exchange. Particular patterns of allocation have, therefore, carried with them implicit decisions as to who should be the immediate beneficiaries of the growth process. This has been exacerbated by the inability of the Government to control the end use of certain strategic inputs in the growth process, such as skilled manpower, steel or cement. Some of the most basic decisions of development strategy – who should be the beneficiaries of the growth process, where are the limited immediate benefits arising out of the growth of the economy most needed and how to ensure that that is where they go – have all been ignored and allowed to go by default. The social and political effects of this act of sophisticated oversight are there today for all to see.

We should add in passing that many important changes have been made to the mechanism for allocation of foreign exchange within the economy since the 1966 devaluation. Indeed, the need for a devaluation was argued to arise as much from the need to rationalize an impossibly cumbersome system of licenses and controls as from a need to promote exports. A detailed study of these developments is to be found in the forthcoming volume by Bhagwati and Desai.[141] Most important among these are the greater freedom from detailed controls offered to producers for imports of current inputs and measures to aid the more efficient producers in getting a larger share of foreign exchange allocations.

In lieu of a summary, it can fairly be said that in Indian experience, the policy of calling on foreign resources to fill a domestic resource gap has turned out to have implications quite unforeseen. The costs of foreign aid have turned out to be higher, its benefits below the expectations of either side. Most important for policy purposes has been the realization that foreign aid is not a homogeneous, pliable substance that can be moulded to one's own requirements. It is an imperfect substitute for free foreign exchange and what it can contribute to an economy's development depends as much on the conditions it carries as on its quantum. Although in recent years there has been some questioning of the policy towards foreign aid, there is as yet no serious attempt to study the social and economic effects, good

[141] Bhagwati and Desai (1970); see also reference to footnote (127) above.

and bad, of foreign aid on Indian economy.[142] The role of foreign aid in Indian economic growth is closely linked with the course and nature of the process of industrial development in India. The two are linked in the realm of strategy, in the role allocated to foreign resources in the industrialization process, and the shape given to that process to conserve scarce foreign exchange. They are linked, too, in the area of tactics, for the process of industrial licensing and foreign exchange control are integral parts of the mechanism through which the Government has tried to control the allocation of resources in a 'mixed economy'. In this concluding section, we shall look at the main features of industrial development during the Plan period, the workings of the licensing system and the rationale of the Government's industrial development policy.[143]

V

In many ways, the development of the industrial sector during the last twenty years is one of the most heartening features of economic development in India. It has attracted much criticism, some of it well merited, much of it ill-informed and ill-conceived. By and large, in terms of technical achievement in a developing country, it is no inconsiderable achievement. In terms of economic performance, if world prices are taken as a guide, it still leaves much to be desired.

In considering the profile of industrial development since 1951, we have to bear in mind both the low level and the relatively narrow degree of specialization of industrial activity in India.[144] Some of the basic statistics relating to both these features are given in Table XII on page 70.

It will be seen from Table XII that the level of industrial production in India has risen consistently since 1951. There was relatively little growth in the early years of the First Plan and the bulk of the increase in industrial production occurred during the Second and the early years of the Third Plan. The rate of growth of industrial production fell from 9·2 per cent in 1963 to 5·0 per cent in 1965. Since then, the level of production remained virtually stagnant until 1968,

[142] See Raj (1969). Patel (1970) raises some questions of fundamental importance in a much wider context.

[143] See the detailed study by Bhagwati and Desai; also India Estimates Committee, *9th Report* (1967), Medhora (1968); a definitive study of industrial concentration is Hazari (1966). One of the few case studies is Baranson (1967), useful as far as it goes but written from an extremely narrow point of view.

[144] Of course, these are relative terms. Even in 1951, India was a very untypical under-developed country, in having a fairly large and diversified industrial sector *compared to other poor countries*.

Table XII

SELECTED INDEXES OF INDUSTRIAL PRODUCTION

Industry	*1951*	*1955*	*1965*	*1967*	*Weights 1956*	*1960*
		(1960 = 100)			%	%
1. Mining	66·6	74·6	131·7	135·8	7·47	9·72
2. Manufacturing	54·6	73·8	153·8	148·8	—	84·91
a. Food processing	66·9	75·9	122·2	111·7	12·58	12·09
b. Textiles	79·7	94·1	114·8	107·3	41·76	27·06
c. Chemicals	42·4	60·1	153·9	172·2	3·56	7·26
incl. Fertilizers			252·3	341·8	0·60	0·46
d. Petroleum	11·0	56·1	158·7	234·2	3·79	1·34
e. Basic metals	46·5	53·3	180·1	181·8	9·25	7·38
incl. Steel	—	—	185·3	177·7	7·48	6·23
f. Machiner (excl. g, h)	22·2	35·5	316·0	299·3	—	3·38
Machine tools	—	—	352·2	321·0	—	0·39
g. Electrical machinery	26·3	49·0	204·4	243·4	—	3·05
h. Transport equipment	19·6	99·2	206·3	144·9	—	7·77
i. Electricity	35·7	51·5	190·9	230·7	3·68	5·37

Source: Revised Index of Industrial Production – from India Planning Commission, *Indicators* (1968).
1956 weights from Reserve Bank of India, *Report on Currency and Finance* (Annual).

when a fairly rapid recovery began in particular sectors of industry. Against this background, three broad patterns of behaviour are discernible. Firstly, mining and the traditional industries like textiles and food processing have increased at a relatively lower rate throughout the period. They have suffered varying but moderate degrees of retardation since 1965. The second group consists of the petroleum-chemical complexes. They have expanded at a higher than average rate, partly illusory because of the low level of production in the early years and they have continued to rise throughout the period. The last group, the largest in terms of new investment, consists of the basic metals, especially iron and steel and the machinery and equipment groups. Although they expanded at a higher than average rate between 1951–65, they have been the most severely hit by the depression. This last factor is of considerable analytical significance and will be referred to later in this section.[145]

The last two columns of the table indicate in a very crude manner

[145] See pp. 83 below.

the change in the degree of specialization that has taken place within the industrial sector. Even within the period 1956–60, we can note the declining importance of textiles as the major sector and the very substantial increase in the shares of the so-called 'heavy industries'. The contrast will be stronger, *a fortiori*, if we compare the pre-1950 pattern to the late 'sixties.

A very important feature of these developments has been felt in the external sector. On the one hand, it has enabled the commodity-composition of exports to be altered away from the traditional exports such as cotton, jute, tea, sugar, etc., towards the new manufactures, such as light engineering goods, iron ore and steel. One cannot be sure at this stage, however, whether this is a trend that is likely to be maintained in the future.[146]

Table XIII

SHARE OF IMPORTS IN TOTAL ESTIMATED SUPPLIES (Per cent)

Commodity	*1950–1*	*1955–6*	*1966–7*
Foodgrains	5·9	1·7	9·7
Raw jute	27·8	12·3	16·9
Textile machinery	N.A.	67·6	58·2
Machine tools (metal working)	89·8	84·8	51·2
Iron and steel	25·2	39·9	9·7
Bicycles	62·5	22·4	neg.
Newsprint	100·0	95·2	78·4

Source: India Ministry of Finance, *Survey* (1967–8), Table 6.9, p. A.64.

The other effect in the external sector has been felt on the side of imports. Import-substitution, as is well known, has played a key role in the formulation of industrial development strategy in India. The quantitative effect of the industrialization policy on import-dependence of the economy is difficult to estimate. At current rupee prices, the level of import has been stabilized around the Rs. 1,100 crores since 1956–7, while national income has risen substantially both in real and money terms. The rise that the level of imports

[146] Supply problems have always played a larger part in determining the level of exports than the official views are ready to admit. There is some indication that the very encouraging foothold gained by India in recent years in export markets for steel and machinery is in danger of being lost through a larger domestic absorption of these goods, as the level of economic activity picks up.

shows in later years, e.g. since 1964–5, is to be attributed largely to a narrow range of commodities, such as foodgrains and fertilizers. This apparent stability of imports in the face of rising levels of output has been achieved only through very rigorous control over imports, involving the virtual exclusion of consumer goods other than foodgrains, and the creation of a high degree of excess demand for a whole range of manufactured goods.[147] The figures given in Table XIII nevertheless give evidence of a lessening dependence of the economy on imported sources which has been a real feature of industrial development in India.[148] Unfortunately, in some ways the foregoing gives too rosy a picture of industrial development in India. The two disquieting features of the pattern of growth in this sector have been the high level of domestic costs, reflecting low productivity and serious shortfalls in strategic sectors, due to errors in project-planning, delays in construction and in foreign aid negotiations.

One of the most important characteristics of the Indian economy since 1956–7 has been the high degree of excess demand that has been allowed to develop as a result of severe import controls and the limited ability or willingness of the Government to use its fiscal and monetary instruments of control to ease pressure on resources originating from non-developmental expenditure in the private and public sectors. The absence of any degree of external competition has enabled the growth of very inefficient firms. In some lines of production, levels of domestic costs two or three times as high as comparable world prices are not unknown. Paradoxically, the almost total prohibition of imports of what are regarded as non-essential commodities, together with the failure of the licensing system to control the growth of domestic capacity for the production of these commodities, have caused very high cost differences to appear precisely in such lines of production.[149] The waste of resources which this

[147] The rise in the level of imports during the last few years, in the face of an almost stationary level of output, is due to the import of a narrow range of commodities, such as foodgrains and fertilizers. During the recession, industrial production has paradoxically been affected both by low levels of demand and low availability of imports.

[148] These figures have to be interpreted with caution, due to the existence of import controls; they are also figures for particular years when special factors might well have influenced available capacity, production or imports. However, they give a substantially accurate picture. See also Robinson (1970), pp. 17–22.

[149] Durable consumer goods are a good example of such a group of industries. It will be naïve to conclude from this that the Government ought to react to this by the decontrol of these commodities, unless the implicit value judgments that such a policy implies in relation to the distribution of benefits in a developing economy were made explicit by the protagonists.

reflects has been allowed to exist in those lines of production which the Government regards as the least essential for development purposes.[150]

As we have said above, a failure to attain a specific set of targets within a given period of time is not by itself a very serious matter.[151] To argue otherwise is to attribute a degree of omniscience to Planners which they seldom merit. However, it *is* important that such shortfalls should not arise so consistently in strategic sectors as to endanger the growth process itself, and impose very high costs on the economy. Unfortunately, this last danger has not always been avoided in India and the failure to do so has not always been due to unavoidable factors. Failure to attain targets set has been a constant feature of planning in India. They have varied in degree from below 25 per cent of targets set to between 75 to 100 per cent.[152] They have related to such key sectors as basic steel, special and alloy steel, pig iron, sulphuric acid, machinery and fertilizers. Shortfalls that were noticed mid-term in the execution of particular Plans have often not been corrected by the end of the Plan period, or its future recurrence avoided. This has also imposed a very heavy cost on the economy, especially in terms of foreign exchange.

Major problems in the field of project preparation have been experienced in the field of estimation of the level of demand, determining the composition of output required of a plant in view of expected composition of demand. Both these factors have led to major changes having to be made in the design and lay-out of the project after work has begun, this in turn increasing the gestation periods for projects where the normal gestation lags are themselves large. It is worth noticing in this respect that the length of these lags does not appear to be significantly different on the average between the private sector and the public sector projects.[153] Another point of criticism is that Indian Planners have often paid what appears to be a too high regard for minimizing long-run average costs in planning the optimum levels of capacity to be created.[154] This has led to an increase in time taken to complete projects as well as a higher level of short-run costs and low profits. In an extremely stimulating study P.N. Mathur and others have drawn attention to what is an important shortcoming of project planning in certain areas. This study attempts to show that in selected machine tools industries, the technical mix of plants has been determined on such a basis as to

[150] See below p. 76 f. for further discussion. [151] p. 21 above.

[152] A very useful summary of the relevant information is Medhora (1968), Ch. 1.

[153] Reserve Bank of India (1968); for other references, see footnote (166) below. [154] See pp. 77 f. below.

allow for substantial idle plant-capacity even for high levels of demand.[155] This factor, of course, does not affect the period of gestation. It does, however, affect levels of costs and profits of the enterprise. Most of these errors in the formulation and completion of projects can be regarded as being 'avoidable' in the sense that they could have been prevented through a greater degree of efficiency in spheres of activity over which Planners have control.[156] Another set of factors which have contributed both to the relatively high cost of industrial development in India and the many delays that it has been subjected to do not fall into this category. We refer to the fact that much of the new investment in this field has had to be financed out of foreign resources. There are substantial delays built into the system by which foreign aid is allocated and administered. These have added substantially in some cases to the delays and costs of projects. Once the basic decision to rely on external resources has been taken, Planners have very limited control in this field and the resulting delays must be counted as one of the indirect costs of the use of foreign resources.[157]

Apart from the development of industries in the public sector, where the Government has direct control over developments within the limits imposed by reliance on foreign aid to finance the import-content of investment, the Government's chief instrument of control in the field of industrial development in the private sector has been the system of industrial and foreign exchange licensing.[158] It is not possible within the space available to give an account of the complexities of the system.[159] We must, therefore, confine ourselves to outlining its very basic characteristics and point out some of its effects upon the economy.

The motive force behind the licensing sytem is the urgent need to conserve the country's scarce foreign exchange resources. It rests on the not unreasonable assumptions that, in the Indian economy, the market processes will neither generate a demand for imports which is within the country's import capacity nor create an industrial structure consistent with the country's long-term requirements. Foreign resources being an essential requirement for industrial development, and limited in amount, the need is felt both for its

[155] Mathur, Valavade, Kirloskar (1967).

[156] It is largely a question of how quickly one feels planners 'ought' to learn to avoid mistakes. Such judgments must to a large degree be subjective to the critic.

[157] See p. 64 above.

[158] On public sector industries, see p. 77 f. below

[159] Such accounts will be found in Bhagwati and Desai (1970), India Estimates Committee, *9th Report* (1967), India Estimates Committee, *11th Report* (1967), India Estimates Committee, *30th Report* (1968) and Medhora (1968).

rationing and for preventing excessive demand made upon it by the private sector for non-essential purposes, which would make the operation of such a rationing system more difficult.

The licensing procedures are extremely complex in detail and call for the co-ordination of the work of a number of Government Ministries and departments, which is not the least of its problems. It applies to industrial units above a certain minimum size and involves the following steps:

1. The purpose for which the licence is sought, i.e. the industry where the capacity is sought to be expanded, must conform to general plan priorities and qualify for inclusion in the private sector under the Industrial Policy Resolutions of 1948 and 1956.[160]
2. The balance between expected demand and output capacity must be such as to make expansion desirable.
3. The project itself must be economically 'viable'.
4. The foreign exchange component must be approved by the relevant ministries, which depends primarily on –
5. the Directorate General of Trade and Development giving it 'clearance fram the indigenous angle'. This is the corner-stone of the policy and involves the issue of a certificate that the materials for which an import licence is sought are not available within the country. This clause is meant to be strictly interpreted and the high cost of domestic supply or the length of order books of domestic firms are not taken into account in giving clearance.
6. Where the expansion involves new issues of capital, this must be approved by the Capital Issues Committee.
7. Any licences issued must be utilized within specified time periods.

Not all industrial expansion will involve expenditure of foreign exchange directly. On the other hand, foreign exchange may have to be allocated for current inputs that do not require an industrial license. However, the majority of the larger schemes have to be approved under the headings 1 to 5. Since devaluation of the rupee in 1966, the procedures have been simplified in various ways but, as far as new investment is concerned, this is how the system roughly works.

Other than the general charge levied against it that it embodies an excessive reliance on controls and that it has led to an inferior

[160] For text, see India Ministry of Finance, *Pocket Book* (1968) and India Planning Commission (1956). The terms of the resolution are very broadly applied.

allocation of resources to that which would have resulted from the market process, how has the operation of the system influenced the pattern of industrial development?

In this connection, we have to bear in mind that the Plan documents lay out the objectives of industrial policy in very general terms and offer no concrete set of criteria by which applications for licenses can be selected or rejected.[161] Applications for licenses have to be considered in a fairly detailed manner, in relation to their technical and economic characteristics. The Plan documents do not lay down any very precise rules of guidance in these fields. The licensing authorities have, therefore, had to devise their own *ad hoc* criteria and these may or may not be entirely in line with the objectives laid down in the Plans.

It has been said before that the *raison d'être* of the licensing system is the foreign exchange scarcity. In practice, the desire to curb the relative growth of the private sector plays a much smaller part in its continuation. In the allocation of licenses, most attention has been given to the import content and the foreign exchange requirements of proposed projects. Where either the foreign exchange content is deemed to be low or where foreign collaboration ensures a supply of foreign exchange, the Government has been more willing to grant licenses, other things being equal. This preoccupation with the necessity to conserve foreign exchange has at times led to a serious neglect of the domestic resource costs of new capacity and the distributive effects of particular patterns of investment in a developing economy.[162] Construction materials, steel, transport facilities and, not least, managerial skills are all scarce resources and their use involves opportunity costs. Moreover, where overall balance between demand and supply has to be maintained through reductions in public expenditure, an additional burden is imposed on the economy. This is because the beneficiaries of public expenditure may be poorer as a class than the consumers of the products of manufactured goods such as synthetic textiles. The net result is a worsening of the distribution of real income within the community. It has to be borne in mind also that the contribution made by an industry to the development process depends on the end use of the product of that industry. Steel that is used to build consumer durables is different from this point of view to that used for building a fertilizer plant or a tractor. As the Government has greater control over the distribution of output of the public sector industries than over those of the private sector, these problems are likely to be exag-

[161] The Planning Commission does issue a guide-line for project evaluation.
[162] See Section IV above.

gerated in the type of cases we are discussing.[163] There is little evidence that this kind of problem has exercised the minds of the licensing authorities to any large extent. This is all the more important because it appears that some industries, which were presumably sanctioned because of their low direct foreign exchange content, appear to have become net consumers of foreign exchange.[164]

It is clear that the 'clearance from indigenous angle' has weighed heavily on the pace of industrial development. It has added to costs and encouraged the development of what are euphemistically called 'unofficial' markets in imported goods. This is because, in considering the domestic availability of particular categories of goods, the licensing authorities have not taken much account of how high the costs of domestic goods were in relation to importables. They have also not considered the problems of availability, where a domestic source can only meet certain demands after an excessively long period of waiting.

Because of the greater availability of project-aid as opposed to non-project-aid, particularly in the early 'sixties, import licenses have tended to be granted more readily for capital goods than for current inputs. As industrial licenses often required an import license to be effectively utilized, this has made it easier to expand capacity than to utilize established capacity. This also has had the twofold effect of increasing import requirements as well as lessening the degree of import-saving achieved in existing lines of production, due to the existence of excess capacity.

A great deal of the new industrial investment in India has been in the public sector. However, the public sector industries are not only important in terms of the volume of investment that they account for. Their qualitative significance is also substantial. They are heavily biased in favour of producer goods industries, such as steel, heavy machinery, machine tools and fertilizers. Out of a total

[163] It is true that in most cases these problems are taken care of by the market mechanism. However, in a developing economy, the existing set of relative prices may not be optimal in terms of the objectives of the Plans. The fact that the administrative resource costs of regulating the system efficiently might be so high as not to make it worth while as an exercise in economic policy does not, however, affect the argument of this paragraph.

[164] Another effect of the preoccupation with this foreign exchange saving is generally felt in developing economies. Restrictions on entry of certain classes of consumer goods and other non-essential commodities puts a premium on these commodities in a 'closed' economy, if nothing is done either to influence the original pattern of demand through redistribution of purchasing power or to reduce the level of demand through taxes or higher savings. This encourages the diversion of domestic resources to the production of these goods. This issue bears certain relevance to the above discussion.

investment of Rs. 3,500 crores until the end of 1968, the major shares were made up as follows:

Hindusthan steel (excluding Bokaro)	Rs. 1,000 crores
Engineering	833
Chemicals (including fertilizer)	350
Petroleum	378
Minerals and metals	273
	Rs. 2,834 crores[165]

A very large proportion of the diversification that has taken place in the industrial sector is due to the development of public sector industries in India. These industries have come in for very heavy criticisms for inefficiency, high costs and low levels of productivity. By inference, many critics would put the blame on the Government for attempting to develop a public sector in India for ideological reasons and ignoring the economic costs of such development. Although it is not clear that the level of efficiency and productivity in private sector industries is all that high, it is quite clear that the performance of the public sector industries has left much to be desired. Yet it is worth pointing out that this generalization covers important differences in the performance of various public sector industries.[166] The main criticism against the public sector industries has been that their costs of construction have greatly exceeded original estimates, that they have made heavy demands on foreign exchange and that they have generated substantial losses.

The latter has been due to low capacity utilization, overmanning and other managerial and technical inefficiencies.[167] The net result of these factors has shown itself in low levels of net value added. Moreover, instead of generating a net flow of resources for development purposes, these industries have had to be subsidized out of government revenue.

During 1967–8, out of fifty-five enterprises that account for 91 per

[165] India Ministry of Finance (1969), pp. 1–2.

[166] Raj (1969); see also p.79 below.

[167] Some of the strongest criticisms have come from within the Indian official circles, especially the Public Accounts and the Estimates Committees of the Lok Sabha. The following sources are the most useful: India Ministry of Finance (1969), India Public Undertaking Committee, *6th Report* (1965), *13th Report* (1965), *15th Report* (1967–8), *30th Report* (1968) and *31st Report* (1968–9).

cent of total investment of Rs. 3,500 crores, twenty-four showed a net loss of Rs. 83 crores. This was only partially offset by a profit of Rs. 48 crores by the other thirty-one.[168] Capacity utilization, for example in the steel sector, has been falling over recent years and in 1967–8 amounted to 87 per cent of hot metal and 69 per cent of saleable steel capacity. Estimates of overmanning have run to two to three times the level of employment required for efficient running of certain enterprises.[169] In addition, numerous examples of excessive levels of stocks and spares carried, avoidable delays in production, and failures to match supply to demand can be provided.

Excess of actual costs over estimates run from around 80 per cent on a vast volume of investment for steel to around 40 to 50 per cent for the major enterprises in fields such as engineering and fertilizers. As the foreign exchange component is high, being typically around 30 to 55 per cent of total estimated cost, there is no doubt that they have made heavy demands on foreign exchange, too. As much of the comments on the behaviour of public sector enterprises has been highly critical and often justly so, it seems worth while to bring out two aspects of the problem. One is that it is not often realized that the experience of the steel industry alone affects to a very large extent the general impression of inefficiency in the public sector. Steel accounts for a little under 33 per cent of total investment in the public sector to date, including expenditure on Bokaro. It is in this area that the largest differences between estimated and final costs have arisen. Capacity utilization has been one of the lowest in the public sector. In the two years 1966–8, the industry made a total net loss to Rs. 58 crores, 38 crores being incurred during 1967–8. If, instead of looking at the overall figures, we look at the experience of the different enterprises, we find a somewhat more cheerful picture. Some enterprises, such as Hindusthan Machine Tools and Indian Telephone Industries yielded rates of return in 1964–5 of around 20 per cent. Out of twenty-four major enterprises in that year with capital invested of over Rs. 8 crores per enterprise, two yielded a net return to the Government of over 10 per cent, twelve yielded rates of between 5 to 10 per cent and seven of less than 5 per cent. The grossest examples of stock-piling and overmanning arise from the experience of one enterprise, the fertilizer plant at Sindri.[170] In many

[168] India Ministry of Finance (1969), p. 1.

[169] India Public Undertakings Committee, *6th Report* (1965), India Public Undertakings Committee, *31st Report* (1968–9).

[170] On rates of return etc., see India Public Undertakings Committee, *13th Report* (1965); on Sindri, India Public Undertakings Committee, *6th Report* (1965).

fields, such as machine tools, transistors, optical glass etc., Indian products are now supposed to be fully competitive in world markets and of good quality. The other is that not all of the problems of the public sector enterprises have risen through inefficiency of management. A great deal of the extra costs of construction of plants and a substantial measure of the delays in project commissioning have arisen because of the problems of negotiating foreign aid, delays in sanctioning of aid and the extra costs of commodity imports from high-cost donor countries owing to country-tied project-aid.[171] To this extent, it gives a somewhat unbalanced picture of developments to lay all the blame for poor performance on the public sector enterprises themselves.

VI

In the previous sections we have tried to give a brief account of the recent experience of economic development under Planning in India. For lack of space we have often compressed arguments to the point of assertions and have offered the bare minimum of empirical confirmation of certain lines of argument. In particular we have said little about important aspects of development such as education, health and transport, as well as the Government's fiscal and monetary policies. It would not be very useful, at this point, to offer a summary of the summary or make policy recommendations. In this section we shall conclude by outlining certain aspects of the Government's policy which have had an important effect on the course of development of the Indian economy.

Much of the criticism directed at the economic policies of the Government relates to the 'basic strategy' followed by the Government, in terms of its efforts to build up an industrial base, the resulting emphasis on investment and foreign aid, and its choice of the industry-mix. To that extent, there is strong pressure on the Government to reverse its strategy, to stress consumer goods output, move resources to agriculture, to go easy on heavy industries and the expansion of the public sector.

As the danger of being misunderstood in this field is the greatest, it should be said here that we believe that many of the arguments in favour of channelling large volumes of resources to agriculture are correct and stress an important sphere of policy where much improvement could be made. Our objection to certain forms in which the argument is put arises from the fact that they ignore the importance

[171] The most noticeable examples are the steel project for Bokaro and various fertilizer projects.

of the technological transformation which has or is taking place in Indian agriculture, without which the progress that could be obtained through additional outlays in that sector would have been very much limited. By emphasizing a nice, commensurable concept such as 'resources' or 'investment' it also tends to divert our attention from the degree of improvement that is required to be made in the organizational structure of the planning process with relation to agriculture. It is true that an increased inflow of resources is necessary to bring about these changes but it is not sufficient by itself. Moreover, by sometimes creating the impression that many of the past problems have been due to a lack of resources or investment, it also under-emphasizes the effects of neglect of institutional reforms in the agricultural sector. Subject to these qualifications, we believe that many of the problems that have arisen can be traced back not to basic errors in strategy but to a failure of the Government to realize clearly the full implications of the strategy to which they have overtly committed themselves. Therefore, the need to alter the basic strategy is less urgent than the need to give effect to the full implications of that strategy. In this context we can say, if somewhat paradoxically, that there are grave dangers in the exercise of hindsight to make up for past policy failures. What would have been wisdom if realized yesterday is not necessarily the wisdom of tomorrow. It is not for nothing that economic policy makers profit so little from experience.

We can start by pointing out that in two important respects the Government did not fully realize the implications of its industrialization strategy.[172] The first is that at the time of Second Plan the strategy was conceived so much in terms of physical resources and physical targets that the Government seriously underestimated the financial implications of such a policy. This has been pointed out by Bhagwati and Chakravarty in their review article and the point has been repeatedly made by economists like Raj.[173] The failure of the Government to mobilize the planned volume of domestic resources through savings and taxation has to be seen in this light.[174] Where the public sector itself was to play a major role in the development process, the failure to channel additional resources into the public sector and the inability to control the use of resources by the private sector between developmental and non-developmental uses have made this failure doubly serious. This is so irrespective of whether the inability to control the private sector arose out of political factors

[172] We use this term in this section as a shorthand term for 'the basic planning strategy'.

[173] See, e.g., Raj (1967).

[174] Bhagwati and Chakravarty (1969), p. 7.

or out of an incorrect appreciation of the costs of domestic resources, or because of the high degree of reliance the Government has placed on a complex system of direct controls, which can be self-defeating in their application.[175] This last set of problems, i.e. those relating to the use of resources by the private sector, relates to the other point that we wish to make in this context. It is that the Planners seriously underestimated the problems of implementing such a strategy in a 'mixed' economy, where a large part of the resource allocation is done through the pricing mechanism. This led to the failure to give detailed consideration to the system of taxes, prices and controls that would be required to implement such a strategy and the ability of the Government machinery to execute such a policy, without major institutional and social reforms. The fact that, under the Constitution, much of the activity in these fields was earmarked for the States, and the failure of the Central Government to work out a viable system of co-operation with the States constitutes an important part of the problem.[176]

A critical distinction in the planning strategy adopted by the Government is that between the consumer goods industries and the producers' goods industries. This is the so-called distinction between 'machines' and 'machines producing machines'. Much of the investment that has taken place has been consciously directed towards the latter group, the capacity of the investment goods producing sectors being rightly regarded as a critical constraint on the rate of growth of the economy. Yet there are two implications to this strategy which are imperfectly realized in official documents. This has implications for future economic policy which are of extreme importance.

These industries are highly capital- and foreign resources-intensive and they involve large volumes of investment. They also have long gestation periods, and therefore impose a high degree of 'waiting' on the economy.[177]

The rate of return which these industries generate and their contribution to the net value added depend critically on the degree of utilization of capacity. This in turn depends on three sets of factors, two of general application and one that applies certainly in India.

[175] On costs of domestic resources, see p. 76 above; on the licensing procedures, pp. 74-77 above and the references cited there.

[176] See, e.g., Hanson (1966), Part 2; Nicolson (1968).

[177] Raj has argued that this gestation lag is not necessarily longer than those relating to certain consumer goods industries. This is partly borne out by the Reserve Bank Study quoted in footnote (153) above (Reserve Bank, 1968). The explanation lies partly in the fact that some of the lag is due to the problems of negotiating foreign aid, where the time taken can be much the same for both types of industries.

These are the level of final demand for their product, the intermediate demand that they generate amongst themselves, being largely buyers of each other's products and the level of public expenditure in the economy.[178] The last factor is important in India, because the bulk of developmental outlay in those sectors which are the substantial users of investment goods comes out of government expenditure. As far as the first two factors are concerned, the level of demand for the products of these industries depends on the rate of investment and the rate of expansion of these industries themselves, because these two factors determine the levels of final and intermediate demands respectively. It is, therefore, not enough for the utilization of capacity in these industries that the rate of growth of the economy is maintained at a high level. It is also necessary that this rate of growth will be accompanied by a high rate of investment. The failure of the Government in the past to realize targets set for investment has to be viewed in this light. Moreover, any attempt to maintain the rate of growth of the economy by cutting down on investment or the rate of public expenditure has serious implications for the economy, which are not sufficiently realized. This is not to argue that a greater emphasis on consumption at this point may or may not be the right policy. It is merely to argue that such a policy has implications for the rest of the economy which have to be explicitly considered. Even more important perhaps is to make the point that it is emphatically not a sensible policy today to cut back on the expansion of the heavy industry sector, however much we might feel that such a policy was ill-conceived in the 1950s. For one implication of its own industrial development policy which neither the Government nor its critics have realized is that a policy stressing the development of an investment goods producing sector as a strategic factor in the development process yields an overall strategy which is to a substantial measure irreversible. It puts a high cost on 'switching' from one growth path to another.

This brings us to the last point on which we wish to conclude. One of the basic issues of a development strategy that recognizes a conflict between short-term and long-term gains is the decision on how the limited short-term gains of the process are to be distributed. In a 'mixed' economy those gains can be distributed either by the creation of substantial volumes of new employment amongst the poorer classes at socially desired rates of real wages, or through a radical reallocation of existing wealth and incomes. The Indian Planners deliberately eschewed the latter. At the same time they have persis-

[178] According to Mathur (1966), the intermediate demand generated by the 'heavy sector industry' within itself is low by international standards.

tently regarded the employment problem as subsidiary to the basic strategy. The need to create new jobs is almost a nuisance because of the conflict it imposes between more jobs and more goods. At the same time there is a certain degree of perplexity that the problem of poverty gets more and more acute and social and political strife is rife. Paradoxically, in some official quarters this leads to the view that concern with 'welfare' objectives has slowed down the 'growth' of the economy. It is time to soft pedal on 'welfare' and to press on with 'growth'. Such are the fruits of acute perception that scorn commonsense.

This strange paradox would make a little more sense if the amount of resources that could be devoted to the production of consumer goods without jeopardizing the future growth of the economy was itself a bottleneck. Yet there is no hard evidence in India that this is so. On the other hand, there is plenty of evidence of resources used in the production of consumer goods being directed towards the production of non-essentials and of serious maldistribution of the available supply of basic consumer goods, such as foodstuff. It is, moreover, not even the result of a failure of the Government to intervene or its unwillingness to do so. It is much more a question perhaps of the political will and of the lack of any clear recognition of where intervention is essential and where it would most bear fruit.

LIST OF WORKS CITED

(Titles are arranged alphabetically according to authors: Government of India publications are listed under INDIA, followed by Ministry; *E.W.* = *Economic Weekly*; *E.P.W.* = *Economic and Political Weekly*; *I.J.A.E.* = *Indian Journal of Agricultural Economics*; *R.B.I.B.* = *Reserve Bank of India Bulletin.*

Bagchi, A.K. 'Concentration of Economic Power in India', *E.P.W.*, August 1967.

'Growth of Agricultural Production: Regional Differences in Rates', *E.W.*, February 1965 (Special number).

Bailey, F.G. *Caste and the Economic Frontier* (Manchester Univ. Press, 1957).

Baranson, J. *Manufacturing Problems in India: The Cummins Diesel Experience* (Syracuse, 1967).

Bardhan, K. 'Do Foodgrains Imports Affect Prices?' *E.P.W.*, November 12, 1966.

Bauer, P. *Indian Economic Policy and Development* (Allen and Unwin, 1961).

Beteille, A. — *Caste, Class and Power* (Cambridge Univ. Press, 1965).

Bettelheim, C. — *India Independent* (MacGibbon and Kee, 1968).

Bhagwati, J. — 'The Tying of Aid', in U.N.C.T.A.D., II, Vol. IV, *Problems of Policies of Financing* (New York, 1968).

Bhagwati, J. and Chakravarty, S. — 'Contributions to Indian Economic Analysis: A Survey', *American Economic Review*, September 1969 (Supplement).

Bhagwati, J. and Desai, P. — *Planning for Industrialization; India's Trade and Industrialization Policies, 1950–66* (Oxford Univ. Press, 1970).

Bhatt, V.V. and Ojha, P. — 'Pattern of Income Distribution in India 1953–4 to 1956–7', *R.B.I.B.*, September 1963.

Blaug, M., Layard, R. and Woodhall, M. — *Causes of Graduate Unemployment in India* (Allen Lane, 1969).

Brecher, M. — *Nehru: A Biography* (Oxford Univ. Press, 1959).

Brown, L. — *The Seeds of Change* (Pall Mall, 1970).

Buchanan, D. — *The Development of Capitalist Enterprise in India* (Cass, 1966).

Coale, A. and Hoover, E. — *Population Growth and Economic Development in Low Income Countries* (Princeton Univ. Press, 1958).

Dandekar, V.M. — 'Planning in Indian Agriculture', *I.J.A.E.*, January–March 1967.

'A Review of Land Reform Studies Sponsored by the Planning Commission', *I.J.A.E.*, October–December 1962.

Dantwala, M.L. — 'Incentives and Disincentives in Indian Agriculture', *I.J.A.E.*, April–June 1967.

Dasgupta, A.K. — 'The Fourth Five-Year Plan', *E.P.W.*, September 24, 1966.

Davis, K. — *Population of India and Pakistan* (Princeton Univ. Press, 1951).

Desai, A.V. — 'Growth and Cycles in the Indian Economy, 1951–64', *E.P.W.*, November 1966.

Desai, D.K. — '—IADP Analysis of Results', *E.P.W.*, June 1969.

Epstein, S. — *Economic Development and Social Change in South India* (Manchester Univ. Press, 1962).

Gadgil, D.R. — *Industrial Evolution of India* (Oxford, 1942).

'Price Policy for Foodgrains: its Implications', *E.W.*, September 1964.

Galbraith, J.K. — *American Capitalism* (Hamish Hamilton, 1957).

Gandhi, V. — *Tax Burden on Indian Agriculture* (Harvard Univ. Press, 1966).

George, P.T.	'Comparative Review of Five Land Reform Studies', *I.J.A.E.*, January–March, July–September 1968.
Gough, K.	'The Social Structure of a Tanjore Village', in McKim Marriott (ed.), *Village India* (Chicago, 1955).
Hanson, A.H.	'Crisis of Indian Planning' in A.H. Hanson, *Planning and the Politicians* (Routledge and Kegan Paul, 1969).
	The Process of Planning (Oxford Univ. Press, 1966).
Hanumantha Rao, C.H.	'Farm Size and Economics of Scale', *E.W.*, December 1963.
	'Agricultural Growth and Stagnation in India', *E.W.*, February 1965 (reprinted in Khusro, 1968).
	'Alternative Explanations of the Inverse Relationship between Farm Size and Output per acre in India', *Indian Economic Review*, October 1966.
Haq, Mahabub Ul	'Tied Credits: A Qualitative Analysis' in J. Adler, ed. *Capital Movements and Economic Development* (Macmillan, 1965).
Hazari, R.K.	*The Corporate Private Sector: Concentration, Ownership and Control* (Asia Publishing House, 1966).
Hazari, R.K. and Oza, A.N.	'Public Sector in India' (in Robinson and Kidron, 1970).
Hone, A.	'Unemployed Engineers', *E.P.W.*, April 13, 1968.
Hopper, W.D.	'Allocation Efficiency in a Traditional Indian Agriculture', *Journal of Farm Economics*, August 1965.
INDIA: Ministry of Finance	*Pocket Book of Economic Information* (1968).
	Economic Survey, 1967–8, 1968–9.
	External Assistance, 1967–8.
	Report of the Committee on Utilization of External Assistance (1964).
	Public Sector Enterprises: A Memorandum (1969).
Ministry of Food and Agriculture	*Indian Agriculture in Brief.*
	Growth Rates in Agriculture (1968).
	Second Report on Intensive Agricultural District Programmes, 1950–65 (1966).
Ministry of Labour	*Pocket Book of Labour Statistics* (1968).
Lok Sabha Estimates Committee	*Rural Works Programme, 1964* (3rd Lok Sabha, 55th report).

Industrial Licensing, 1967 (4th Lok Sabha, 9th report).

Utilization of External Assistance, 1967 (4th Lok Sabha, 11th report).

Foreign Exchange, 1968 (4th Lok Sabha, 30th report).

Lok Sabha Committee on Public Undertakings — *Fertilizer Corporation of India 1965* (3rd Lok Sabha, 6th report).

Management and Administration of Public Undertakings, 1965 (3rd Lok Sabha, 13th report).

Financial Management of Public Undertakings, 1967–8 (4th Lok Sabha, 15th report).

Indian Drugs and Pharmaceuticals, 1968 (4th Lok Sabha, 30th report).

Hindusthan Steel Ltd., 1968–9 (4th Lok Sabha, 31st report).

Planning Commission — *The Second Five-Year Plan, 1956.*

The Third Five-Year Plan, 1961.

The Fourth Five-Year Plan (1967–8) Plan, 1966.

The Fourth Five-Year Plan 1969–74 (draft) (1969).

Material and Financial Balances, 1964–5, 1970–1, 1975–6 (1966).

Regional Variation in Social Development and Levels of Living, Vols. I and II (1967–8).

Indicators of Progress (mimeo, 1968).

Macro-economic models of self-reliant growth (mimeo, 1968).

Report of the Committee on Distribution of Income and Levels of Living (1964).

Khusro, A.M. — 'Returns to Scale in Indian Agriculture', *I.J.A.E.*, (ed.) October–December 1964.

Readings in Agricultural Development (Allied Publishers, 1968).

Kidron, M. — *Foreign Investments in India* (Oxford Univ. Press, 1965).

Krishnan, T.N. — 'Marketed Surplus of Foodgrains', *E.W.*, February, Annual, 1965.

Kuznets, S. — *Six Lectures on Economic Growth* (F. Cass, 1959).

Ladejinsky, W. — *A Study of Tenurial Conditions in Package Districts* (Government of India Planning Commission, 1965).

'Punjab's Green Revolution', *E.P.W.*, June 28, 1969.

Lal, D. — 'A Quantitative Analysis of Aid-financed Imports

of Certain Chemicals into India', U.N.C.T.A.D., TD/B/C.3/59 (mimeo, 1968).

Lewis, J.P. — *Quiet Crisis in India* (Brookings Institution, 1962).

Lipton, M. — 'Strategy for Agriculture: Urban Bias and Rural Planning' (in Streeten and Lipton, 1968).
'Transfer of Resources from Agricultural Sector to Non-agricultural Sector in India', U.N.–E.C.A.F.E. (mimeo, 1969).

Lydall, H. — 'The Inequality of Indian Incomes', *E.W.*, June 1960.

MacDougall, Sir Donald — 'India's Balance of Payments Problem', in P. Rosenstein-Rodan (ed.), *Pricing and Fiscal Policies* (Allen and Unwin, 1964).

Mahalanobis, P.C. — *An Approach of Operation Research to Planning in India* (Asia Publishing House, 1963).

Malenbaum, W. — *Prospects for Indian Development* (Allen and Unwin, 1962).

Manne, A. and Rudra, A. — 'A Consistency Model of India's Fourth Plan', *Sankhya* (Series B) February 1965.

Marglin, S. — *Public Investment Criteria* (Allen and Unwin, 1967).

Mason, E.S. — *Economic Development in India and Pakistan* (Harvard Univ. Press, 1966).

Mathur, G. — 'Growth under Parasitic Conditions', *Seminar*, 1966.

Mathur, P.N. Valavade, S.P. and Kirkoskar, M.V. — 'Optimum Capacity and Imbalance of Capital Structure: the Case of Machine Manufacturing Industries', *Arthavijnana*, September–December 1967.

Mazumdar, D. — 'On the Economics of Relative Efficiency of Small Farmers', *E.W.*, July 1963.

Meade, J.E. — *The Theory of International Economic Policy:* Vol. II: *Balance of Payments* (Oxford, 1951).

Medhora, P. — *Industrial Growth since 1950 – An Assessment* (Bombay, 1968).

Millikan, M. — 'India in Transition: Economic Development', *Foreign Affairs*, April 1968.

Minhas, B.S. — 'Objectives and Policy Frame of the Fourth Plan' (mimeo, New Delhi, 1969).

Minhas, B.S. and Srinivasan, T.N. — 'New Agricultural Production Strategy: Some Policy Issues' (in Khusro, 1968).

Minhas, B.S. and Vaidyanathan, A. — 'Growth of Crop Output in India', *Journal of the Indian Society of Agricultural Statistics*, Vol. XVIII, 2, 1965.

Mitra, A. — 'Population and Foodgrain Output of India: A

Note on Disparate Growth Rates' (——) (in Robinson and Kidron, 1970).

Mukherji, K. *Levels of Economic Activity and Public Expenditure in India* (Asia Publishing House, 1965).

Myrdal, G. *Asian Drama*, Vol. III (Allen Lane, 1968).

Nehru, J. *Autobiography* (Allied Publishers, 1962).

Speeches, Vol. III (Government of India, n.d.).

Nicolson, N.K. 'Political Aspects of Indian Food Policy', *Pacific Affairs*, Spring 1968.

Nurkse, R. 'Domestic and International Equilibrium', in R. Nurkse, *Equilibrium and Growth in the World Economy* (Harvard Univ. Press, 1962).

Panse, V.G. 'Critical Study of New Food Strategy', *Yojana*, August 21, 1966.

Parikh, A. 'Statewise Growth Rates in Agricultural Output: An Econometric Study', *Arthavijnana*, March 1966.

Patel, I.G. 'Aid Relationship for the Seventies—a Comment on the Report of the Commission on International Development' (mimeo, 1970).

'Foreign Aid: Retrospect and Prospect', *Commerce*, March 30, 1968.

'The Strategy of Indian Planning' in C.R. Rao (ed.), *Essays in Econometrics and Planning* (Pergamon, 1963).

Patel, S.J. 'Export Prospects and Economic Growth: India', *Economic Journal*, September 1960.

Pocock, D. 'Social Anthropology: its Contribution to Planning' (in Streeten and Lipton, 1968).

Raj, K.N. 'Employment and Unemployment in the Indian Economy; Problems of Classification, Measurement and Policy', *Economic Development and Cultural Change* (1959).

'The Fourth Plan and Future Economic Policy', *E.P.W.*, March 1967.

Indian Economic Growth: Performance and Prospects (Allied Publishers, 1965).

Lectures delivered at the University of McGill, Parts II and IV (mimeo, 1969).

'Price Behaviour in India 1949–66: An Explanatory Hypothesis', *Indian Economic Review*, October 1966.

'Regional Variations in Foodgrains Prices', *E.P.W.*, August 20, 1966.

Raj, K.N. and Sen, A.K. 'Alternative Patterns of Growth under Conditions of Stagnant Export Earnings', *Oxford Economic Papers*, February 1961.

Raj Krishna — 'Farm Supply Response in India–Pakistan: A Case Study of the Punjab Region', *Economic Journal*, September 1963.
'Government Operations in Foodgrains', *E.P.W.*, September 16, 1967.
'Agrarian Reform: The Debate on Ceilings', in *Economic Development and Cultural Change* (1959).

Ranadive, K.R. — 'Pattern of Income Distribution in India, 1953–54 to 1959–60', *Oxford Institute of Economics and Statistics Bulletin*, August 1968.

Rao, V.K.R.V. — 'Agricultural Production and Productivity During the Plan Periods', *I.J.A.E.*, January–March 1962.

Rath, N. and Patvardhan, V.S. — *Impact of Assistance under PL 480 in the Indian Economy* (Asia Publishing House, 1967).

Reddaway, W.B. — *The Development of the Indian Economy* (Allen and Unwin, 1962).

Reserve Bank of India Bulletin — 'Time lags in Implementation of Development Projects' (March 1968).

Reserve Bank of India — *Report on Currency and Finance*, Annual.

Robertson, C.R., Saini, G.R. and Sharma, P.K. — 'The Package Programme, I and II', *E.P.W.*, August 27, September 3, 1966.

Robinson, E.A.G. — 'Economic Progress in India', *Three Banks Review*, March 1970.

Robinson, E.A.G. and Kidron, M. (eds.) — *Economic Development in South Asia* (Macmillan, 1970).

Rudra, A. — 'Agriculture and Industry; Relative Rates of Growth', *E.W.*, November 7, 1964.

Rudra, A. — 'More on Returns to Scale in Indian Agriculture', *E.P.W.*, October 26, 1968.

Sen, A.K. — 'Strategies of Economic Development: Feasibility Constraints and Planning' (in Robinson and Kidron, 1970).
'Size and Holdings of Productivity', *E.W.*, February 1964.

Sen, A.K. and Varghese, T. — 'Tenancy and Resource Allocation', *Seminar*, 1966.

Singh, Manmohan — *India's Export Trends and the Prospects for Self-sustained Growth* (October 1964).

Streeten, P. and Hill, R. — 'Aid to India' (in Streeten and Lipton, 1968).

Streeten, P. and Lipton, M. (eds.) — *The Crisis of Indian Planning* (Oxford Univ. Press, 1968).

Sundaram, K. — 'P.L. 480 Imports: Efficiency in Purchase and Distribution', *E.P.W.*, March 4, 1967.

Thamarajakshi, R.	'Urban–rural Terms of Trade', *E.P.W.*, June 1969.
Thorner, D.	'Coastal Andhra: An Affluent Society', *E.P.W.*, February 1967.
Thorner, D. and Thorner, A.	*Land and Labour in India* (Asia Publishing House, 1962).
Wharton, C.R., jun.	'The Green Revolution: Cornucopia or Pandora's Box', *Foreign Affairs*, April 1969.

2

ECONOMIC PROGRESS IN INDIA*

by Austin Robinson

Emeritus Professor of Economics at the University of Cambridge

I

This is a difficult moment at which to appraise the economic progress of India. Most readers of the newspapers are much more aware of the internal divisions of the Congress Party than of the underlying economic changes in the Indian economy; more conscious of the riots and hartals promoted by a generation that believes that progress is to be achieved by confrontation and violence rather than by compromise and collaboration; less certain that the very concept of a united India, itself an artificial outcome of British rule, can survive the growing divisions between linguistic and racial groups; less certain that centrally planned development, presupposing as it does a strong and effective central government, will continue to have reality.

Yet paradoxically in the last three or four years India can be regarded as having reached an important turning point in her economic development. It is much too early to say with any certainty that India can from now on progress more rapidly and more steadily than in the past. Political difficulties may be more potent than economic improvements. But at least it is important to understand and assess what has been happening on the economic side.

If one is to judge progress in this respect, one must begin by considering what have been the limiting factors on Indian development in the past. There have been five major limitations:

1. Expansion of the Indian economy, when combined with population growth, has generated incomes of which a large proportion has been spent on increases of food consumption; any brave attempt to speed up economic growth has run into the limits of food supply and has caused inflation of food prices. Any shortfall in food supplies has had to be made good by import; this has added to the already existing balance of payments difficulties.

2. Economic expansion and the capital investment which it has

* In *Three Banks Review*, March 1970.

required has in the past involved additional imports; the import-content of fixed capital investment has been high, and higher, except in years of acute food shortage, than the marginal import content of consumption, so that a switch of expenditure from consumption to fixed capital formation was likely to increase balance of payments difficulties.

3. Any growth of consumer demand, so far as it did not fall on food consumption, was likely to fall on consumption goods which, apart possibly from textiles, were principally met by import; thus expansion of demand was likely to impose immediate strains on the balance of payments; this added to the difficulty of absorbing the unemployed and expanding activity to do so.

4. The Indian economic structure was adapted to the economic pattern of activity of the nineteenth century; exports of a few traditional products had then sufficed to pay for low levels of imports of simple machinery and for a modest level of consumption goods; the structure and levels of imports and exports needed to be adapted to the current requirements of a more rapidly growing economy, including increased requirements of materials and intermediate products necessitated by new industrial developments.

5. The volume of savings, though hitherto supplemented by foreign aid, has been doubtfully adequate to sustain, without considerable inflationary pressures, the levels of growth that have been attempted.

All of these limitations have exercised themselves at some time during the past decade. The order in which they have been listed reflects neither their past nor their present relative importance. In subsequent sections of this article progress will be examined in overcoming each of these limitations. There is, however, one potential limitation, familiar in the analysis of the problems of growth in any western country, which is almost irrelevant in India. The economy is not up against the limitations of labour supply, though from time to time there may be a shortage of particular skills. Indeed, one of the acute problems of India is that of creating sufficient jobs for those who are likely to be entering the labour market and for the already numerous unemployed.

II

Some attempt will first be made to outline as a background the actual progress of the Indian economy over the eight years 1960 to 1968. Table 1 brings out certain essentials. First over the years 1960–1 to 1964–5 (a year that benefited by an exceptionally large

Table 1

GROWTH OF REAL NATIONAL INCOME AT PRICES OF 1960–1

	1960–1	*1961–2*	*1962–3*	*1963–4*	*1964–5*	*1965–6*	*1966–7*	*1967–8*	*1968–9*
National Income	100·0	103·9	106·0	112·1	120·1	113·3	114·6	124·7	128·4
Population mid-year	100·0	102·3	104·8	107·3	109·9	113·4	116·2	119·1	122·1
Income per Head	100·0	101·6	101·2	104·5	109·3	99·9	98·6	104·7	105·2
Private Consumption	100·0	—	—	—	112·9	—	—	—	(120·0)
Private Consumption per Head	100·0	—	—	—	102·7	—	—	—	(98·3)

Note: The estimates of private consumption and private consumption per head in 1968–9 have been made by the present author for purposes of this article. Private consumption has been estimated by the Perspective Planning Division of the Planning Commission to have been 85·6 per cent of net national product in 1960–1 and 80·5 per cent in 1964–5. It has been assumed that it was 80 per cent in 1968–9.

agricultural output) progress was rapid. National income grew by an average of 4·7 per cent per annum. There followed the disastrous years 1965–6 and 1966–7 when agricultural output as a whole, which in 1964–5 had been 11 per cent higher than in 1960–1, fell 16–17 per cent below that of 1964–5 and that of the essential food grains was down by 19 per cent and 8 per cent in the two respective years.[1] The repercussions of the monsoon failures together with the wars against China and Pakistan, on the balance of payments and on the economy generally were severe. National income fell by 6 per cent in 1965–6 and in 1966–7 was still nearly 5 per cent below the level of 1964–5.

In the two subsequent years there has been a marked recovery. By 1968–9 the level of real national income is estimated to have been 28·4 per cent higher than in 1960–1, an average rate of growth of 3·2 per cent per annum over the eight-year period as a whole. But for reasons that will be explained below, this aggregate for all the activities of the economy is very misleading.

The second thing that Table 1 brings out is that this not inconsiderable increase in total national income has hitherto meant little increase in average income per head, and when allowance is made for increased expenditures on fixed capital investment, probably a slight fall in real consumption per head. The average annual growth of real income from 1960–1 to 1968–9 by 3·2 per cent has been very largely offset by a population growth of 2·5 per cent, so that the average increase of income per head has been no more than 0·7 per cent per annum. Once again the improvement was much greater over the years down to 1964–5; over those years income per head was growing by 2·3 per cent per annum and income per head was higher in 1964–5 than in any subsequent year; in only four of the subsequent eight years was income per head more than 2 per cent higher than in 1960–1.

This emphasizes, if emphasis is necessary, the immense effect on Indian development exercised by population growth. Indian vital statistics are so imperfect and births so incompletely recorded that present birth rates are largely a matter of guesswork. The Fourth Five-Year Plan as finally revised describes the increase of population as having been the result of a sharp fall in the mortality rate without any significant change in the birth rate 'which appears to have

[1] The two years of crop failure were extraordinarily different. In 1965–6 failure was widespread and almost every State was 15–20 per cent below the level of 1964–5. In 1966–7 few States were more than 5-10 per cent below the level of 1964–5; disaster was concentrated in Bihar, West Bengal, U.P., Madhya Pradesh, Gujarat.

remained unchanged around 41 per thousand population during the greater part of the past two decades up to 1965–6' but since then 'has come down to 39 per thousand for the country as a whole, the rate being somewhat higher in rural areas than in the urban'. It has set the objective of bringing the birth rate down to 25 per thousand within the next ten or twelve years and has provided funds to spread contraceptive facilities and propaganda for the small family. All this is as it should be. But it remains that Indian birth rates have fallen less during the past twenty-five years than those of most other Asian countries – notably those of Japan – and that population growth is at present the greatest obstacle to increasing welfare: increased production serves principally to keep output per head constant; increased investment serves principally to keep capital per head constant rather than to increase it.

Table 2

POPULATION GROWTH IN ASIAN COUNTRIES

	Population 1957	*Population 1967*	*Live birth rate 1957*	*Live birth rate 1967*
Japan	100·0	110·1	17·2	18·3
Singapore	100·0	135·3	43·4	25·9
Philippines	100·0	138·5	29·9	22·0
Taiwan	100·0	137·2	41·4	28·5
Ceylon	100·0	127·7	36·4	31·6
India	100·0	127·1	41·0	39·0

III

May I turn now to the first of the limiting factors on Indian development – the limitation imposed by the agricultural sector and food supplies? If one takes a longer view, Indian agricultural output had shown a surprising capacity for growth. If one goes back as far as 1950–1, the rate of growth of all agricultural production down to 1964–5 was about 3·6 per cent per annum. If one takes the whole period down to 1968–9, the growth was 3·2 per cent. For the all-important foodgrains the growth of domestic production from 1950–1 to 1964–5 was also 3·6 per cent per annum; for the whole period to 1968–9 it was 3·5 per cent. This is about sufficient to cover population growth of 2·5 per cent per annum and an expenditure elasticity of demand for foodgrains of the order of 0·5 per cent if total consumption per head is growing by 2·1 per cent per annum, as forecast by the Fourth Plan. For food as a whole budget inquiries have shown expenditure elasticities ranging from as high as 1·0 in the

Table 3

SUPPLY OF FOODGRAINS, 1950–69
(million tons)

	1950–1	*1960–1*	*1963–4*	*1964–5*	*1965–6*	*1966–7*	*1967–8*	*1968–9*
Domestic Production	55	81	81	89	72	74	96	98
Imports	5	3	6	7	10	9	6	4
Total Supply	60	85	87	96	82	83	102	102
Seed, Feed and Wastage	7	10	10	11	9	9	11	11
Final Consumption and Stock Change	53	75	77	85	73	74	91	91
Final Consumption and Stock Change per head of Population (1950–1 = 100)	100	116	110	121	102	101	119	116

Note: The allowances for seed, feed and wastage is a round figure based on estimates for 1964–5 and a provision for 1970–1 made by the Perspective Planning Division of the Planning Commission, and on estimates of net availability after allowing both for the above factors and for changes in government but not private stocks made in the *Economic Survey*, 1968–9, p. 62.

The first estimate of domestic production in 1969–70 is 105 million tons.

lower income groups to 0·5 in the middle income groups, but that for foodgrains will be somewhat lower.

Table 3 shows the domestic production and imports of foodgrains over the period 1950 to 1969. It will be seen that total availability to cover both consumption and stock change rose considerably between 1950–1 and 1960–1, even if allowance is made for the fact that the latter year was a year of good crops with one to two million of probable stock building. Availability per head, including stock change, has since then risen little. But it has depended until the last year or two increasingly on import.

Down to 1965–6, food prices were remarkably stable, considering the general inflationary pressures of India. Rice prices, which were 100 in 1952–3 were 101 in 1960–1 and were up to 128 in 1964–5. Wheat prices, again taking 1952–3 as 100, were 92 in 1960–1 and 136 in 1965–6. In both cases it was in the years 1966–7 and 1967–8 that, after the shortages of the previous crop years, prices bounded up and reached 208 and 186 respectively in 1967–8.

The higher crops of 1967–8 and 1968–9 have been due in part to more normal rains than in the two very exceptional previous years, partly to the normal upward trend, partly to the phenomenon which is commonly described in the countries of South Asia as 'the green revolution'. The normal upward trend has been the consequence partly of increases of productivity, partly of increases of area. For the years 1949–50 to 1964–5, before the green revolution made itself felt, the Fourth Five-Year Plan analyses the sources of increased production both by crops and – very important – by States.

Two things are immediately obvious from Tables 4 and 5. First, for all crops and all India the increase of agricultural production has come almost equally from increases of area and increases of productivity. The total increase of output of all foodgrains over these years has come in greater measure from productivity than from area. This

Table 4

COMPOUND RATES OF GROWTH FOR VARIOUS CROPS IN ALL INDIA 1949–50 TO 1964–5
(per cent per annum)

	Production	*Area*	*Productivity*
Rice	3·37	1·26	2·09
Wheat	3·97	2·70	1·24
Pulses	1·62	1·87	−0·24
All foodgrains	2·98	1·34	1·61
All crops	3·19	1·55	1·60

Table 5

COMPOUND RATES OF GROWTH OF AGRICULTURAL PRODUCTION IN VARIOUS STATES 1952–3 TO 1964–5 (per cent per annum)

	Production	*Area*	*Productivity*
Punjab	4·56	1·90	2·61
Gujarat	4·55	0·45	4·09
Madras	4·17	1·10	3·04
Mysore	3·54	0·81	2·71
Mahashtra	2·93	0·44	2·45
Madhya Pradesh	2·49	1·28	1·21
Orissa	2·48	0·81	1·66
Uttar Pradesh	1·66	0·72	0·94

has been particularly true of rice. Second, the increases of production have been very unevenly distributed over India as a whole. There are three States of notable advance – Punjab, Gujarat and Madras; certain other States follow not far behind them in growth of productivity. There are other parts of India – and notably the agriculturally important U.P. – where increases of productivity have been very small. In part the explanation is that the three States of notable advance have been able to make better use of their available water supplies by irrigation, tubewells and other facilities. In part they would seem to have been more receptive of new methods and more vigorous in applying them.

All this was happening before the coming of the 'green revolution'. This revolution is composed of a package of four improvements, none of which is wholly effective without the others: improved varieties, increased use of fertilizers, improved water supplies, better cultivation. The improved varieties are principally of rice and wheat, deriving either directly or as hybrids from the Philippine rices or the Mexican wheats; in both cases hybrids making use of the resistant powers of existing indigenous improved varieties to Indian diseases and environments would appear to be better than the original foreign importations. The improved varieties of wheat have shown themselves better suited in the first stages to Indian conditions than those of rice; for rice, further work on adaptation is still necessary, but proceeding intensively; work on the pulses is equally necessary and is now proceeding, but is behind that on wheat and rice. The virtue of these improved varieties is that they are more responsive to high inputs of fertilizer and water than the existing Indian varieties.[2] At

[2] Other improved varieties are 'short-duration' rather than primarily 'high-yield' varieties and make their contribution by permitting shorter use of land and more multi-cropping.

the same time they are more exigent of both the care and the timing of cultivation, and impose added work and new problems on the cultivator.

The new varieties have made it possible, and in suitable conditions highly profitable, to use much more fertilizer than was profitable to use with existing varieties. But again the successful use of more fertilizer has depended not only on the new input-responsive varieties but also on the availability at the right times of adequate supplies of water. This has been made possible in part by improved irrigation facilities; in part by the explosive growth of tubewells, pumped in most cases by electricity, but in some cases by small diesel engines. The tubewell is, however, a fairly considerable item of investment. A large farmer can afford such an investment and control the use of the water to fit in with his own plans and needs. The small farmer cannot afford this big investment. He either lacks the sufficient water supply to make effective use of improved varieties and more fertilizer, or if, through some co-operative arrangements, he has access to tubewell or other water supply, he may have insufficient control over the timing of his water supplies to produce fully satisfactory results.

Thus in its first phases the 'green revolution' has favoured the larger and richer farmer. Response to the new techniques has, moreover, been unevenly spread over India. Once again the Punjab, Gujarat and Madras have been in the van. Again the U.P. has been laggard, though in many respects it seems well placed to share in the benefits. The problems are really two. Much more is known about the response of alluvial soils to large use of fertilizers than is known about the response of the upland soils. The sub-soil water supplies for exploitation by tubewells are predominantly in the Ganges–Jumna plains to the south of the Himalayas, in the river estuaries of Gujarat, in the plains to the east of the Ghats in Southern India. The uplands that compose the greater part of Central India have no similar water resources for ready exploitation.

The expansion of this group of improved techniques has been rapid, as is shown in Table 6.

There remain, however, a number of uncertainties. How far and how fast will the 'green revolution' spread? Are there institutional changes in respect of land-ownership which must be overcome before it can go very much further? How can it be made available to the small cultivator as well as to the big? Are the momentary failures to expand faster the result of lack of availabilities of inputs, of lack of capital for small improvements, of lack of responsiveness in traditionally-minded and financially cautious small cultivators, anxious to wait and see the results of the experiments of others? And why

Table 6

THE GREEN REVOLUTION

	1964–5	*1966–7*	*1967–8*	*1968–9*	*Target for 1973–4*
Nitrogenous fertilizer available (thousand tons N)	450	940	1235	1400	3700
Areas covered by:					
High yielding varieties (m. acres)	nil	4·8	6·3	21·0	60·0
Other improved varieties (m. acres)	99·3	108·4	—	—	—
Plant protection (m. acres)	38·0	59·0	—	—	—
Tubewells (thousands)	—	—	—	1069	1799

have certain States lagged? Is it a result of differences of physical environment or of differences in the vigour with which administrations have pressed the new possibilities? And, most important from the point of view of any economic planner or forecaster, does the 'green revolution' mean a once-for-all step forward, leaving unchanged after a few years the underlying trend of growth of agricultural output? Or does it mean that, as the improved methods progressively spread and traditional agriculture is progressively replaced by the more modern techniques used in other countries, the rate of growth of agricultural output will over a considerable period be raised?

At present it is difficult to answer any of these questions with certainty. Expert opinion in India ranges from exaggerated optimism to extreme caution. The most that one can say with reasonable certainty is that the chances of agricultural production maintaining the growth of 3·5–4·0 per cent or thereabouts which is necessary to keep abreast of population growth and growth of consumption per head, and of thus relieving the inflationary pressures in the food sector and the strains on the balance of payments are very much brighter than they were even five years ago. Thus this particular limitation on Indian growth is likely to be less dominant.

The Fourth Plan has set the target for the compound growth of total agricultural production at 5 per cent for the decade; this is by no means unrealistic if the momentum of the green revolution can be maintained and the necessary inputs provided. For foodgrains the Fourth Plan target for 1973–4 is 129 million tons, implying an annual growth of about 5·0 per cent. It is hoped to increase the area under high-yielding varieties during this period from 21 million to 60 million acres; to increase fertilizer supplies from 1·4 million tons of N to 3·7 million tons; to increase tubewells from 1·06 million to 1·80 million; to make corresponding provision for machinery and other inputs and for financial facilities. At the same time, through the new Food Corporation of India, efforts are being made to develop a better agricultural marketing system with guaranteed minimum prices for the main crops and facilities for acquiring and storing operational and buffer stocks for foodgrains; already capacity exists to store about 4·5 million tons of which about 2 million tons is available for buffer stocks. It is hoped to increase this capacity during the Plan period sufficiently to carry a buffer stock of 5 million tons.

IV

The second main limitation on Indian economic development has been the fact that new fixed capital formation has hitherto depended very heavily on the import of capital equipment. Of the total of fixed capital formation about 45 per cent has been in the form of building and construction, with a low import-content; about 55 per cent has been in the form of non-building inputs, with a high import-content. The past first phase of development has involved an exceptionally high import-content because it has been mainly composed of investment in infrastructure, and particularly of investment in electricity generation and distribution, and in establishing a steel industry and machinery-building industries. The great steel plants at Bhilai, Rourkela, Durgapur and Bokaro, the heavy electrical plants at Bhopal, Hardwar and Ramachandrapuram, the heavy machine tools plants at Ranchi and elsewhere, the big fertilizer plants at Sindri and elsewhere have inevitably involved in the first stages large imports of equipment which India was then unable to produce. In a number of such cases the import-content of capital formation was well over 50 per cent. The Fourth Five-Year Plan reminds one that as late as 1967–8 as much as 30 per cent of the country's machinery requirements had to be met by imports, and that 70 per cent of alloy and special steel was then being imported.

But this situation is changing very rapidly. Already by 1968–9 90 per cent of mild steel requirements were being met from internal sources. As the main emphasis in investment progressively moves on from creating and expanding the heavy industries to creating and expanding lighter consumer good industries, the investment in the heavy industries will pay off and a very much larger proportion of the equipment required for such industries can and will now be made in India. Thus the import-content of investment may be expected to fall progressively. Precise estimates are not available but some rough calculations made for the purpose of this article suggest that the overall import-content of investment in machinery and equipment may fall from around 19 per cent in 1965–6 to around 11 per cent at the end of the Plan period in 1973–4. Table 7 shows the changing proportions of various supplies of plant, intermediate products and finished goods in recent years and the rapid decline in some cases of the share of imports.

Table 7

SHARE OF IMPORTS IN TOTAL ESTIMATED SUPPLIES
(percentages)

	1950–1	*1955–6*	*1960–1*	*1965–6*	*1967–8*
Textile machinery	—	67·6	69·1	56·8	56·5
Sugar mill machinery	100·0	95·2	19·3	0·8	0·9
Metal working machine tools	89·8	84·8	64·8	61·8	53·8
Iron and steel	25·2	39·9	35·7	16·7	11·5
Aluminium	72·8	68·5	58·1	25·1	27·9
Man-made fibre and yarn	—	20·7	25·4	6·0	2·9
Caustic soda	64·7	62·5	27·7	25·4	2·8
Bicycles	62·5	22·4	—	—	—
Sewing machines	41·1	11·2	0·3	0·7	0·5

Notes: (1) Source is *Indian Economic Survey*, 1968–9, pp. 112–13.
(2) For comparability with earlier years the value of imported supplies in 1967–8 are measured in pre-devaluation rupees, using figures given *loc. cit.*, p. 113.
(3) The ratio of imported supplies to domestic supplies does not, of course, give in the strict sense the full import-content of investment or expenditure; the domestic supplies usually have an import-content of raw materials or components which are not here calculated.

In less precise terms it can now be said that India can build for herself, if it is desired, complete cement plants, sugar mills, cotton textile mills. The Ranchi plant could build a steel works of moderate size. Bhopal can now build electricity generating plant of up to 120 MW. and will be moving on to larger sizes. The import-content of a fertilizer plant is currently about 30 per cent and of a plant to produce other chemicals about 50 per cent. The import-content of

Indian-built automobiles, electric appliances, and radio is of the order of 5–10 per cent.

This means that from now onwards India will be increasingly able to start and carry through considerable development projects without the constraints and delay involved in trying to secure (as was necessary until recently) project aid from some source, or at least an assurance that total aid would be sufficient to permit the financing of a project with a high import-content. Many valuable forms of investment now have a relatively low import-content.

This does not mean that India will import less. Indeed it is expected that imports will remain approximately constant in volume from 1967–8 to 1973–4 and thereafter increase some 24 per cent by 1978–9; in the period 1973–4 to 1978–9 there is likely to be a further round of investment in expanding heavy industry. It means rather that the character of the imports will change. India will require increasing imports of materials and intermediate goods that she cannot produce for herself. In the field of machinery and equipment she will require increased imports of more sophisticated plant that she cannot yet produce; she will require less of the simpler and less sophisticated plant that Britain in particular has exported to India in the past. Whether Britain can hold her present share of the Indian market will depend on our success in developing capacity to make and export these new types of equipment (which in the past we ourselves have largely imported from America and other countries), as competitively as we have exported the simpler equipment that India has needed in the past.

It would be ingenuous and misleading to suggest that this great structural change in the Indian economy and introduction of a whole range of new industries has been achieved smoothly and without acute growing-pains. In the early stages India was very short of trained and experienced engineers and technicians qualified to handle the very difficult tasks of building plants and getting them into production in a country with no past experience of tackling these problems. Foreign experts, knowledgeable about the gestation periods and tempos of their own countries, have proved very fallible in their predictions of the gestation periods and tempos of India. Attempts to achieve these results in conditions of balance of payment strain have meant an over-centralization of decision-making in Delhi and delays in ordering equipment for which there were long waiting lists of orders in the supplying countries. The anxiety of Indian planners to achieve results quickly and relieve poverty and unemployment quickly has led to unrealistic planning, not so much in respect of the desirable balance of investment, as in respect of the timing of completions, the periods of running in and the rates of possible build up of production. There have been a large number of cases, only too well known to all Indian observers, of major technical mistakes in construction or operation, which have led to temporary breakdowns. If one compares the achievements with the promises and prognostications it is very easy to feel disappointment. A nation must learn, it has been said, by making its own mistakes. It is much more relevant to compare what exists today with what existed twenty years ago and to feel admiration. There exists today in India the beginnings of a great industrial state, and over the past twenty years a new generation of younger engineers, technicians and scientists has grown up which is far more qualified to carry through the next round of developments.

These mistakes, and particularly the misjudgments of the practicable tempo of development, have had one predictable consequence. In some branches of the heavy industries, of the machine-building industries, and of electricity supply, capacity has been built up faster than has yet been justified by demand from new expanding industries. A study recently made for the *Reserve Bank of India Bulletin* has shown that, if shift-working was adopted in industries in which it was desirable, a very big increase of production could be achieved (the article put it as high as 61 per cent) above the depressed level of 1967, without any further investment; what is less clear is that the production would be properly balanced as between different products. Growth of demand in 1968 and 1969 has absorbed much of the over-capacity. But it remains that the steel industry and a number of branches of the machine-building industries can meet the growth of the next few years without more investment than is already in train. Thus the capital/output ratio of the next stage of expansion is likely to be lower.

V

The consequences of the transformation of the Indian economy that have been described in the last section are to be seen in the structure of the economy and the relative growth of its various components. The changes are best stated in terms of the composition of the national income. Table 8 shows what has happened:

It will be seen that, as in all countries as they develop, the share of agriculture at constant prices has been falling; because of the shift in the internal terms of trade favourable to agriculture this phenomenon is concealed when measured at current prices. The share of large scale manufacturing, though rising steadily, except for the set-

Table 8

CONTRIBUTIONS OF VARIOUS ACTIVITIES TO NET DOMESTIC PRODUCT
(at prices of 1960–1)

	1960–1 %	*1964–5* %	*1967–8* %	*1968–9* %
Agriculture, Forestry and Fishing	51·0	46·7	45·3	44·6
Manufacturing, Construction Mining and Utilities	20·1	22·3	22·1	22·8
of which: large scale manufacturing	8·0	9·6	9·4	10·0
Transport and Distribution	14·1	15·1	15·6	15·5
Banking, Dwelling, Public Administration, Defence and other Services	14·8	15·9	17·0	17·1
Net Domestic Product	100·0	100·0	100·0	100·0
N.D.P. (1960–1 = 100)	100·0	120·3	124·8	128·4

Source: Reserve Bank of India Bulletin, June 1969: figures for 1968–9 projected on the basis of indices and other evidence of production by the author of this article.

back of 1966–7 and 1967–8, is still relatively small. Transport, distribution, banking and other services have, as in most countries, been increasing slowly their share in the total of activities.

Within the total of industrial production, it is the capital goods industries and the basic industries providing the necessary materials for them which have been growing most rapidly. Table 9 shows, however, that down to the first quarter of 1969 production in the

Table 9

INDICES OF INDUSTRIAL PRODUCTION
(1960–1 = 100)

	1960	*1964*	*1965*	*1966*	*1967*	*1968*	*1969* (1st Qr.)
General Index	100·0	140·9	153·7	152·4	151·4	160·9	168·3
Basic Industries	100·0	152·1	164·3	172·9	176·4	193·9	205·9
Capital Goods Industries	100·0	206·1	244·2	210·1	205·2	210·9	224·5
Intermediate Goods	100·0	132·2	140·1	136·7	139·6	148·2	153·0
Consumer Goods	100·0	118·6	127·5	131·3	125·6	131·9	142·6

capital goods industries, though recovering, was still below the peak of 1965.

The rate of growth of net domestic product as a whole from 1960–1 to 1968–9 was 3·2 per cent per annum; down to 1964–5 it was 4·8 per cent. For the whole period to 1968–9 the growth of the contribution of manufacturing, construction, mining and the associated public utilities was 5·7 per cent; down to 1964–5 it was as high as 7·5 per cent. In considering what is practicable for the future if the constraints imposed by food supply are less severe, this much higher performance of the industrial sector needs to be borne in mind.

VI

I come now to the balance of payments and the problems of imports and exports which determine it. If one goes back to the close balance of the year 1950–1, when the series of development plans started, this was achieved with a volume of imports at constant prices about 45 per cent of the level of 1968–9 and with a volume of exports about 70 per cent of the 1968–9 level. The problems of the balance have arisen, as was said earlier, because capital development in India has had a high import-content, and because actual production (both the raw material and the fuel endowments of India are lacking in important requirements of the needs of an industrialized economy) has involved added imports. The problem has been and remains one of modifying the structure of the economy sufficiently to provide a satisfactory balance on the new basis.

In more normal years, as represented best by 1960–1, 1964–5 and 1968–9 India's total deficit on both current and capital accounts, requiring to be financed, has been equivalent to about 41–2 per cent of the total of imports measured c.i.f., or about 4 per cent of the national income. In the years of crop failure and recovery, as represented by 1965–6, 1966–7 and 1967–8 the amount requiring to be financed was equivalent to about 54–6 per cent of imports or about 5 per cent of the national income.

May I start with the pattern of imports in recent years? Table 10 is presented for convenience in dollars rather than rupees since devaluation makes a series in rupees more difficult to interpret. It shows the large share of imports of foodgrains and cereal products in the total during the crisis years. The value of cereals imported in 1968–9 was little more than half that of 1966–7 but still accounted for 18 per cent of the total. The import of raw materials and intermediate products, as was to be expected, mounts steadily and now makes up 43 per cent of the total. The import of capital goods is now well below the peak of 1965–6.

Table 10

THE COMPOSITION OF IMPORTS 1960–1 TO 1968–9
($ millions)

	1960–1	*1965–6*	*1966–7*	*1967–8*	*1968–9*
Cereals	380·9	676·3	867·8	690·8	448·7
Raw materials and intermediate manufactures	973·3	1005·7	892·1	1043·3	1040·0
Capital goods	747·6	1071·4	791·2	680·4	698·3
Others unclassified	291·5	204·5	219·4	217·2	253·3
Total imports	2393·3	2957·9	2770·5	2631·7	2440·3
Percentage shares of:					
cereals	15·9	22·9	31·3	26·2	18·4
materials and intermediates	40·7	34·0	32·2	39·6	42·6
capital goods	31·2	36·2	28·6	25·9	28·6
others	12·2	6·9	7·9	8·3	10·4
Volumes of imports (1960–1 = 100)	100	120	116	130	118

While the volume of imports has risen from 1950–1 to 1968–9 by about 4·0 per cent per annum or 1·3 times the growth of national income, the volume of exports has increased by only 1·8 per cent per annum – less than 0·6 of the growth of national income and only about 0·4 of the rate of growth of trade of similar developing countries over the period.

For this disappointing performance there have been many explanations and excuses provided – some good, some less cogent. Of the total of exports in 1950–1, tea, jute manufactures and cotton manufactures – India's traditional exports – represented 56 per cent. Exports of engineering products and of iron-ore and concentrates were then negligible. Another 18 per cent were largely made up of a variety of oils, spices, ores, tobacco and similar primary products which had also traditionally contributed to India's exports. For many of these the demand in world markets had a low income-elasticity and India already produced a large proportion of the total supply. The volume at constant prices of the traditional exports of tea, jute manufactures and cotton manufactures has fallen since 1950–1 by a little over 10 per cent, or about 0·6 per cent per annum, in some

Table 11

INDIAN EXPORTS 1960–1 TO 1968–9
(U.S. $ millions)

	1960–1	*1965–6*	*1966–7*	*1967–8*	*1968–9*
1. Jute manufactures	283·8	383·9	332·6	312·1	290·6
2. Tea	259·5	241·1	211·1	240·2	208·7
3. Cotton fabrics	120·8	116·5	84·9	87·1	94·0
Total of traditional exports	664·1	741·5	628·6	639·4	593·3
4. Iron ore	35·7	88·4	93·6	99·7	117·8
5. Manganese ore	29·5	23·2	18·9	14·8	18·0
6. Iron and steel	11·6	17·5	31·6	69·2	99·2
7. Engineering goods	17·9	34·9	30·7	43·6	89·9
Total of 4–7	94·7	164·0	174·8	227·3	324·9
8. Chemicals and allied products	7·2	19·2	14·5	15·9	23·4
9. Leather and manufactures	52·4	59·7	82·8	71·3	96·9
10. All others	568·0	707·4	640·9	644·1	774·6
Total Exports	1,386·4	1,691·8	1,541·6	1,598·0	1,813·1
Percentage shares of:					
traditional exports	47·9	43·8	40·8	40·0	32·7
items 4–7	6·8	9·7	11·3	14·2	17·9
other exports	45·3	46·5	47·9	45·8	49·4
Volume of exports (1960–1 = 100)	100	124	119	122	142

Notes: (1) Source: *Indian Economic Survey*, 1968–9, pp. 110–11 for years to 1967–8; year 1968–9 from *Basic Statistical Material Relating to Foreign Trade Production and Prices.*

(2) Values are throughout in US $ at current prices and exchange rates.

cases because agricultural difficulties have limited supplies. The remaining exports have increased over the same period by 138 per cent, or about 5·0 per cent per annum. The low base from which they started has, however, precluded hitherto a satisfactory total growth of total exports.

Some part of the loss of traditional exports is, however, less easily justified. An interesting recent analysis of Indian export performance by Professor Benjamin Cohen[3] has shown that while imports from

[3] Paper for the International Economic Association Conference on *Economic Development of South Asia* to be published during 1970 by Macmillan.

all sources of India's traditional exports by North America, Europe and Japan increased in value during the period 1960 to 1967 by 19 per cent, those from India declined by 3 per cent. On the other hand, Pakistan's share rose by 13 per cent. If India had remained as competitive as in 1960 – Professor Cohen argues – she could at least have added some 23 per cent to her traditional exports. Such an increase would have eliminated about 30 per cent of the 1968–9 trade gap.

Table 12

BALANCES OF PAYMENTS, 1960–1 TO 1968–9
($ millions)

	1960–1	*1965–6*	*1966–7*	*1967–8*	*1968–9*
Current Account					
Imports (cif)	2,393	2,958	2,771	2,632	2,440
Exports (fob)	1,386	1,692	1,542	1,598	1,813
Trade Balance	−1,007	−1,266	−1,229	−1,034	−627
Adjustment to Balance of Payment Basis	60	76	70	−16	(–)
Invisibles (net)	−2	−153	−214	−214	(−213)
Current Account Balance	−949	−1,343	−1,373	−1,264	(−840)
Capital Transactions					
Private (net)	+35	−31	−28	−20	
Government (net)	+9	+23	+119	+187	
Amortisation Payments	−79	−178	−202	−249	
Repurchase of Rupees from I.M.F.	−23	−75	−58	−58	
Banking Capital	+20	−18	+3	+24	
Errors and Omissions	−13	+19	+37	−114	
Balance of Capital Transactions	−51	−260	−129	−229	(−160)
Total Deficit	−999	−1,602	−1,502	−1,494	(−1,000)
Financing					
External Assistance:					
Loans	416	968	792	990	
Grants	70	73	87	117	
P.L. 480	389	525	447	391	
Drawings from I.M.F.	—	137	188	90	
Decline in Reserves (+) Increase (–)	124	−101	−12	−94	
Total of Financing	+999	+1,602	+1,502	+1,494	(+1,000)

Note: Figures in brackets are rough estimates for 1968–9.

The resulting balance of payments and the methods of financing it are shown in Table 12. For purposes of consistency with Tables 10 and 11 it starts with the trade figures for imports and exports rather than with the slightly differing balance of payments calculations which make deductions from recorded imports where goods are in part received without foreign payment and allow for other minor differences. It will be seen that not only current transactions but also normal capital transactions are in deficit; the inflow of capital for Indian development on private account has been small and capital movements have been almost wholly in the form of government financing. The amount requiring to be financed has been of the order of \$1·0 billion, which rose to \$1·5 to \$1·6 billion in the years 1965–6 to 1967–8.

A policy of eliminating the gap must clearly start on the export side. A continued growth of non-traditional exports by 5·0 per cent per annum combined with stability in traditional exports could add by 1973–4 some \$330 million to exports; more competitive costs of the traditional exports might possibly add another \$120 million to exports. This would imply, if the gap were to be reduced to about \$250 million per annum which might be covered by more normal capital inflow, a level of imports \$300 million (or if one is sceptical about recovering traditional exports \$400 million) below that of 1967–8 – an almost impossible task of import-saving. For it would imply reducing imports by these amounts in circumstances in which, with growth but the present propensities to import, the non-cereals imports might be expected to increase by something like \$800 million.

Turning to imports one may, perhaps, begin by assuming that, with the green revolution, cereals imports can be reduced over a year or two by a further \$250 million below the level of 1968–9; to eliminate them completely may raise problems of how some of India's customers for engineering goods and consumer goods are to pay for them, but it is obviously India's policy to become self-supporting in food. This would leave the problem of saving some \$600 to \$700 million out of an import bill which would otherwise have been about \$2,800 million – a reduction of about 20 per cent to 25 per cent.

This would be an almost impossible task. It would involve exploiting to the utmost the two gains which India has achieved: that the import-content of capital formation can now be greatly reduced; that the capital/output ratio for future development is likely to be very appreciably lower than it has been in the first phase. But its accomplishment would put severe strains on the Indian economy and revive the shortages of spare parts, components and materials, from which India has only partly escaped since devaluation, to an extent that would be almost certainly self-frustrating. It is more sensible to set a less heroic objective of financial independence for the next five years.

VII

Thus far I have been concerned to show the actual changes that have been achieved in the Indian economy and have deliberately eschewed discussion of the present plans and forecasts for the future. It is interesting in the light of what has been achieved to go on now to the plans for the future.

It has been emphasized that the two major constraints on Indian development hitherto – the propensity to inflation in the food sector and the high import-content of capital formation – are now less potent than in the past. The problems of the balance of payments remain formidable but perhaps seem a little less insoluble than they did three or four years ago.

The weakening of these constraints (though the balance of payments constraint is still very powerful) has made the ability to find savings to finance the planned investment the dominant constraint for the near future. The question that economists, both academic and government, are now asking themselves with increasing urgency is what level of saving – and particularly what marginal level of saving – can realistically be assumed for the future. In the past rather high marginal savings ratios have been assumed. The abortive first draft of the Fourth Plan assumed that out of the expected addition to real gross domestic product a little over 24 per cent would be able to be devoted to increased capital expenditure. Such a high ratio presupposes to an extent now possibly unrealistic a strong government prepared to tax heavily and a united nation prepared to accept taxation for the future benefits it would bring. However clear the benefits may be to the outside observer, it is a little uncertain whether today the conditions are such that they can be achieved.

The high marginal savings ratio represented the implications of raising the ratio of net investment to net national income from 13·8 per cent in 1965–6 to 17·5 per cent for 1970–1. The actual ratios of recent years would appear to have been progressively rising; estimates of them[4] are as follows:

[4] I owe those for 1950–1 to 1965–6 Mr Mozoomdar of the Indian High Commission in London; they represent his own unofficial estimates based on official sources. The two last years are estimated from the Fourth Plan and the

Table 13

RATIOS OF NET INVESTMENT TO NET NATIONAL INCOME
(all figures as percentages of net national income)

	1950–1	*1955–6*	*1960–1*	*1965–6*	*1967–8*	*1973–4*
Total Investment	5·0	7·0	11·5	13·8	11·4	13·8
Domestic Savings	—	—	8·0	10·5	8·0	12·6
Foreign Savings	—	—	3·5	3·3	3·4	1·2

The new revised Fourth Plan, covering the period 1969–74 aims to raise the national income by 5·5 per cent a year over the period of the Plan and to make possible continued growth at 6 per cent. This 5·5 per cent is the resultant of 4·0 per cent expected growth in agriculture, 8·2 per cent in manufacturing, mining, construction and utilities, 5·6 per cent in services. Between 1967–8, which is used throughout as the base year, and 1973–4, it is hoped to raise net investment about 6·2 per cent per year and to restore the ratio of investment to about the level it reached at the peak in 1965–6.

The crucial balance of payments forecasts and plans assume that that total imports in 1973–4 will be 1·4 per cent lower than in 1967–8 (that year is in fact 6·4 per cent or $155 million higher than in 1968–9). To balance payments it is calculated that exports must grow by 7 per cent or more a year. By 1973–4 it is argued that they must be 59 per cent higher than in 1967–8 or 42 per cent higher than in the good year 1968–9. The Plan comments that 'this rate of growth does not appear to be out of reach if proper re-orientation of policies and institutional arrangements for export promotion is brought about.' These should, it is argued, include measures to restrain domestic consumption and expand investment in exportable goods.

In this way it is hoped to reduce the level of net aid receipts, after payment of amortization and interest, by a half below the very constant levels of the Third Plan and of the past three years. This, if it can be achieved, is a sensible policy. The Achilles heel is obviously the high rate of growth of exports assumed. One has learned by hard experience the dangers of treating export targets as a blancing factor rather than realistic export forecasts as an ingredient of one's planning.

The Plan, with its growth rate of 5·5 per cent per annum is the outcome, most would now say the satisfactory outcome, of long tussles in Delhi between two schools of thought: those who have believed that only by bold plans, aimed to achieve 7·0 per cent growth,

division between sources of savings is derived from the Plan and other official sources.

could sufficiently rapid assaults be made on poverty and unemployment; and those who have held that the savings ratios and taxation levels implied were unrealistic and would lead again to failures of fulfilment and thus to unbalanced and wasteful development. Most would now agree that a plan of this order of magnitude is better, and may even end in greater growth, than a larger but over-ambitious one. The Plan retains, however, the high marginal savings ratio of about 24 per cent which has worried a number of critics. The Planning Commission is satisfied that a more severe taxation policy can and will provide the necessary increase in public savings.

VIII

But the great problems remain. The first is that of population growth. So long as India continues to grow as in the past decade – from 439 millions in 1961 to over 560 millions by 1971, and (as has been pointed out by Professor Reddaway) continues to require provision for housing, feeding, clothing and equipping an additional 120 millions a decade from a national income under half that of the United Kingdom, so long it will be a great achievement if standards of living do not fall, and a near miracle if they are made to rise significantly. There is no problem as urgent in India as that of reducing birth rates to a level compatible with the greatly reduced death rates.

The second problem – arising in large part from the first – is that of employment. Progress in any nation has largely taken the form of releasing manpower from agriculture and other occupations of low productivity and, by absorbing it into new activities, thus adding to the national product. This process of transfer and reabsorption has hardly begun in India. Statistics do not exist to measure the problems with any exactitude. But their broad orders of magnitude can be seen. About 43 per cent of the population described themselves at the 1961 Census as workers. On that basis between 1961 and 1968 the number of available workers must have increased by about 37 millions. Of these, after allowing for the migration to the towns, some 30 millions are in rural areas.

To this problem of reabsorption of present and future unemployed, industrialization has made hitherto relatively small contribution. Between 1961 and 1968 employment in industrial activities rose by about 4 millions, to which large scale manufacturing contributed barely 1 million. Trade, administration, defence and services have probably absorbed a further 5 millions. About 1 million were added to the urban unemployed. But something like 27 million potential workers have probably been added to the population living from agriculture – an increase of about 21 per cent since 1960–1. During the same period agricultural output has grown by about 14 per cent. Productivity in agriculture measured in terms of output per head of available rural workers has fallen rather than risen. Of the total of workers a slightly larger rather than a smaller proportion than in 1960 are probably now dependent on agriculture. And already several years ago the National Sample Survey estimated rural unemployment at 5·7 millions.

It is such frightening calculations as these which, however inaccurate they may be in detail, make one wonder whether enough is yet being done to devise more capital-saving forms of development and to expand employment to the greatest extent that is economically possible. It is these great issues, and not the problems of inflation and the balance of payments, which breed revolutions and provide the major headaches of the Indian Planner.

3
THE STRATEGY OF INDIAN PLANNING*

by I. G. Patel

Secretary, Ministry of Finance, Government of India, New Delhi

1. INTRODUCTION

1.1. Any society which aims at economic progress must strive for an increase in the rate of saving and investment, a widespread diffusion of technical skills among its people and a framework of leadership that permits a reasonable degree of coherence in its efforts. These and many other aspects of national endeavour which are a necessary and integral part of the process of development cannot nevertheless be dignified to the status of a 'strategy'. For strategy implies essentially a deliberate choice – a choice of the point and timing and manner of attack on the problem at hand.

1.2. It is generally assumed that Indian Planning, at any rate since the publication of Professor Mahalanobis's plan-frame in 1955, is based on a specific strategy. What precisely is this strategy of Indian Planning? What is the particular element of choice that it embodies? What are the underlying assumptions that impart rationality to the choice? And if these assumptions are not satisfied in Indian conditions, is it possible to evolve an alternative strategy? Some of these questions are discussed in the present note in the hope that it might help clarify issues of significance in future planning.

2. THE STRATEGY

2.1. Perhaps the most frequently encountered description of the strategy of Indian Planning is that it seeks to lay particular emphasis on 'heavy' or 'basic' or 'producer goods' or 'capital goods' or 'machine building' industries. The reason for this emphasis most generally given is that it quickens the pace of capital formation.

2.2. An industry may be considered 'heavy' either because its product is not light or because it requires heavy investment per unit of output. But we cannot assign any overriding economic significance to industries simply in terms of criteria such as the weight of their product or the scale of investment they call for. At best, if

* In C.R. Rao (ed.), *Essays in Econometrics and Planning* (Pergamon, 1969).

the industries we seek to emphasize happen to be 'heavy', by and large, the term might help in conjuring up the right image. Similarly, industries or facilities which form the 'basis' for the growth of other industries derive their significance from these 'other' industries and it does not advance matters much in determining priorities to say that the 'base' must come before the 'superstructure'. The priority or the emphasis must be in terms of the final products, although it goes without saying that whatever is essential for the production of the particular final products – be it power or transport or skilled labour or steel or other materials – must be produced in the right proportion and at the right time.

2.3. The same consideration applies to singling out 'producer goods' industries for special emphasis. In common economic usage, 'producer goods' are distinguished from final goods in the sense that unlike the latter which are directly consumed or invested, the former are necessary for the production of final goods. Needless to say, things overlap; what is directly consumed or invested may also in part be used for producing consumer goods and investment goods. But one cannot assign a priority to producer goods *per se* any more than one can do so in respect of basic facilities such as power or transport.

2.4. The question is not simply one of semantics, as failure to distinguish clearly between that which is sought to be emphasized and what is essentially a means to that which is desired makes for shortcomings in policy. Thus the emphasis simply on steel may well obscure the fact that production of steel for the manufacture of motor cars (rather than for the fabrication of machines) might in fact be a negation of the basic strategy.

2.5. In terms of final goods, then, one can speak of emphasis on investment goods as distinguished from consumer goods – and going a step further, on those investment goods which are intended for augmenting the capacity of the investment goods industries themselves. Assuming for a moment that the Indian strategy of economic development consists of growing emphasis on the machine-building industry (with a growing proportion of the machines devoted to the investment goods industries), what would be the rationale of such a strategy?

3. RATIONALE IN A CLOSED ECONOMY

3.1. In a closed economy, a relatively greater emphasis on investment goods as distinguished from consumer goods is synonymous with a higher *ratio* of saving and investment in total national income; and if the output of investment goods is directed towards the investment goods industries themselves, the ratio of savings and investment to income would also rise at a faster rate than would be otherwise possible. In the extreme case, if all increments in output are in the nature of investment goods and all additional investment goods are reserved for the investment goods industries, barring what may be required to maintain the output of consumer goods, the transition from a low ratio of savings and investment to national income (say 6 per cent) to the desired rate (say 20 per cent) would be reached sooner than would otherwise be the case. If a rate of investment of 20 per cent is deemed sufficient to yield the desired rate of growth of output as a whole (say 5 to 6 per cent), the process or strategy may be reversed thereafter in the sense that the total output of investment goods may then be distributed between the consumer goods industries and the investment goods industries in whatever proportion that would be required to enable consumer goods output and investment goods output to grow at the same rate – keeping the ratio of both consumption and investment in national income more or less constant (say 80 per cent and 20 per cent respectively).

3.2. If consumer goods and investment goods industries (each taken together with their respective constellation of producer goods, basic facilities and the like) require the same amount of capital per unit of output, the total production of investment goods will need to be distributed between consumer goods industries and investment goods industries in the same proportion as is desired between consumption and investment (80:20). If, as is more likely, the investment goods are more capital-intensive, the investment goods industries would claim that much higher share in the allocation of investment goods (say 40 per cent, leaving 60 per cent, for the consumer goods industries).

3.3. The basic strategy we are considering and its rationale in a closed economy may be described, therefore, as follows. If a minimum growth rate of say, 5 per cent per annum is desired, it would require a ratio of investment to income of, say, 20 per cent. To maintain this rate of investment and this rate of growth would require a certain distribution of investment goods output between consumer goods and investment goods industries (say, 60:40). The higher the proportion of investment goods output that is reserved for the investment goods industries, the sooner would the desired ration of investment be reached. The growth in consumption (i.e. the output of consumer goods) would necessarily be smaller in the meanwhile – and perhaps the growth in output as a whole as well if the capital requirements of the investment goods industries are larger per unit of output than those for consumer goods industries. But the loss in consumption or in output as a whole would be made good over a time, as the day when the desired rate of increase in overall output (and in each constituent thereof) would begin to materialize, would come sooner. If the need to permit a certain increase in consumption – say at least to match the growth in population – limits the extent to which this strategy can be followed, there is, nevertheless, no escape from raising the ratio of investment goods going to the investment goods industries to a certain level, however gradually. This level is the one that should obtain when the desired ratio of investment in national income is reached and has to be maintained.

3.4. In short, given the assumption of a closed economy and given the technical relations between investment and output in different industries, there is a structure of production that is implicit in the objective of a desired rate of growth. The sooner this structure begins to be approximated, the sooner will the desired rate of growth be achieved. But the pace at which the structure can be approached will be a function of – and indeed be synonymous with – how fast the rate of saving (and investment) can be stepped up; and a faster pace of approaching what may be called the balanced structure of production might necessitate not only a quicker step-up in the rate of saving but also an acceptance of a lower rate of growth in the meanwhile.

4. AN OPEN ECONOMY

4.1. The case for investment goods industries in India, however, cannot be made to rest on the identity between investment and the output of investment goods which must prevail in a closed economy. Should not the fact that it is possible for India to take advantage of international division of labour make any difference to the kind of strategy it might follow in its planning?

4.2. If the ultimate objective is to attain a rate of investment high enough (20 per cent) to permit a satisfactory rate of growth (5 to 6 per cent per annum) in as short a time as possible, the structure of availabilities at India's command – sooner or later – must be the same as would obtain under the structure of production in a closed economy to which we have already referred. The difference that the possibility of international trade makes would, therefore, be in putting the same basket of consumer goods, investment goods for consumer goods industries and investment goods for investment goods industries (with their concomitant producer goods) at the disposal of India on the basis of a structure of production that would or could be different from that in a closed economy. Given the possibility of international trade, India could concentrate on the production of goods in which she had a comparative advantage and thereby achieve a somewhat higher rate of growth without having to forego that complex of availabilities which is pertinent to sustaining the tempo of further growth. International trade would thus be a liberating factor in the sense that it makes it possible to obtain that which is scarce in exchange for something which is not so scarce.

4.3. Two reasons might be given why, despite the consideration just mentioned, it would still make sense to try and erect a structure of production as if India were a closed economy. It might be argued that a country like India must have the capacity to produce all kinds of machines so that its growth would not be interrupted even when it is denied access to world markets for a time. An argument for autarky of this kind can lay little claim to rationality for it does not make much sense to determine one's day-to-day behaviour on the basis of what might be required in an ultimate emergency; and if the case is one of relative self-sufficiency in some line as a measure of insurance, it is at least arguable that there should be less emphasis on self-sufficiency in the case of things like machinery which can be run down for a few years than in regard to materials and essential consumer goods which exhaust their usefulness over a shorter span of time.

4.4. Alternatively, it might be argued that even if a realistic assessment of the possibility of international trade is made, the structure of production that would best assure the inevitable pattern of availabilities would not be materially different from the structure of production that must prevail in a closed economy. This may be for two reasons. First, the possibilities of increasing exports may be so limited that there is no escape from having to satisfy the bulk of the requirements of continuing development at a satisfactory pace from domestic production as distinguished from imports. Alternatively, it may be that while possibilities of trade are not inherently limited, they lie in the direction of a sufficiently broad-based structure of production which would correspond in broad outlines to the kind of structure that must prevail in a closed economy. In other words, the country's resource base might dictate a diversified economy which produces something of practically everything even if at each stage it would find it profitable to export some items from each category of production in return for similar items of import. Which of these two assumptions would be valid in India and what precisely are their implications? Or could it be that India's export possibilities are not only limited but are also to be found, such as they are, in the direction of an economy which is more or less fully diversified?

4.5. It could, of course, be argued that the possibilities of enlarging India's *present* exports are limited. The demand for tea or jute products around the world may not reasonably be expected to grow rapidly, whereas facilities for the manufacture of simple consumers' goods like cotton textiles might become so generally available among all countries that it would not be safe to rely on exports of such items for any length of time. It may also be that many of our present exports are particularly vulnerable in the face of growing protectionism or technical change abroad. The combination of all these factors could be shown to produce a strong presumption that, on the basis of the present range of exports, we would be faced with steadily adverse terms of trade or a slow rate of growth in the volume of exports – or both.

4.6. But arguments of the kind just presented with reference to existing exports do not warrant the conclusion that export possibilities *in general* would also be limited. Nor can one readily take it for granted that there are insuperable factors which must necessarily limit the demand or the competitive position of all existing exports. If development is a matter of more and more investment and progressively improved techniques, it would stand to reason that there would be scope for investing the growing resources in a manner which would enlarge export possibilities. There are a large number of commodities – in all fields of production – for which international demand would grow more than in others; and with ingenuity, demand could be created for many others. There is no reason to believe that a society which can successfully replace the imports of complicated products cannot nevertheless find export markets for a growing range of commodities if it sets out to do so. And it is not as if the only category of goods in which international trade is growing is that of investment goods. Fruits, processed foodstuffs, ordinary hospitality to tourists, synthetic fibres, minerals, producer goods such as fertilizers or steel, bicycles, automobiles and even cosmetics and handloom fabrics are items for which demand abroad will grow and can be stimulated. Whether conditions in world markets are such that the ratio of exports to national income must necessarily fall so that the ratio of imports to national income must also be brought down are ultimately semi-philosophical questions to which precise answers are neither possible nor necessary. The important fact is that there are no inherent limitations to exports in a developing economy so that it would be both unnecessary and wasteful to try and erect a structure of production with an accent on self-sufficiency from the outset.

4.7. Even if export possibilities are limited, what is the meaning of saying that this limitation must be overcome by trying to erect a self-sufficient economy? One may safely assume that whatever it is that limits exports will also limit the creation of a broad-based economic structure capable of delivering all the consumer goods, producer goods and investment goods necessary for rapid and continuing growth. More likely than not, lack of export opportunity or possibility will be only a reflection of the general lack of growth potential. And in any event, if export opportunities are limited, the attempt to press ahead with broad-based development will lead to balance of payments difficulties which can be overcome either by slowing down the rate of growth even when internal savings would be available or by relying on external capital. Even if external assistance is available, there would in practice be an understandable insistence on the part of both the giver and the receiver that the scope of such assistance be limited as far as possible. In other words, by the time a country comes to rely on external assistance to a significant extent, it would be called upon to exploit the possibilities of exports even if these possibilities are limited and could be exploited only at a price, i.e. by accepting less favourable terms of trade.

4.8. It might be argued that available resources should not be devoted to exploitation of export possibilities at less favourable terms of trade and should be devoted instead to activities which would ultimately save much more in imports (or earn much more by way of exports). But in practice, a strategy of this kind could be pursued with the help of external assistance only if there is considerable statesmanship and forbearance among the aid-giving countries. Even for the aid-receiving countries, it would require virtually an act of faith to forego even limited export possibilities in the present for the sake of much larger possibilities of import substitution (or of exports) at a later stage *if* external capital has to be paid back with interest. The wiser course, if export possibilities are really limited, would be not to rely on external capital and face the consequences thereof or to rely on external assistance only to the extent that it is available on terms which square with a realistic assessment of its future balance of payments.

4.9. Yet another version of the hypothesis of inherent limitation on exports may be that there is a degree of uncertainty that attaches to export promotion which does not apply to import-substitution so that the latter must be given a margin of preference in planning. Exports might be shut off by the trade policies of others, whereas what is saved on imports is secure. This is, of course, one of those propositions which gain in validity the more widely they are accepted as axiomatic. But it cannot alter one's view as to what would be more rational if it were possible.

4.10. The alternative hypothesis, viz. that while export possibilities exist and could be created and exploited, they lie essentially in the direction of establishing a broad-based industrial and economic structure, certainly fits the facts about a large continental country like India which has a diversified resource base. Given the fact that India has abundant resources of iron ore, coal, and other minerals, there is no reason why it could not, in time, be proficient in the manufacture of steel or engineering goods or machinery. Similarly, given its rich soil and low yields at present, it could add substantially to its output of many agricultural products; and the same would be true of a large variety of manufactured consumer goods. While India would export and import growing amounts of a large variety of goods, the general drift of the economy would be towards a well-diversified structure of production.

4.11. But where exactly does the line of reasoning just outlined lead us in the matter of priorities in planning? Granted that agricultural output on a wide front can be increased, it does not follow that it should be increased in the direction of substituting for imports rather than of increasing exports. Granted that steel can be competitively produced, it does not follow that exports of iron-ore should not be increased. And indeed, once steel begins to be produced in large quantity and efficiently, it does not follow that it should be better to employ the steel for producing machinery rather than exchange it directly for machinery. And when machines are produced (or indeed obtained by exchange), they may yield more if applied to consumer goods industries where export-potential (or indeed import-substitution) has reached a certain momentum rather than to developing import-substitution in new lines. At each stage of development, a choice will have to be made between consolidating and enlarging existing export opportunities and developing new export-potential, between consolidating and enlarging capacity for import substitution in existing lines and developing a similar capacity in new lines. The simple rule of going in for import-substitution all along the line cannot yield the best answer if only because it would spread the total effort too thinly. Nor can one claim any merit in merely minimizing total imports over a period as there is no virtue in minimizing imports if exports can be increased even more by not doing so.

4.12. At best one can argue that if a country's comparative advantage is likely to lie over a wide field and if some of these fields are such as to require a considerable time for this advantage to be developed fully, it should take action well in advance to be able to exploit this advantage. But even advance action which looks to the future involves a choice – a choice, first between immediate gain and larger future gain and, again, a choice between advance action of one kind and another. By all means, within limits, at each stage of development a country should try to keep a step ahead, so to speak, by investing in ventures that take time to fructify; but such ventures would be as much in the field of export-promotion as import-substitution – as indeed in the field of basic facilities and services which would be necessary for both. The necessity to look ahead, therefore, does not by itself imply that a structure of production more akin to that in a closed economy will happen to be the most desirable if we do look ahead. And even if this is the case, it does not necessarily follow that the best approach to the final structure that is likely to emerge is by trying to skip stages all the time rather than by advancing in uneven but measured steps in different directions at different times.

4.13. Once we embark on the high seas of international exchange and discard the shelter of the hypothesis of limited export possibilities, we cannot seek anchor in simple rules like import-substitution all along the line or the development of machine-building capacity for the investment goods industries at the fastest possible pace. The simple world of a strategy drawn from the model of a closed economy must give place to measurement and assessment of costs and benefits over time with due allowance for at least the interest one has to pay on foreign debt for buying time. The broad outlines of policy may resemble somewhat the dictates of a simple strategy; but the differences may be just as vital if not more. In actual practice, Indian Planning today steers clear from *excessive preoccupation with self-sufficiency as a result of the necessity to export more.* But between these conflicting pulls, the actual course of the economy needs to be charted more precisely with reference to detailed assessment of available alternatives.

4.14. Whatever the allocation of resources that might turn out to be most appropriate from time to time, the basic necessity of increasing savings and investment and of enlarging technical skills and the organizational base would, of course, remain. But with these, we are back from the realm of strategy and choice to what is imperative and implicit in any plan of development.

4
POPULATION CONTROL: AIMS AND POLICIES*†

by Robert Cassen

Economist, I.B.R.D., Washington D.C.

1. Few people would deny that the rapid rate of population growth in India is one of the greatest threats – if not the greatest – to her hopes of prosperity. The total population almost certainly passed the 500 million mark before the end of 1966, and at the estimated rate of 2·4 per cent, is currently growing by 1 million a month. There is not much evidence that would offer the expectation of any decline in fertility in the near future, while the death rate is expected to continue to fall. In the absence of any decline in fertility, the rate of population growth may be expected to increase, reaching, according to one estimate,[1] 3·1 per cent in 1985. At that rate, the population would double in less than twenty-three years.

2. Given what seems almost to be a law of demography in developing countries – that all population estimates are underestimates – one can hardly feel that this forecast is too gloomy. The emphasis given to population control in the Plans and the tremendous effort which is now being made in India, are therefore both very natural and very welcome.

* In P. Streeten and M. Lipton (ed.), *Crisis of Indian Planning* (Oxford Univ. Press, 1968). (This article was first published in 1968. If time had allowed, the author would have wished to revise it in some parts. In particular, he would wish to have paid closer attention to the question of the cost of a prevented birth and to the critical relationship between expenditure on family planning and the actual prevention of births – Ed.)

† This chapter was written while the author was employed by the U.K. Ministry of Overseas Development. No part of its contents should be taken necessarily to reflect official policy. The author is indebted to his colleagues there for comments on this and connected work, and particularly to Mr D. Seers and Mr W.A.B. Hopkin. I have benefited greatly from discussion at the Conference, and most especially from the comments of Professor Paul Streeten and Michael Lipton. The customary absolution from responsibility applies.

[1] U.N. Dept. Economic and Social Affairs, *Report on the Family Planning Programme in India* (February 1966), U.N. doc. (T.A.O./I.N.D./48, Photo-offset), p. 95 (henceforth 'U.N. *Report*'). For trends in total population etc., see Appendix, Table 1, pp. 142-3.

3. This chapter has three main sections. In the first there is some discussion of factors other than birth-control measures and their possible influences on the growth of Indian population. In the second the economics of reducing the birth rate are examined in general terms. In the third, the current programme is considered.*

1. THE INFLUENCE OF FACTORS OTHER THAN BIRTH CONTROL

4. The view has been expressed that the population problems of developing countries may 'solve themselves'. Although there is no satisfactory quantitative explanation of the decline in birth rates experienced by the developed countries, the list of contributory factors believed to be the causes of the decline is fairly well defined. It has even been graced with the title of the 'theory of demographic transition',[2] though as more and better historical demographic data are compiled, this theory becomes more rather than less puzzling.

5. At any rate, there is agreement among demographers that fertility decline is associated with economic development, and in particular with 'modernization'. The growth of urban industrial society makes itself felt as an influence in the direction of changing social customs which affect fertility – most particularly in raising the marriage age – and of raising the economic cost of having children.

6. As far as India is concerned, there is little basis to hope that such factors will operate significantly in the near future. Urbanization, which figures importantly in the theory of demographic transition, does not yet appear to be having much effect on the overall birth rate. The urbanization which has taken place in India has not been accompanied by the types of social change which favour lower birth rates. Indeed, the social system and family structure of rural life seem to survive transplantation to the town or city quite remarkably, according to sociological studies. Marital fertility is somewhat lower in cities than in rural areas, and urban birth rates are lower than rural rates, in part as a consequence of the high male–female ratio in cities.[3] But the differences are not very great, and the rural-urban distribution of population has changed little between the 1951 and 1961 censuses.

7. As far as marriage age is concerned, the U.N. Report on the

* [I.e. *circa* 1967 – Ed.]

[2] For a discussion of this theory, see D.M. Heer, 'Economic Development and Fertility', *Demography*, III, No. 2 (Chicago, 1966), and works there cited.

[3] See Appendix, Table 2, p. 143.

Family Planning Programme in India calculates[4] that if the average age at marriage rose from 16 to 20 over the period up to 1985, the birth rate would fall by about 7 per 1,000 – that is, from 41·4 in 1965 to 34·4 in 1985. This by itself would be only a slight contribution to the solution of the population problem. And, as the Report emphasizes, this is not an extrapolation of any trend, but an upper limit to the results both of changes which are occurring and of possible policies to be pursued by the Government of India to raise the marriage age.

8. One aspect of the 'transition', possibly more hopeful than those mentioned hitherto and largely neglected by the U.N. Report, is the relation between death rates and birth rates. A commonly quoted cause of high birth-rates in developing countries is the combination of high death rates and no social security, or, to put it another way, the desire of parents to ensure that some at least of their children will survive as long as they themselves do. Demographers at the Harvard School of Public Health have produced studies showing that, in a cross section of forty-one countries, the strongest relation among numerous variables with fertility was that of infant mortality – where one was high, so was the other.[5] They could, of course, be positively correlated simply as a result of some other factor or factors acting on both. But simulation studies of mathematical population models have yielded results described as 'generally realistic', showing slower population growth rates, over a range of mortality rates, the lower the mortality.[6]

9. Of course, there are historical cases of simultaneously falling death rates and rising birth rates. To treat death rate reductions as a hopeful source of fertility reductions in India, one would need

[4] U.N. *Report*, pp. 97–8. More precisely, the Report estimates such a reduction in the birth rate on the basis of assumptions that by 1985 no girls will marry before 18, 15 per cent will be married at 18, 30 per cent at 19, 60 per cent at 20 'and so on', making an allowance for increased marital fertility as a consequence of the likely reduction in the period of delayed consummation of marriage.

[5] D.M. Heer, *op. cit.*

[6] D.M. Heer and D.O. Smith, *Mortality Level and Desired Family Size*, Contrib., No. 26 (Harvard Centre for Population Studies, 1966). Another simulation study has, however, found, on the basis of different assumptions, an increase in the population growth rate, the decline in the death rate outweighing the associated decline in the birth rate. Cf. J.C. Ridley and others, 'Effects of Changing Mortality on Natality: Some Estimates from a Simulation Model', *Milbank Memorial Fund Q.*, January 1967 (New York), pp. 77–97. This study, emphasizing the effects of increased marital duration and increased intervals between births resulting from lower death rates and lower infant mortality (unlike Heer and Smith's study, which emphasizes desired family size) is based on parameters derived from Indian demographic data, and may well be the more realistic as regards the near future of the Indian population.

to know something of the time lags involved, or threshold values of death rates, or changes in death rates that would support the case. Historically, the time lags appear to have been rather long.

10. This is not an adequate discussion of autonomous factors influencing the rate of growth of population in India. It has only attempted to draw out one or two important points. The U.N. Report concludes that some decline in fertility would undoubtedly take place in the future, even in the absence of a birth control programme, 'as a result of modernization and changes in customs and social factors, particularly a slow but steady rise in the average age at marriage'. However, it goes on to say, it is not excluded 'that this decline in fertility will, at least partly, be counter-balanced by an increase in fecundity,[7] and by an increase in the proportion of live births to total births, as a result of improved health conditions. Future decline in adult mortality may also reduce the frequency of widowhood and keep a larger proportion of women in marital status; and a weakening of taboos against re-marriage might tend to raise the present relatively low level of fertility in India.'

11. It is this analysis, together with the expectation of a continued decline in death rates, which led the Report to project an increase in the growth rate of the population in the absence of any measures to control it. We have not found much, if any, cause to challenge this view. One last point, however, may be of some significance. Although such social and economic change as has been occurring in India may not have brought with it any fall in fertility, this may in part be due to a lack of knowledge of, and means for, birth control. It may well be that this change is nevertheless engendering a sharpening of the motivation to adopt measures of birth control when these are made available.

2. THE ECONOMICS OF REDUCING THE BIRTH-RATE

(*a*) *The General Argument*

12. We consider the question first quite generally, with the proviso that we are referring to countries where the pressure of population

[7] 'Fecundity' in demographic parlance refers to the biological potential for reproduction, while 'fertility' is simply the number of births expressed (usually) as a rate per 1,000 women. The latter is distinguished from the (crude) birth rate, which is the number of births per 1,000 people. A factor of some importance, which the U.N. *Report* has not taken into account, is the impact of the eradication of malaria in 1945–55. This considerably reduced child mortality, and results currently in a rising share of women of child-bearing age, making the task of achieving an actual fall in the birth rate, even with a successful family planning programme, a very daunting one, at least before the mid-1970s.

on resources is already considerable. In crude aggregate terms one can set out the problem quite simply. A fall in the birth rate reduces the number of children in the year in which it occurs relative to the number there would otherwise have been (and in subsequent years if the lower birth rate continues – we will assume that it does). If we assume – which may not be entirely correct – that a child performs no productive service until the age of fifteen, then we can be confident that income per head during those fifteen years will be higher than it would otherwise have been, if only because there are less heads. (This will be true provided that, as seems plausible, the reduction of numbers of people of non-working age does not affect output. Though it is of course possible that, had there been more children, their parents would have made greater efforts.) But the effect on growth is more complicated than this. The increase in income per head through the reduction of numbers[8] in early years may itself lead to additional increases in incomes. What happens will depend on how the resources, released by the relative reduction in the number of children, are used.

13. These resources may be used in a number of ways. They may simply be consumed – if so, the consequences for economic growth are hard to calculate. There is some effect of consumption on productivity in developing countries, but it would be a major task requiring original research to quantify it. Nevertheless, even if all the released resources are consumed, there is likely to be some improvement of economic performances. The resources may also be saved and invested, though once again only a firm believer in aggregate capital–output ratios would put a definite quantity on the effect of this investment on growth, except to say that it would be positive.

14. Further to this, as well as the resources directly released through the reduction of the number of children to be clothed and fed, there are likely to be investment resources shifted from the social uses encouraged by a growing population to the provision of productive equipment. It is possible that the contribution of this effect to economic growth may be at least as significant as those mentioned in the previous paragraph.

15. It is, then, fairly clear that for the early years after the fall in the birth rate there are unambiguous gains in income per head (*a*) simply as a result of the reduction of numbers, with no loss of output, and (*b*) as a result of the application of the resources made

[8] Here and at other points in the paper 'reduction in numbers' should be read as an elliptical expression for 'reduction in numbers relative to those which would have occurred otherwise'.

available by the reduction of numbers. But, after fifteen years or so, the reduction of numbers affects the size of the labour force, and calculation becomes difficult. One can put the question simply: will the relative loss of labour offset the gains during the early years?

16. We shall not attempt to pursue this question in full. We shall ignore the arguments which purport to show the economic advantages of rapid population growth, since they are hardly relevant to the Indian case. But reference should be made to two important features of the problem. The first is unemployment. Clearly, in a country which has difficulties in absorbing its existing labour force, additions to the labour force cannot be of immediate benefit. Thus, while it is fifteen years before the labour force is affected by a reduction in the birth rate, it may be twenty or thirty years before the numbers actually employed are significantly affected. The second is the so-called 'burden of dependency'. As can be seen from the Appendix (Table 1) fertility decline has the effect of raising quite sharply the proportion of people of working age in the population. These points imply that, whatever sacrifices of output are made by a reduction in labour-force size, they occur a long way in the future and are partially cancelled out by changes in the age distribution. The benefits of reduced numbers, however, occur immediately.

17. (Strictly speaking, the presence of unemployment means that one is concerned with the absolute number of dependants, adult or child, rather than the ratio of people of working and non-working age. A constant dependency ratio as indicated by the size of age groups may conceal a worsening or an improving situation, depending on what is happening to employment. One should add that, for precise calculation, two further aspects at least should be taken into account: (*a*) the fact that declining fertility increases the participation of women in the labour force; and (*b*) the relative consumption standards of children and adults. If welfare is a matter of consumption per head and not output per head, one should note that the dependency ratio need only be corrected for a participation rate to estimate changes in output per head, but further correction is required for estimating the effect of a change in the dependency ratio on consumption per equivalent adult. See also the quotation from Coale and Hoover in note 9.)

(*b*) *The Indian Case*

18. Let us now consider these arguments in the Indian case. The purpose of doing so is not to demonstrate that the gains from reducing the birth rate in India outweigh the losses. It is rather to see what steps would be necessary to calculate the economic effects of reducing

the birth rate, and thereby to evaluate the return to expenditure on birth control.

19. Unfortunately, as we shall see, it is not possible to estimate at all accurately the 'returns' to birth control, if the above general argument is roughly correct, since on almost all points where quantitative estimates are necessary, they are lacking in the literature known to the author, and it is beyond the scope of this study to provide them.

20. In particular, an estimate of the effect on income per head of a reduced birth rate would require at least: (*a*) an estimate of the marginal propensity to save, not out of aggregate income, but out of income per head. It may be that studies exist for areas of India showing savings at different levels of income and family size, which would go some way towards assisting a calculation of the additional savings that could be expected from growing incomes with lower, as compared with higher, population growth; but the author has been unable to locate any such studies; (*b*) in so far as additions to income per head are consumed, an estimate of the effect of increased consumption on productivity. Although this effect may be substantial, the author has not found any quantitative work on this subject in India adequate for the purpose; (*c*) an estimate of the extent to which the composition of investment as between social overhead capital and productive equipment might be affected by a reduction in the rate of growth of population. In this case it would be hard to provide a quantitative estimate, since public policy would weigh so heavily as a determinant. In the case of India it might be argued that, in the short run at least, a reduction of the rate of growth of population would not have much effect on the composition of investment, on the grounds that the need for social investment is already far from being met, and that a small reduction in this need is unlikely to reduce to any significant extent the pressure for social investment, at least in the public sector. On private sector housing, there might be some effect.[9]

[9] One might compare A.J. Coale and E.M. Hoover, *Population Growth and Economic Development in Low-Income Countries* (Princeton Univ. Press, 1958) – still the most painstaking attempt at an estimate of the economic consequences of reduced fertility in India, even if its demographic basis has been overtaken by the 1961 Census. They allow for increased savings, but the main difference between the high-fertility and low-fertility income projections comes from the change in the composition of investment. Over numerous variations in the values of parameters, they estimate that the low-fertility case typically shows a 1 per cent gain in the annual growth of *total* output over a thirty-year period, so that gains in consumption per head are very considerable. (Another interesting feature of their analysis is an estimate of the very long run; using a Cobb–Douglas

21. What we have in mind here is a model of economic-demographic growth, in which the marginal propensity to save is a function both of income and of population; output is a function of consumption per head, as well as the usual variables; and the capital–output ratio is a function of population (this would seem to be the simplest way of taking account of the effect of population change on the composition of investment). But since we cannot estimate, or even guess intelligently, many of the coefficients involved, further elaboration of such a model would not be useful for present purposes. Nevertheless, spelling this out does achieve one thing: it introduces a criticism of one aspect of those cost–benefit analyses of birth control which include in their estimate of benefits no recognition of the interactions of population change and economic growth. (This is one of many criticisms to which Enke's celebrated analysis[10] is subject, concentrating, as it does, simply on the discounted present value of an individual 'life'.)

22. Without some such model as above described, it is hard to make an accurate assessment of the effect of reducing the rate of growth of population on income per head. However, since these considerations all work in the direction of raising income per head (there are others, not yet considered in this section, which work in the opposite direction, which will be mentioned below), a cruder calculation may suggest a lower limit to this effect.

23. For reasons which will be made clear in the last section, we will examine here the effects of a programme which would effectively reduce the 1975 population by 40 million over the ten years from 1965, relative to what it would otherwise have been; that is, we will compare the alternatives of 630 million people and 590 million people in 1975.

24. The simplest calculation is the effect on income per head of the fact of there being less heads. If income growth were entirely independent of population growth, income per head in 1975 with a population of 590 million would be approximately 6·8 per cent higher than with a population of 630 million. As has been suggested, the effect of a reduced birth rate on economic growth is likely to

---

production function, which allows for substitution between labour and capital, they estimate income per consumer in the low-fertility case to be nearly double that in the high-fertility case after fifty-five years, claiming that 'the economic advantages of reduced fertility are distinctly *not* limited to a transition period before labour force growth is affected' (p. 327).) We cannot here attempt any critique of their approach.

[10] S. Enke, 'The Economic Aspects of Slowing Population Growth', *Economic Journal*, March 1966.

raise this figure within the ten-year period, but we were, for reasons explained, unable to make this calculation.

25. However, there is some cost involved in achieving the lower population. An acceptable figure for the upper limit of the cost of a 'prevented birth' is \$10.[11] With an average of 4 million prevented births per year, this gives an annual expenditure of \$40 million per year, or Rs. 300 million (post-devaluation). Assuming an incremental capital–output ratio of 4, and a marginal savings rate of 0·16, and no depreciation of capital, the increment to total income in 1975 of an annual investment of Rs. 300 million for ten years is about Rs. 800 million, or less than Rs. 1·5 per head.[12] Let us say Rs. 2, to err on the side of caution.

26. At the time of writing, no estimate was available of Indian national income in 1975. The Draft Fourth Plan[13] indicated that work on such estimates was still in progress. But taking the target income for 1970–1 of Rs. 231,000 million and assuming a growth rate of 5 per cent per year gives roughly Rs. 300,000 million for 1975, or about Rs. 508 per head at 590 million population, and about Rs. 476 per head at 630 million. (Our calculation is, in any case, insensitive to changes in the estimate of 1975 income.)

27. We have still to allow for the alternative use of resources. Correctly, we should not have calculated the growth of total incomes at the same rates, since the high-population total income should be greater to allow for the use of resources not devoted to family

[11] The figure is taken from G. Ohlin, *Population Control and Economic Development*, O.E.C.D., Development Centre Studies, No. 8, p. 138. This implies another criticism of Enke, whose much lower figure comes from estimating only the medical charges involved, omitting organizational and educational costs.

[12] We have calculated this in the following way. If an amount C is invested each year, with capital–output ratio k, and marginal savings ratio m, the addition to the capital stock after T years is given by the formula

$$C\frac{(1+m/k)^T-1}{m/k}$$

assuming no depreciation, and assuming that all savings are invested. Since, however, we are interested in the income generated by this investment in year T, we should not include in the formula for the relevant capital stock the capital generated indirectly by year T's investment, so that the formula should become

$$C\left[1+\frac{(1+m/k)^{T-1}-1}{m/k}\right]$$

Dividing the resulting capital stock estimate by k, estimated income in year T from the stream of investments is derived. (This is an improvement on the formulation in Ohlin, p. 149, where the increments to the capital stock due to the savings generated by each year's investment are neglected.)

[13] *The Fourth Five-Year Plan*, 1966, p. 28 [this Plan was later abandoned].

planning. But Rs. 300 million is a very small fraction of total investment (less than 1 per cent of total annual investment as projected in the Draft Plan). An acceptable, if rough and ready, way of making this allowance might therefore be to subtract the increment in income per head due to the alternative use of resources from the higher figure, giving Rs. 506 and Rs. 476 respectively, or a net increase in income per head due to birth control of over 6 per cent. Over ten years, this represents somewhat more than an additional ½ per cent per year on the rate of growth of income per head.[14] The above calculation can be summarized as follows:

ALTERNATIVE SITUATIONS IN 1975

Population	*Cost of E.P. Programme in foregone 1975 income*	*Total income*	*Income per head*
630	Rs. (nil)	Rs. 300,000 m.	Rs. 476
590	Rs. 1,500 m.	Rs. 298,500 m.	Rs. 506

28. It must be emphasized that we have been trying to calculate the *lower limit* of the net increase. At every stage of the calculation we have adopted figures which favour the return to the 'alternative use of resources' and diminish the return to birth control. We have ignored the positive effect on growth of reducing the birth rate; we have taken the highest suggested figure for the cost of preventing a birth; we have ignored depreciation and gestation lags in calculating the return to the alternative use of resources. This has been done partly because no figures are available, and partly because, where a range of figures is given, one has often no particular reason for choosing the higher or lower end of the range. But we have also been motivated by the existence of some suspiciously high estimates, and a desire to produce another estimate which commands some confidence.

29. It may be useful to compare our result with the kind of calculation made by Enke. As is well known, his conclusion was that the return to investment in birth control may be as much as a hundred times as high as the return to other forms of investment. We

[14] This analysis is challengeable at many points. We have made a set of calculations with various levels of marginal savings rates and capital–output ratios: see Appendix, Table 3. It is obvious that, at any reasonable values of these parameters, the superiority of investment in birth control is unchallenged. As one would expect, the calculation is more sensitive to changes in k than changes in m.

have not in fact calculated a 'return to investment', but rather have attempted to assess the difference in *per capita* income after ten years with and without a programme comparable to that being undertaken by the Government of India. In our calculation, the net gain from birth control of *per capita* income in 1975 is Rs. 30, representing fifteen times as large a return as that from other investment. A true cost–benefit analysis would of course take the annual stream of benefits and costs and compare their discounted values. The 'value' of a prevented birth diminishes over time with the increase in the probability of death, as well as from possible effects of changes in the size of the labour force in later years, so that a great deal depends on the discount rate employed. We have preferred to avoid introducing yet more untrustworthy numbers into the calculation.

30. An interesting point, raised by Michael Lipton, is the implication of the difference between the average and the marginal investment in birth control. Although the average return is very high, the costs of extending particular aspects of the programme in particular areas may be very considerable – sufficient possibly to compare unfavourably with alternative uses of resources. In fact, if one disaggregated the programme on a local basis, one would have a series of programmes, the cost curve of each of which would probably have the shape of an inverted, recumbent 'S', rising at first as the programme spreads to remote areas and people unfamiliar with birth control, then falling, as with 'contagion' models of disease or information, as widespread knowledge makes acceptance simpler, and finally rising again as it attempts to reach the most scattered or most uninterested inhabitants of the area. This last phase of an area programme might well lack economic justification, but one would expect the bulk of the population to be reached on the declining-cost part of the curve in each area. It is nevertheless an important qualification to our argument that not all expenditures on birth control are justified. In defence of our analysis, however, it can be said that we were using the U.N. Report's maximum feasible programme, whose feasibility should in part have depended on considerations of the costs of further extension.

31. One could go deeper still, and examine the sensitivity of the results of given outlays on birth-control measures to variations in complementary educational and medical measures, in rural and urban demographic patterns, in income distribution, in administrative expenditure and techniques, and so on.[15] Information on some of these questions is available from studies of programmes in other countries; and it is to be hoped that the continuous evaluation

[15] The author is indebted to Professor Paul Streeten for these points.

proposed in the Indian programme will not lose sight of these points. Certainly an analysis of returns to expenditure, with medical, administrative, and educational charges lumped together in a figure for 'cost per prevented birth', gives little guidance for the detailed preparation of a programme. Our intention, though, has been mainly to give substantive justification to the overall policy decision to spend very large sums of money on family planning, and give some indication of the likely return.

32. The effect on the labour force is worth a further mention. It has been assumed throughout that there are no adverse effects on economic growth of a reduced rate of growth of population. This is roughly correct for the early period, since the reduction in the birth rate does not affect the size of the labour force for fifteen years or so after its onset. But here we see the importance of the age distribution. Even with a rate of fertility decline slightly greater than the one we have postulated (44 million prevented births by 1975), the difference between the 15–59 age groups in the populations with constant and with declining fertility is about 36 million in 1990. (50·4 per cent of 983 million, compared with 68·0 per cent of 668 million.) Assuming 0·7 of this age group to be the labour force, one could expect a substantial proportion of these 25 million extra workers to be unemployed. But even if they were all employed, the productivity of the labour force as a whole in the higher population would have to be about 37 per cent greater than that in the lower population, just in order to provide the same income per head. If one were to talk of consumption standards rather than income per head, this figure would be substantially reduced, since the bulk of the difference between the two populations consists of children whose consumption is much lower than that of adults.

33. However, as has been suggested, the lower population is more likely to enjoy greater productivity of the employed than the higher one. It is as much due to this, as to the fact that even if there were gains from the higher population their present value at twenty-five years' distance would still be insignificant, that we feel justified in ignoring any possibility of an adverse effect on fertility decline on income per head.

3. FAMILY PLANNING IN THE PLANS

34. The precise programme envisaged during the 'sixties is still under review at the time of writing; the details of the programme as set out in the Draft Fourth Plan, 1966, are no longer the basis of policy. A paper prepared by the State and Central health authorities,

however, gives an indication of the scale of programme which is likely to emerge.[16] The details given there are of a plan for 1967–8, and some broad targets for the remainder of the period. The plan for 1967–8 comprises the following targets (as far as concerns numbers of people to be reached with birth control measures):

I.U.D.s	2 m. people
Sterilizations	1·5 m. people
Conventional contraceptives	2 m. people

The goal for the plan period as a whole is 'to expose at least 50 per cent of the 90 million couples in the age-group 15–45 to one or other method of contraception'.

35. Since a great deal of emphasis is placed on the I.U.D. programme, it may be as well to discuss this first. On the basis of trials in various countries, it is believed that two out of every five loops inserted in every year will be expelled or removed before having much effect, while each loop which remains in position might (in India) prevent an average of 1·3 births over a five-year period. This implies that 'for every five loops inserted, four births will be prevented over a five-year period'.[17] The 1967–8 target for I.U.D.s implies, on these assumptions, about 1·6 million prevented births over the five years.

36. On the basis of assumptions of effectiveness as used by the U.N. Report, the whole 1967–8 programme would imply about 3 million prevented births. If the programme were to expand with the same proportionate emphasis on the different techniques of contraception, and 45 million couples were reached within the Plan period, this would imply more than 25 million prevented births as a result of action taken within the period (though some of the 'prevented births' would occur outside the period). In Section II above, we discussed the possibility of 40 million prevented births in ten years on the basis of equal annual numbers of prevented births. In fact, we may expect an accelerating programme. Even so, the tentative figures outlined here are ambitious; our target figure of 40 million prevented births would be passed before 1975.

37. The U.N. Report concluded that a programme rising to 9 million prevented births in 1975 would achieve the target, and estimated that this might be managed in the following way:

[16] 'Family Planning Programme' (1967, mimeo).

[17] U.N. *Report*, p. 101. The expulsion/removal rate may be pessimistic, though recent research may bear it out.

Method	*Number in 1975*	*Prevented births*
Rise in age at marriage	—	1·9 m.
Sterilization	3 m.	2·1 m.
I.U.D.	5 m. (insertions)	4·0 m.
Condoms	300 m. (pieces)	1·0 m.[18]

38. The Report felt that this target might be reached as the result of very vigorous government action. Evidently the authorities have felt that the target was too low, since, although they do not mention any efforts to raise the age at marriage (the Report on *this* issue may well have been optimistic), they do indicate an intention to make substantially greater efforts with the main birth control methods.

39. The Planners are undoubtedly right to raise their sights, though there may be some doubt as to whether performance better than that indicated in the U.N. Report will be attainable. The U.N. Report assesses the need for additional trained personnel of various kinds before the end of the current plan period to be over 70,000. The Indian document above has much higher targets: 40,000 additional auxiliary nurse midwives (A.N.M.s) alone, compared with the Report's 30,000. It is virtually impossible for an outsider to evaluate what the Draft Plan proposes about training, other than to say the obvious: the training requirements are immense on any assumptions, and may well prove a bottleneck.

40. Concerning training, one difficult question deserves attention: namely the distribution of operations between doctors and medical auxiliaries in the I.U.D. programme. Extensive medical training is not required for insertion of the I.U.D.; but it is far from being a trouble-free device, and failure in even a few cases can lead to adverse public opinion which might discredit the family planning effort over a wide area. Doctors are important both for the pre-insertion check-up, and in general as confidence creators. This is why, in some countries, family planning has progressed most satisfactorily in relation to a general public health programme, which has the additional advantage of relieving a 'family planning' doctor from the claims of other kinds of medical attention which arise where medical facilities are poor. As against this, the greater the

[18] *Ibid.*, p. 103. Some of these 'prevented births' occur after 1975. The *Report* does not give figures for all intervening years, and is ambiguous as to whether 40 million births *which would have occurred by 1975* are prevented by the programme, or 40 million births some of which would have occurred after 1975. We have assumed the former, which is not impossible on the basis of the figures given, and compares with the low fertility case of Table A.

share of highly-trained medical personnel in the programme, the slower is its possible rate of expansion.

41. Fundamentally the problem is one of weighing risks – the risks of medical complications or failure (leading to the possible disruption of a programme) which one would expect to increase with the less highly skilled people that are employed – against the possible gains to be derived from faster implementation of the programme. This is one of the more complex questions in the whole field of the training, pay, and employment of medical personnel, which will probably (and certainly should) be one of the first tasks of the committee set up to evaluate the programme. As more reliable information comes to hand concerning the first years of activity, it should be possible to come to some conclusions on the subject.

42. A few words about sterilization and other birth control methods may be of use. To date (June 1967) there have been approximately 2·34 million sterilizations (male and female).[19] The 1967–8 target looks feasible by past standards of performance. The demographic effect of sterilization is hard to assess; it depends on the age and fertility of couples, and the existing family size when the operation is performed. Condoms appear to be a cumbersome method for a large-scale programme, an estimated 300–475 being required per prevented birth.[20]

43. The relative costs of different methods are:

Method	*Rs.*
I.U.D.s	20–35 per insertion (mainly medical costs)
Condoms	20–30 (?) (year's supply)
Sterilization	40 (of which Rs. 30 are for publicity, transport, and compensation)[21]

Given the rates of demographic effectiveness, the cost per prevented birth favours the I.U.D. There are, of course, 'programme costs' on top of the above figures. The usual estimate of a prevented birth is Rs. 35–75 (post-devaluation).

44. Without any knowledge of the details beyond 1967–8, it is clear that either the cost of preventing a birth is higher than is customarily believed, or that a great deal of this expenditure is an investment for future acceleration of the programme (presumably much of it in training). Otherwise the implied scale of expenditure

[19] 'Family Planning Programme.'
[20] U.N. *Report*, p. 102.
[21] Ohlin, pp. 136–8. These figures are an international average, and should be treated as a rough guide only.

would be sufficient to prevent from 35 to 60 million births in the period up to 1975 (independently of any expenditure after 1970), or between one- and two-thirds of the 100 million births expected in the period, which even in the lower case is an extremely ambitious aim. The rate of expansion of the programme as a whole is colossal. Some 4–5 million couples have been reached already; the 1967–8 programme should bring this to 10 million. That leaves 35 million to be reached in the ensuing three years if the target of 45 million couples is to be attained.[22]

45. The Government of India has repeatedly said that finance will be made available up to any amount that can be usefully spent. As far as the physical aspects of the programme are concerned, this is undoubtedly a sensible policy. It is fairly obvious that the availability of physical resources will limit expenditure within what could or should be made available. The question of incentive expenditures, however, does remain open. But it can only be settled on an area basis. In many areas experience shows that all facilities offered are utilized, indeed demand is often greater than supply. Thus the amount of useful incentive payments may also be limited by physical availabilities, especially if the programme were concentrated in areas

[22] Since writing this paper, the author has had an opportunity to collect some more up-to-date information in India. As of October 1967 the figures for achievement of the programme are as follows:

Loops in place	1·5 m.
Effectively sterilized couples	2·6 m.
Couples employing conventional contraceptives	0·8 m.

The programme is stated not to be going well in Assam, Bihar, Rajasthan, and Uttar Pradesh. Plans have been issued for the year 1967–8 as follows:

I.U.D. insertions	4·1 m.
Sterilization	2·0 m.
Conventional contraceptives	3·1 m.

There is said to be an acute shortage of contraceptive supplies, particularly those of a conventional nature. A total of Rs. 310 million has been voted by Parliament for family planning during 1967–8, Rs. 256 million of which is for expenditure by State Governments. One or two details may be of particular interest; for example the State Government of Maharashtra has passed legislation depriving families who do not restrict themselves to three children, or to their present size, of various fiscal and welfare benefits. In some States, incentive programmes have been adopted for the employment of part-time doctors. As regards the I.U.D. – most controversial part of the programme – there is a vast variety of experience; it is by no means the case that the I.U.D. is a failure, but future plans for this method of contraception remain open to change. The plans referred to above for 1967–8 may look ambitious, but they could be attainable. In 1966–7, for example, sterilizations numbered over 860,000, and may soon become the programme's leading sector.

where problems of popular response are less of an obstacle to it.[23]

46. (There is also the question of removing fiscal and other assistance to childbearing. The Indian tax system gives concessions for the first two children. But the vast majority of the Indian population, and particularly that part of the population which is prone to having large families, is outside the tax net. There are also maternity and child benefits for an estimated 3 million workers under the Employee's State Insurance Scheme, and in some other conditions of employment. The abolition of all such allowances and benefits, although politically awkward and unlikely to have any large impact on the birth rate, would accord with the spirit of the family planning programme and the climate of opinion related to childbearing which the Government of India is trying to create.)

4. CONCLUSIONS

47. A considerable effort will be required even to prevent an increase in the rate of growth of population. The challenge of bringing this rate within bounds that promise prosperity for India is indeed enormous. Our examination suggests that autonomous factors – other than Malthusian ones, which we have avoided examining – do not promise any reduction. Prospects for reducing the rate of growth rest with distributing and encouraging the use of birth-control facilities, and perhaps with attempts to raise the marriage age.

48. There is some indication that the programme is not yet progressing very fast. Although the authorities give the highest priority to it, evidence suggests that the programme has not until very recently had the attention it deserves – particularly as regards its administration. Plans for production of materials, training of personnel, and the organization of distributional and educational facilities down to the village level appear to be adequate, as does the financial provision. It is therefore mainly on the administration of the programme that its success now depends.

49. One aspect we have not covered is the question of external assistance for the programme. Several Governments (the United Kingdom's now among them) are willing to provide personnel, contraceptive materials, and other forms of assistance for population control policies. The major role for aid donors is unlikely to be the actual provision of medical personnel, since these are scarce even in

[23] This is to speak only of incentives for the clients of the programme. There is also a complex question of incentive payments to employees of the programme, which we have not gone into here. At the time of writing, there is no published data on the success of the programme on an area basis.

the developed countries, and in any case may be less suitable than indigenous doctors and auxiliaries. But they can do a great deal in the field of training. As far as contraceptive supplies are concerned, one would hope that India will soon become self-sufficient, though in the meantime, donors should be willing to provide supplies and assistance for their production in India. It should not be forgotten that technical progress in family planning is very rapid, and improved methods are currently being tested; here again donors can assist in the rapid diffusion of new techniques. Finally, there is a range of ancillary equipment (mobile film units, clinics, and so forth) for which donors can provide assistance. In the current state of opinion among donors, no part of the Indian programme should be held back for want of foreign exchange. If, as now seems likely, the facilities of the World Health Organization can be made available for family planning, that would be a very suitable body through which assistance could be channelled.

STATISTICAL APPENDIX

Table 1

PROSPECTIVE TRENDS IN TOTAL POP., BIRTH RATES, RATE OF POP. GROWTH, NO. OF BIRTHS AND AGE DISTRIBUTION IN INDIA, 1965–90

Year	Mid-year total pop. (m.)	Crude birth-rate (m.)	Rate of pop. growth (per 1,000)	No. of births (m.)	Pop. by broad age groups (per cent): Under 15	15–59	60 & over
I. *Constant fertility*							
1965	484·3	41·4	24·1	20·0	40·7	53·8	5·5
1970	548·8	40·5	26·5	22·2	41·5	52·8	5·7
1975	629·0	40·1	28·2	25·2	41·9	52·1	6·0
1980	725·0	40·0	29·5	29·0	42·3	51·6	6·1
1985	841·4	39·9	30·9	33·6	42·8	51·0	6·2
1990	983·2	39·9	32·1	39·2	43·4	50·4	6·2
II. *Moderate fertility decline* (birth-rate 25 in 1985)							
1965	484·3	41·4	23·3	20·0	40·7	53·8	5·5
1970	544·1	36·5	22·9	19·9	41·0	53·2	5·8
1975	607·3	32·2	20·9	19·5	39·8	54·0	6·2
1980	669·1	28·4	18·4	19·0	37·5	55·8	6·7
1985	729·0	*25·0*	16·2	18·2	34·6	52·2	7·2
1990	785·8	22·0	15·1	17·3	31·8	60·4	7·8

III. *Rapid fertility decline* (birth-rate 25 in 1975)

1965	484·3	41·3	24·1	20·0	40·7	53·8	5·5
1970	538·7	32·2	19·2	17·3	40·4	53·8	5·8
1975	585·7	*25·0*	14·4	14·6	37·6	56·0	6·4
1980	621·6	19·4	10·0	12·1	32·7	60·1	7·2
1985	647·0	15·1	7·3	9·8	27·1	64·8	8·1
1990	668·2	15·1	6·5	10·1	22·9	68·0	9·1

Source: UN *Report*, p.123.

Table 2

	Birth rate (per 1,000 people)		*Marital fertility* (per 1,000 once-married women)	
	Rural	*Urban*	*Rural*	*Urban*
Assam	44·9	42·3	271	268
Jammu and Kashmir	33·5	25·5	165	146
Kerala	36·2	31·3	229	203
Madhya Pradesh	n.a.	n.a.	188	199
Mysore	34·2	31·3	182	178
Orissa	36·5	31·9	173	160
Punjab	39·2	34·5	232	207
Rajasthan	40·4	41·1	200	209
Uttar Pradesh	36·8	32·7	179	179
Delhi	41·9	36·7	225	216

Source: Min. of Home Affairs, *Vital Statistics of India for 1961* (1964), Table 29A, pp. L–LI. As the text makes clear, the figures are not very trustworthy. Some States were not included for lack of data. The figures for marital fertility are based on sample surveys and census data. In all cases the figures quoted are less than 'computed' figures, i.e. those rates implied by the growth of numbers between the 1951 and 1961 Censuses.

Table 3

CALCULATED ADDITIONAL INCOME PER HEAD IN 1975 FROM NON-BIRTH CONTROL INVESTMENT

(various values of marginal savings rate and capital output ratio)

Extra savings per rupee of extra income	*Extra capital requirements per rupee of extra annual output*		
	2 Rs.	*3 Rs.*	*4 Rs.*
m.	*Extra income per person*		
(Rs.)	(Rs.)		
0·1	2·86	1·80	1·30
0·15	3·16	1·90	1·32
0·2	3·49	2·03	1·43
0·3	4·24	2·33	1·58

5
THE ASPECTS OF INDIAN EDUCATION*

by A. K. Sen

Professor of Economics, London School of Economics

In 1950–1, when the First Five-Year Plan was launched, the total direct expenditure on education in India was a little over 1 per cent of the national income. It rose steadily and by 1968–9 this was well over 3 per cent. The question is asked from time to time: is this enough, or should the share of educational expenditure in national income go up even further? Or is this too much already? This is not a very useful way of looking at the problem of allocating resources to education. The advisability of putting money into education depends clearly on the precise field into which it is expected to go. While there are sectors with severe shortages there are also areas with much slack within the education system in India. An expansion of the total educational budget may be a good thing or may not be, depending on precisely where the money is to go. It also follows that much may be achieved by reallocating the educational funds differently. Indeed, the scope for such adjustment is considerable, especially with the developmental part of the funds as opposed to the maintenance part.

For discussing this problem of allocation we have to go into the relative costs and relative contributions of different types of education. It is, of course, true that most people will concede the compelling social need for literacy and primary education. And it is also accepted that unemployment of highly educated people is an expensive waste of money. Further, we found that educated unemployment was likely to grow even more with our present trend of expansion even if we did not exceed the limits laid down by the Education Commission. While the picture may look clear enough from these broad points of view, the requirements of policy-making should compel us to consider in detail the different types of gains and losses in pursuing different policies. And we also have to supplement general social considerations by detailed economic ones.

* Part Two of the Lal Bahadur Shastri Memorial Lectures delivered during March, 1970, in New Delhi. The original series entitled 'The Crisis in Indian Education'. [Some of the conclusions derived at the end of this lecture follow from the arguments developed in the first lecture, which is not included, and are discussed fully there – Ed.]

There has been much discussion in recent years on the evaluation of the economic rates of return from investment in different fields of education. There have been various attempts in India to calculate these rates, in particular by Harberger,[1] Nalla Gounden,[2] and Blaug, Layard and Woodhall.[3] Before going into the actual numbers, some preliminary points are worth making.

First, the rate of return from the private individual's point of view will typically be different from that from the point of view of the society as a whole. For one thing, some of the costs of education are borne by the Government rather than by the individual, since the fees represent only a small part of the total cost of running schools and colleges. For another, some of the benefits from education accrue not to the person being educated but to the society, e.g. the advantages that the people derive from having educated neighbours. On the other hand, some of the benefits may be purely personal without helping the society as such. For example, a person may improve his chances of employment at the cost of others by acquiring an additional academic degree, but from the point of view of the society the losses of the others have to be subtracted from the gains to this person. Considerations of this kind may be very important in an economy with unemployment.

A second preliminary clarification concerns the problem of measuring the impact of education on the productivity of a person. It is, in general, very difficult to measure such differences in productivity directly, and the convention is to measure it indirectly through the rise in a person's salary or wages as a consequence of his acquiring the additional bit of education. If a person earns Rs. 300 per month in the absence of a certain training and his earning goes up to Rs. 400 when he does receive this training, then Rs. 100 is taken to be the productivity difference caused by the additional education received. This approach to the estimation of the impact of education on productivity is based on the notion that the operation of the market ensures that a person will receive remuneration equal to his productivity at the margin. The limitations of this approach are, however, very serious since the market may fail to perform this precise function.[4] The methodology here is based on a certain

[1] A.C. Harberger, 'Investment in Men versus Investment in Machines: the Case of India' in *Education and Economic Development*, ed. C.A. Anderson and M.J. Bowman (Frank Cass, London, 1966).

[2] A.M. Nalla Gounden, 'Investment in Education in India', *Journal of Human Resources*, Summer 1967.

[3] M. Blaug, P.R.G. Layard and M. Woodhall, *The Causes of Educated Unemployment in India* (Allen Lane, 1969).

[4] I have discussed this problem in some detail in 'Economic Approaches to

theory of market operations which are by no means universally accepted. It is possible to argue that salary differences do not represent differences in productivity but merely reflect certain conventional differentials. In any case, the wages may at most represent productivity from the point of view of the employers, without taking account of the impact of education on the rest of the society operating outside the market mechanism. All the estimations of returns to education in India that have been done so far are based on working on wage differences. It is worth remembering that this implies a certain view of the market mechanism which is very much open to question, even though it may be interesting to see what figures we arrive at if we proceed on this line.

A third point concerns the interpretation of salary differences when one is looking at the salaries of different individuals with different educational attainments. Do we assume that but for the educational difference their other abilities are the same? It may be thought that when dealing with large groups personal variations may not be important, and this is indeed so if we expect that the process of selection for further education is unrelated to the person's abilities. If it is thought, however, that a more able person has a better chance of getting higher education, then an average group of more educated persons will have greater intelligence and other native talents.

This problem of isolating the contribution of education from productivity differences has turned out in general to be a major headache in calculations of returns to education, and the Indian case is not any less difficult. Indeed there are some additional complications in the Indian case compared with the cases of the more advanced countries. One of the major factors in the possibility of having higher education is the economic status of the family, so that even a very talented person may be left out of the system of further education because of economic pressures. This happens even in the more advanced countries, but it seems to happen much more often in India. Further, even when selection is on the basis of performance at the earlier stages of education, this performance may be a poor guide to native abilities. For the same level of intelligence and innate talents a person from a poorer family will tend to be at a disadvantage because of having poorer facilities for study in the shape of books, leisure, accommodation, and such things. While this is true everywhere, it seems to be, once again, a more important

---

Education and Manpower Planning', *Indian Economic Review*, New Series, Vol. I, 1966.

factor in India. It should also be added that the concept of innate ability is itself a rather complex notion to deal with. Abilities as student are not the same as abilities as a worker, for the two may require very different types of talents, and good students are often terrible flops in real life. Also the talents required vary from job to job. All this should make it clear why the problem of isolating the contribution of education is a rather difficult one to resolve. It is naïve to assume that the different education groups have exactly the same talents, but at the same time it is difficult to pinpoint the exact differences and to decide precisely on the extent to which meritocracy has superseded traditional immobilities.

Harberger assumes that the entire salary difference reflects the contribution of education. Nalla Gounden, on the other hand, assumes that 50 per cent of the difference is due to educational difference, while the other 50 per cent is attributed to differences in ability. Blaug and his colleagues use two ratios, viz. 50 per cent and 65 per cent, as alternative assumptions of the share of educational differences in the salary differentials. This is a tricky problem and arbitrariness is difficult to avoid in this field. Luckily the broad conclusions are not much affected by the precise assumption we choose.

Of the various estimates made of the alternative rates of return, those by Blaug and his colleagues are the latest and incorporate the important features outlined by the earlier authors. They also take explicit account of certain other features such as the problem of wastage in the form of drop-outs. I would very briefly state their results on the social rates of return on investment in education. There is a general decline in the rate of return as we move to higher stages of education. The rate of return of primary education for an illiterate person is found to be about 15 per cent, that of going through middle school after completing primary education is about 14 per cent, and the return on completing secondary school following middle school is 10·5 per cent. This decline continues at the next stage and the average rate of return on doing the bachelor's degree in Arts, Science or Commerce is estimated to be a little less than 9 per cent. If we use a rate of interest of 10 per cent as the minimum acceptable, then primary education would be found to be very profitable, middle school to be quite profitable though less so than primary education, and secondary school would be found to be worth it though not by a big margin. In contrast, general university education would appear to be decidedly unprofitable.

To avoid a possible misunderstanding I should explain that these rates of return relate to expansion of the different types of education in question. The intention is not to suggest that all university education is unprofitable at 10 per cent rate of interest, but only that the further expansion at this stage will be unprofitable, and a reduction up to a point will make things better. I should also explain that what precise rate of interest we use to determine our policy choice is itself a matter of some considerable controversy and 10 per cent may not be necessarily accepted as the figure to choose. Blaug and others themselves use a set of assumptions which make them treat 12·5 per cent as the minimum acceptable rate of return to investment in education. If such a rate is chosen, then not merely university education but also secondary schooling will be found to be over-expanded. The important point to note is that the rate of return systematically declines as we go from lower to higher stages of education. The precise figures depend also on the assumption of the relative contribution of education to salary differential; the figures quoted assume a 65 per cent share of education. A variation of this assumption will alter the actual figures, but as long as we assume the same ratio for all levels of education the tendency of the rate of return to decline as we move from lower to higher stages will certainly remain valid.

There are two questions of educational investment which are worth separating out, viz. (*a*) the question of the comparison of rates of return in education with those in other fields, and (*b*) the question of the relative rates of return within the broad area of education. I have commented so far on the former by choosing a rate of return from outside, but we can also pose the problem of how best to allocate a given sum of money that may be available for educational expansion of all kinds. From the latter point of view an expansion of primary education yielding more than 15 per cent return at the cost of reducing university education yielding less than 9 per cent return would appear to be socially desirable if the figures quoted are accepted. The general conclusion that we arrived at on the basis of broad reasoning in the last lecture seems to survive the more detailed argumentation using the rates of return approach.

These works on rates of return are extremely interesting and Blaug and others have been careful and wise in their pioneering work. I would, however, like to express a general reservation about taking these numbers too seriously. Indeed, the entire approach is based on a number of assumptions about market operations that may or may not hold, and while Blaug's may be the best estimates of rates of return, they may not be generally accepted as sufficient for policy making. But it is interesting to note that if we accepted the general approach incorporated in these estimates of rates of return – and this is an approach that has been widely used in recent years in many countries of the world – then we would arrive at conclusions rather similar to the ones we arrived at on the basis of broader reasoning.

There is, in fact, one respect in which, in my opinion, Blaug and his colleagues tend to overestimate the social rates of return. This concerns the question of corrections for unemployment. If there is 10 per cent unemployment in a certain category of jobs and 90 per cent of the people with that qualification are employed, then Blaug takes 90 per cent of average earnings in that field as the relevant productivity figure. This is based on a certain hypothesis about the operation of the economy and the determination of employment. An alternative assumption may be that adding another qualified person to the already available pool may not add to the jobs at all, and if that view is taken then the social gain from having one more man added to the pool would tend to be zero. Suppose there are 90 employed people and 10 unemployed in this category in the absence of a certain educational expansion, and when that expansion takes place one more person is added to the pool. If the number of jobs remains the same, then we shall have now 90 employed people and 11 unemployed. The additional man would have produced nothing. Thus, whether there is any social gain from having more educated people when some are already unemployed depends on how we expect the total employment to change as a consequence of an expansion of the number of job seekers in that category. An expansion of job seekers can increase employment mainly through a reduction in the wage rate, and whether this will happen and with what effect will depend on a variety of economic and social considerations. Blaug's estimates assume an adjustment process such that when expansion takes place the probability of employment remains unchanged. The market is taken to be adjustable. But is this a fair assumption, since it is evidently not so adjustable that it can eliminate unemployment altogether? If such adjustability is not assumed and Blaug's figures are thought to be overestimates, this will reduce the overall rates of return to education.

The whole question of educated unemployed is a rather complex one in an economy like India. It has been pointed out that unemployment mainly takes the form of a long period of waiting before a person emerging from the education system finds a job. Blaug estimates the average waiting period of a graduate to be about 6·5 months, and the average waiting period of a matriculate to be about 17 months. It might, incidentally, be added that the tendency to remain unemployed for a considerable period of time after completing matriculation is a strong incentive for going into higher education. This is an important factor in India in adding to the demand for university education in contrast with countries where a matriculate finds jobs easily, thereby making him relatively more reluctant to go in for further studies, rather than having some immediate income.

For the motivation of students, rates of return from a private (as opposed to social) point of view is relevant. As might be expected, the private rates of return are considerably higher than the figures of social rates of return which were quoted earlier. There is the same tendency for the decline of the rate of return as we move from lower to higher stages, but even at higher stages of education the absolute rate of return remains quite high, and for the general bachelor's degree (i.e. B.A., B.Sc., or B.Com.) Blaug and his colleagues estimate the average private rate of return to be 10·4 per cent. The private rates of return tend to be higher than the social rates largely because the student bears only a small part of the cost of education, since the Government subsidizes education heavily. The vast demand for higher education in spite of its social unprofitability springs partly from this purely economic reasoning.

These figures take into account the actual probability of employment. It may be argued that a student contemplating further education typically tends to take a relatively more optimistic view of job opportunities than what the hard-headed statistician would estimate. If so, the student's subjective impression of profitability of higher education would tend to be more than what these calculations on rates of return yield. It may, therefore, be argued that just as Blaug's figures may overstate the social rates of return, they possibly understate the subjective private rates of return which motivate the students. If this is accepted, then the dichotomy between private demands and social needs would appear to be even more severe than these rates of return indicate.

I have so far been concerned mostly with general categories of education. I should now look at specific fields such as engineering and medicine. Of these fields Blaug estimates the rate of return for engineering education and finds it to be higher than for B.A., B.Sc. or B.Com. This figure of 10·5 per cent is also higher than the rate of return in secondary education. If this estimate is accepted, then there will be relatively little reason to believe in the over-expansion of engineering education, at least compared with the more general branches of higher education. This is probably right, but even here there may be problems. The reservation that we had about Blaug's treatment of unemployment applies here too and, from the social point of view, adding to the supply of engineers may not easily add to the number of jobs as implied in these estimates. And if the number of jobs is taken to be given, then at the margin expansion of engineering education would hardly produce any social gain while it will certainly involve the economy in considerable cost. A more pessimistic view like this seems to get some support from the steadily rising proportion of unemployment among engineers in India with the growth of the supply of engineers. It is, in fact reported that the number of engineers without a job has increased in the last three years from 4,000 to 50,000 and it appears that the Union Minister for Education is advising the universities and State Governments to limit admission to engineering courses.[5]

But if our analysis is right, the problem is not confined to engineers alone. There is a general tendency of public policy to produce more highly educated and trained people than are necessary for the growth and development of the economy. As in the argued first lecture, this arises largely from a difference in social and private profitability of higher education and from the Government's tendency to base educational policies on public pressures. In spite of the large number of highly trained people who are unemployed, it may be worth while for a person to become an engineer or a lawyer or a doctor. He bears only a small part of the total cost of education, the society bearing the rest of it. Further, the society has to take into account the loss of others from the reduction in employment prospects as a consequence of an increase in the numbers of job seekers; the individual, in contrast, need be concerned only with his own prospects. I have already discussed this problem in the first lecture, so that I shall not go into it further.

There is some evidence that a situation of widespread unemployment is developing in the field of medicine and may become more and more obvious as time goes on. Mr P.N. Mathur, who is researching on this problem for his doctoral dissertation at the Delhi School of Economics, has gone into the demand and supply of doctors for the coming two decades in some detail.[6] There are alternative assumptions that one can make about demand depending on the economic relationships that are held to be valid. There are also alternative supply projections depending on the expansion plans of the Government. The extent of surplus or shortage should depend upon the precise estimates that one chooses from the set of alternatives. However, interestingly enough even the *highest* estimate of demand for 1975–6 or 1985–6 seems to fall substantially short of the *lowest*

[5] *The Times of India*, Delhi, Sunday September 28, 1969, p. 8.

[6] P.N. Mathur, 'Supply and Demand for Critical Human Skills in India's Developing Economy: A Case Study for Doctors', Ph.D. thesis draft, unpublished.

estimates of supply, so that a surplus seems to be definitely developing. The lowest estimates of supply are based on the assumption of no expansion whatever in the number and size of medical schools, which is certainly very conservative. The extent of surplus is likely to be quite substantial, even though a precise estimate may be hazardous because of various possible alternative assumptions. The employment situation of doctors will thus become extremely disturbing in the not too distant future, unless specific actions are taken to counter this.

It is worth noting that unemployment of doctors is usually not visible. This is because many of them live on private practice as opposed to having a fixed job in a government hospital or in a private institution. One impact of unemployment is a reduction in the clientele and consequently in the level of earnings of the doctors, and it may not take the form of a number of people being *fully* unemployed. In this respect the unemployment of doctors is rather like that of peasants, and the theory of 'disguised unemployment', which has been much discussed in the context of peasant agriculture, holds also for certain self-employing professions like doctors and lawyers.

This persistent tendency of over-producing highly educated people in several fields may largely arise from a difference in private and social profitability, but on top of that there is also the problem of miscalculation of demand by the Government.[7] For theservice sectors certain arbitrary 'norms' are used. In the case of doctors the demand is taken to be that required in having one doctor per 3,000 inhabitants in 1975–6 and one per 2,000 in 1985–6. The Planning Commission and the Union Government's Department of Labour and Employment[7] have used a norm of one per 3,500 in 1973–4. *Actual* demand, however, will depend on other more concrete considerations like purchasing power of the people. The private demands are, of course, supplemented by the Government's own programmes of public health and community medication, and in India this is indeed a substantial proportion of the total demand. The fact that these programmes as announced would not meet the gap between the supply of doctors and the private demand for doctors indicates a failure on the part of the Government to have a consistent policy of medical education and utilization of doctors.

The normative considerations determining the medical expansion plans seem to be running ahead of the actual actions of the Government in terms of expanding hospitals and other medical services. If the normative figures are used to determine the expansion schemes

[7] [This problem was discussed at length in the first lecture, excluded here—Ed.]

in medical education, then the Government should also carry through the hospital programme which will make these normative assumptions actually valid. If, on the other hand, the Government wants to stick to its hospitalization programme, given the sluggish growth of private purchasing power, it must slow down the expansion of the supply of doctors. Which of these two alternative policies should be pursued is a matter on which disputation is possible, since hospital programmes are expensive and may cut out other useful programmes of the Government, but at the same time they are also extremely important for a poor inequitable society. But no matter which of these approaches are taken by the Government there is no argument whatever for gearing the education programme to certain lofty ideals which bear little relation to the Government's own hospital programme.

I turn now to the problems of primary education. The discussion so far has had an urban bias. Even rates of return from primary education that I have quoted were based largely on employment opportunities in the urban areas. The impact of education on the rural economy, in particular on agriculture, has been a matter of debate for some time now. This is a field where the amount of work done is still inadequate and much public thinking is based on hunches of one kind or another. The traditional view is to regard formal education, including literacy, to be unimportant from the point of view of agricultural productivity, and to argue that all that matters is the traditional wisdom of the peasant. This glib view has been successfully challenged by a variety of studies recently, notably in a Ph.D. thesis by Dr D.P. Chaudhri recently completed at the Delhi School of Economics.[8] Dr Chaudhri used inter-state data, inter-district data, inter-village data and inter-family data to see how differences in educational levels related to differences in productivity, and found in most cases a significant positive association. This association survives even when due account is taken of variations in other economic features. It would appear from this that educational differences do affect agricultural productivity and schooling is a relevant constituent of a programme of agricultural expansion.

In this context I should explain three special aspects of the impact of education on agricultural production that have not attracted much attention. First, in traditional studies of economics of education it is often assumed that education is another input like any other such as fertilizer, pesticide, seeds, or water. On this assumption one might

[8] D.P. Chaudhri, 'Education and Agricultural Productivity in India', unpublished Ph.D. thesis. Department of Economics, University of Delhi, Aprii 1968.

try to find out how output would increase if the educational level of the cultivators rose, *given* the other factors of production, and that would be a way of isolating the contribution of education to productivity. It might, of course, be the case that having more education would increase the profitability of applying other factors of production. But on this approach it is assumed that in each case all factors are applied up to the point that maximizes profits so that in each case the additional costs and additional benefits from the use of each input are exactly balanced. This view, I would argue, is too mechanical to be used for observing the impact of education on agricultural productivity. Education affects a person's horizon of vision, it is not just like any other input. The main point is not that, given other factors of production, having more education increases the yield of output, though education may also do this. The real point is that education affects the way the cultivator thinks about everything, including production, and it also affects his attitude towards other inputs. For example, the profitability of using fertilizers may become clear to a peasant if he can read a hand-bill on it rather than relying solely on verbal communication. Furthermore, the thoroughness with which the cultivator can investigate the economic opportunities of using modern inputs may vary greatly with the extent of education, so that in viewing the impact of education a broader view will have to be taken. The impact of more education, *given* all other factors of production, may be small, but we are concerned also with how the other factors change in response to education.

My second observation concerns the use of inter-family data in studying the effect of education on the use of modern inputs. The evidence here is conflicting, though certainly the hypothesis that education affects the use of modern inputs gets some support and certainly cannot be rejected on the basis of the available data. But what is more important is the necessity to consider this relationship not in the context of inter-family variations but in terms of larger groups and classes. The advantages of schooling, especially of secondary schooling, apply not merely to the person who goes through this but spread also to his neighbours. Treating families as completely isolated is not a very good assumption, even for the rural communities in Europe or America, but in India it is fatal. The entire organization of rural society and economy is such that on a variety of matters, including the use of modern inputs and new varieties of seeds, communication between different members of the same village or community is extensive and the influence on one another is great. Therefore the right units for study are not families but communities, classes or villages. In fact sometimes even villages may be too small as units. The picture emerging from inter-family data should not, therefore, be taken too seriously even if it were conclusive. It is very important to be careful about units of influence and communication in dealing with a factor like education. Neither is education an input in the mechanical sense in which it is sometimes taken, nor is it a factor that influences only its owner. Externalities, as economists call them, are significant aspects of the problem.

My third point concerns the impact of school education on economic operations *through* changes in social and political elements in the system. Administrative factors are becoming increasingly important in the operation of Indian agriculture; this may extend not merely to the channelling of credit but also to the systematic use of irrigation water, the division of scarce fertilizers, the supply of new varieties of seeds, and other group activities. The administrative possibilities are, of course, substantially affected by the educational background of the villages. But more than this, even the political organization of the village or of the society at large may depend substantially on educational factors. There have been observations on the correlation between literacy rates and the pattern of voting. These studies which seem to give positive results are, however, in their infancy. It is difficult to say how strong these considerations might be, but it is important to recognize that a study of the impact of education must go into these broader considerations in order to be complete. If, for example, having a more literate or educated rural population makes it easier for the Government to carry through a vigorous policy of land reform based on an active co-operation of the villagers in exposing evasion of the reform legislations, this is certainly relevant. If educational expansion helps social workers or political activists to mobilize the rural population into being more conscious of their rights, and less tolerant of social inequities and of administrative abuse and corruption, that is relevant also. It would be idle to pretend that we know precisely how these factors work, but it would be foolish to assume that relations of this kind do not exist.

Coming back to rather more concrete estimations, it would appear that even in the absence of going into the details of these indirect features it can be said that education does have a substantial impact on agricultural productivity. The extent of the return is also significantly high, particularly when the readjustment of other factors of production are taken into account in the light of what has been discussed earlier. It is, therefore, worth noting that the compulsion for the expansion of rural school education is not based merely on social objectives; it relates concretely to economic production as well. In my last lecture, the main argument was largely from the point of view of the compelling social need for literacy and schooling; that argument becomes stronger if it is supplemented by the relevant economic considerations just outlined.

Primary education is neglected in terms of the low allocation of public expenditure into that field, but there is a substantial possibility of expanding the level of expenditure on primary education by economizing on wasteful investments in some branches of higher education. There is also scope for a general expansion of the budget. But this is not the whole story. There have also been significant non-financial failures, especially in the failure to relate rural schooling to the requirements of the rural economy. There has been a fair amount of discussion recently on the content of the curriculum in school education in the rural areas, and its remoteness to the life of the peasants has been widely noted. I would, therefore, not go into this here; the importance of these considerations are well known. I would, however, like to go into one particular problem of co-ordination that we have found to be very important in the context of a study undertaken at the Agricultural Economics Research Centre at the University of Delhi.[9]

It is generally known that one reason for the failure of primary education in rural areas is a very high ratio of drop-outs. The ratio of drop-outs in India is one of the highest in the world, and in some parts of India the figures are fantastic, especially for girls. It would appear from the *Second All-India Education Survey Report*[10] that while 70 per cent of the boys and 66 per cent of the girls in Kerala see their way through from Class I to Class IV in primary schools, only 27 per cent of the boys and 15 per cent of the girls do this in Bihar. The position varies greatly from State to State but the overall rate of drop-out is very high. In trying to relate drop-outs to various factors including facilities provided in the schools, it was found that the relationship was not very strong, so that the problem cannot be easily handled by the expansion of such things as playground facilities, nearness to the place of residence etc., even though these may be desirable for their own sake. An important factor in drop-out is the income level of the child's family; the poorer a peasant is the more likely he is to dropout, given other things. Caste also seems to be a relevant factor and lower caste people have a greater tendency to dropout, which is probably partly a reflection of the relation between income and caste, but may also be partly independent of

[9] *Primary Education in Rural India: Participation and Wastage*, Agricultural Economics Research Centre, University of Delhi, Delhi, May 1968.

[10] Conducted by the National Council of Educational Research and Training.

income. The question thus relates to the general social and economic structure of the village community. In this field possibilities of change have well-known hindrances. There is, however, one very simple factor that seems to be crucial to the question of dropout. There is fairly strong evidence that the tendency to drop-out is very much sharper when the seasonal peaks of agricultural activity are reached. In Uttar Pradesh and Punjab, to which our study was confined, the drop-out was significant both at the Kharif season as well as at the Rabi season during sowing and harvesting, though in Punjab the drop-out seemed to be greater in Kharif than in Rabi. Some school teachers even reported 40 to 50 per cent drop-out at the time of sowing and harvesting of Kharif crops. While drop-outs referred to here may be of a short-term nature to start with, nevertheless short-term drop-outs frequently trigger off a long-run stay away. Thus, the agricultural activity peaks may initiate a departure from the school altogether.

Unfortunately the timing of the academic year in the rural schools does not seem to be at all integrated with the agricultural activities. In fact, the examinations frequently coincide with peak harvesting activity, as for example in U.P. where examinations are held in April when Rabi harvesting is at its peak. In so far as the children of many families help out at the time of peak activities of agriculture there is a built-in bias in the system towards a high proportion of drop-outs and wastage. It is perhaps one more reflection of our inability to relate educational arrangements to the overall nature of the society and the economy, and the unfortunate results are very serious indeed. A rearrangement of the school year and a change in the timing of examinations are typical ways through which education could be more fully integrated into the Indian rural economy.

I have moved over a wide range of issues in discussing problems of educational planning in India. It is not easy to summarize the results of our analysis in a few sentences. I would, however, list a few of the more important points that seem to have emerged; this will be done in deliberately bald terms, even at the risk of being misunderstood.

First, considerations of *social* profitability of education differ substantially from those underlying *private* profitability. An inadequate recognition of this distinction seems to have been a source of some confusion in public policy making in the field of education.

Second, another source of difficulty is the use of inefficient and antiquated techniques in forecasting manpower requirements of the Indian economy as a basis for educational policy. The Education Commission, which produced an otherwise excellent report full of insight and wisdom, did however make rather disastrous manpower estimates, which had several biases all working in the direction of overestimating the requirements of highly educated manpower. The use of inflated fixed coefficients, the inadequate recognition of educated unemployment, the total neglect of the current prevalence in the Indian economy of 'over-qualified appointments', the assumption of unrealistically high growth rates, and the use of arbitrary 'norms' for doctors and other professions, are cases in point. Similar criticisms apply to the estimation of the Planning Commission and the Union Government's Department of Labour and Employment. All this has contributed towards a wasteful growth of expensive higher education in several fields.

Third, there has been a failure of leadership in withstanding political pressure for over-expansion of higher education. For a variety of reasons that I have tried to spell out, the individuals' demand for higher education tends to exceed considerably the requirements of the country, and rather than standing for social interests, public policy has been drifting in response to political winds. Even the Government's own calculations of educational implications of the manpower estimates, unnecessarily high as they are, have been systematically exceeded by actual expansion policies in several fields.[11]

Fourth, primary education has been relatively neglected in terms of social needs as well as in terms of economic returns, estimated through various methods. The allocation of public funds has been severely biased in the direction of catering to the vocal urban middle classes and neglecting the inarticulate requirements of basic education in the rural community. The relevance of primary education to the rural economy has tended to be ignored because of a narrow framework of economic analysis.

Fifth, there has also been a general failure in relating education to the economic life of the nation. An example of this is to be found in the arrangement of rural schools in many parts of India such that the vacations do not coincide with the busy seasons of agricultural activity and much of the drop-out seems to originate then. Further, the timing of school examinations often coincides with a seasonal peak, as in the U.P. in April, which is the time of rabi harvesting. Education has been viewed as an activity governed by rigid rules unrelated to the economic life of the community.

Sixth, the growing unemployment of engineers is only a reflection of the tendency of public policy to over-expand higher education and specialized training on the basis of poor estimations of demand, with

[11] [These three points were discussed at length in the first lecture – Ed.]

a built-in upward bias reinforced by the failure of leadership to withstand political pressures unrelated to social needs. As such the problem is not peculiar to engineers and is present in other fields as well. With self-employed professionals unemployment is 'disguised' rather than 'visible', but is no less real, and for some professions such as doctors the situation is likely to get much worse in the coming decade or so unless drastic measures are taken.

The diagnosis of these ailments immediately points ways towards possible cure. Better estimation of manpower by avoiding the existing biases, recognition of the dichotomy between private and social profitability of education, and relating educational organization to the economic life of the community, especially in the rural areas, are obvious recommendations to make. There also has to be a major shift in emphasis from over-expansion of higher education towards a more balanced pattern of educational growth with much greater emphasis on basic schooling.

The expansion policies in different fields must take a more explicit account of economic considerations, and the antiquated basis of the conventional estimates of enrolment requirements must be fully recognized. Economic arguments must, of course, be tempered by other factors, but as it happens the direction of change required by economic considerations is exactly the same as the pointer we got from our analysis yesterday of the broad social considerations.

The most important characteristic of public policy on Indian education has been one of drift – a drift in response to the wind from whichever direction it might be blowing. The direction of the wind has been largely determined, naturally enough, by the existing stratification of Indian society. Bending to the pressures of vocal groups and powerful classes has contributed to the perpetuation – and indeed intensification – of the social inequities. The rot in Indian education is, thus, ultimately related to the structure of Indian society.

While I have tried to pinpoint the areas in which Indian educational planning requires better technical work, especially related to economic considerations, I have little confidence that correct calculation and efficient estimation can, on their own, save the situation. The most spectacular deficiency has been one of commitment. The failure of leadership in policy-making is as much due to this deficiency as due to technical errors and mistakes. In the last analysis educational transformation in India is not merely a matter of clear thinking but also of courage and determination. A radical reorganization of Indian educational structure, the need for which I have tried to demonstrate, will demand a lot more than technical expertise. To ignore this will be escapism.

6

AID TO INDIA*

by Paul Streeten
Queen Elizabeth House, University of Oxford

and Roger Hill
University of Kent

. . . .

1. REVIEW OF PAST AID TO INDIA

Up to the end of March 1966 aid authorizations from all sources amounted to Rs. 58,015 million, of which 77 per cent (Rs. 44,818 million) had been utilized. Only Rs. 290 million of the authorized aid and Rs. 220 million of the utilized aid were received prior to the First Plan.

Table 1 shows external assistance by sources. The doonors' list is

Table 1

(Rs. m.)

Sources of aid	*Aggregate external assistance since independence*			
	Authorized up to March 1966		*Utilized up to March 1966*	
	Amount	*% of Total*	*Amount*	*% of Total*
I.B.R.D./I.D.A.	7,415	12·8	5,815	13·0
US	30,487	52·5	26,052	58·1
USSR	4,855	8·4	2,833	6·3
W. Germany	4,444	7·7	3,417	7·6
UK	3,660	6·3	2,931	6·6
Others	7,154	12·3	3,770	8·4
Total	58,015	100·0	44,818	100·0

Source: Reserve Bank of India, *Report on Currency and Finance 1965–6* (1966), p. 28, Table 28.

* In P. Streeten and M. Lipton (ed.), *Crisis of Indian Planning* (Oxford Univ. Press, 1968). An introductory section dealing with the Terminology of Aid and one dealing with the provisional Fourth Plan, 1966, have been excluded, together with a concluding section on policy – Editor.)

dominated by the U.S., which provided over half the authorized aid, and a little under three-fifths of the utilized aid. Aid authorizations under P.L. 480 accounted for 51 per cent (Rs. 13,860 million) of U.S. aid. I.B.R.D. and I.D.A., the main multilateral donors, have been responsible for just over 12 per cent of the aid received by India. Table 2 provides a more detailed breakdown of the sources of aid.

Table 3 breaks down external assistance by form. The outstanding feature here is the decline in grants: from 36 per cent of authorizations in the First Plan to 3 per cent in the Third Plan. Loans amounted to Rs. 22,690 million during the First Plan, but the 1951 U.S. Wheat Loan accounted for Rs. 9,030 million (40 per cent) of this figure. Over two-thirds of the aid utilized in the Third Plan has been in loan form. Authorizations of P.L. 480 aid reached very high levels during the Second Plan and provided a large 'carry-over' into the Third Plan. For this reason utilization of P.L. 480 aid between 1961–6 was nearly double the authorization during the same period.

2. EXTERNAL DEBT

External debt servicing charges rose from $250 million in the Second Plan (just under 4 per cent of export earnings) to $1,150 million during the Third Plan (about 14 per cent of merchandise export earnings) and to 22 per cent in 1966. During the period 1966–70 these charges are estimated as $3,050 million – 28 per cent of estimated export earnings and 36 per cent of aid requirements. The total outstanding external public debt has risen from $400 million in 1955 to $6,900 million in June 1966.[1] The problem of external debt is a major one in the late 1960s. While debt servicing obligations rose by 84 per cent between 1962 and 1966, exports increased by only 14 per cent. This is the legacy of past loans. However, a marked softening of aid terms has taken place recently. The average rate of interest on new external debt contracted during 1960 was 4·19 per cent, the average grace period 4·0 years and the average term to maturity 16·7 years.[2] In 1965 the corresponding figures were 3·18 per cent interest rate, 7·4 years grace period, and 31·3 years to maturity.[3] This reflects an even greater improvement if account is taken of the general rise in commercial interest rates. Nevertheless, further renegotiations, rescheduling, consolidations and waivers of loans must be expected during the Fourth Plan period, for servicing charges are likely to account for 28 per cent of a very optimistic

[1] I.B.R.D., *Ann. Rep., 1965–6* (1967), p. 33, Table 5, and *1966–7*, p. 31, Table 6
[2] *Ibid.*, p. 36, Tables 7 and 8.
[3] *Ibid.*, p. 35, Table 9.

Table 2

SOURCES OF EXTERNAL ASSISTANCE

(Rs. m.)

	Aid authorized up to end of 1st Plan	*Aid authorized during 2nd Plan*	*Aid authorized during 3rd Plan*
I. Loans			
(1) Repayable in foreign currencies			
(i) International institutions	572	2,612	4,231
(ii) U.S.	903	1,085	7,917
(iii) Canada	—	157	310
(iv) U.K.	—	1,226	2,420
(v) W. Germany	—	1,342	3,081
(vi) Japan	—	268	1,381
(vii) U.S.S.R.	648	3,190	1,005
(viii) Switzerland	—	65	180
(ix) France	—	—	571
(x) Italy	—	—	813
(xi) Poland	—	143	270
(xii) Yugoslavia	—	190	24
(xiii) Czechoslovakia	—	231	400
(xiv) Austria	—	—	85
(xv) Belgium	—	—	114
(xvi) Netherlands	—	—	219
(xvii) Sweden	—	—	22
(xviii) Denmark	—	—	14
Total	2,123	10,509	23,057
(2) Repayable in Rupees			
(i) Denmark	—	—	10
(ii) U.S.	146	2,304	486
Total	146	2,304	496
II. Grants			
(i) U.S.	918	546	200
(ii) Canada	323	571	551
(iii) Australia	111	22	22
(iv) New Zealand	17	17	7
(v) U.K.	4	4	6
(vi) W. Germany	—	21	—
(vii) Norway	7	19	20
(viii) U.S.S.R.	—	12	—
Total	1,380	1,212	806

III. P.L. 480, 665, and Third Country Currency Assistance	169	11,307	4,506
Grand Total	3,818	25,335	28,865

Source: Reserve Bank of India, *Report on Currency and Finance 1965–6* (1966), Statement 82.

Table 3

EXTERNAL ASSISTANCE BY FORM

(Rs. m.)

	Authorizations			*Utilization*		
	Up to end of 1st Plan	*During 2nd Plan*	*During 3rd Plan*	*Up to end of 1st Plan*	*During 2nd Plan*	*During 3rd Plan*
1. Loans	2,269	12,813	23,553	1,264	7,247	19,094
(i) Repayable in foreign currencies	2,123	10,509	23,057	1,241	6,709	17,530
(ii) Repayable in rupees	146	2,304	496	23	1,168	1,564
2. Grants	1,380	1,212	806	702	1,603	877
3. P.L. 480 and P.L. 665 aid and Third Country Assistance (gross)	169	11,280	4,506	51	5,423	8,532
4. Total	3,818	25,305	28,865	2,017	14,273	28,503
Debt Servicing Payments	n.a.	n.a.	n.a.	n.a.	1,192	5,470
Net Aid					13,081	23,033
Net Aid at 1965–6 import prices					13,769	25,403
5. I.M.F.	476	952		476	952	
Percentage Distribution						
1. Loans	59·5	50·7	81·6	62·7	50·7	67·0
2. Grants	36·2	4·8	2·8	34·8	11·2	3·0
3. P.L. 480 and 664 aid and Third Country Assistance (gross)	4·3	44·5	15·6	2·5	38·1	30·0
4. Total	100·0	100·0	100·0	100·0	100·0	100·0

n.a. = not available.

Source: Reserve Bank of India, *Report on Currency and Finance 1965–6* (1966), Statement 82.

export projection of Rs. 80,330 million (Rs. 51,000 million in pre-devaluation rupees).

The problem of debt service has several aspects.

(i) In the 1970s the debt servicing problem will become even more serious. From 1966–7 to 1980–1 India will require some $18,000 million of foreign aid but her debt servicing liability will come to $14,000 million. After 1975 the Planners expect repayments to outstrip inflows of capital.

(ii) Next, there are the terms on which loans are incurred and renewed. India herself has in the past declared that she does not wish to receive grants. Some donors believe that soft terms discourage economic use and encourage waste. There cannot be much in this argument because the Government of India can lend on at appropriate interest rates, and can require these rates of return for its own projects. Soft terms are intended to get over the foreign exchange difficulty and do not reduce the need to calculate adequate domestic returns on expenditure. Whether local currency counterpart funds for interest receipts should be accumulated by the creditor country is another question.

(iii) Most bilateral aid is tied to procurement from the donor and often tied to projects as well. Repayment, on the other hand, is demanded in convertible currency, and the use of such funds is not tied to Indian exports. This asymmetry introduces an additional element of hardness. The exception is aid from Russia and certain European countries which is usually repaid in the recipient's traditional exports; thus, in effect, repayment is in the borrower's own currency.

(iv) It is not sufficient to give debt relief when the time for debt repayment arrives. Foreign exchange has to be accumulated in the form of extra reserves, and hence diverted from development imports well in advance of the date when debt payments are due, and debt relief promised in advance is worth more than relief that comes later.

(v) From the point of view of any one creditor, debt relief should be given by all creditors. Otherwise the relief given by one can be regarded as being used to pay the obligations to others. (The same applies to giving aid on soft terms.) The World Bank, because of its need to raise money in the capital markets of the West, is in a special position and may not be able to give relief without impairing its impeccable credit standing. But bilateral Consortium donors normally consider that they must act in consort.

3. THE SLOW UTILIZATION OF AID

Until recently, a characteristic of Indian aid was the large proportion authorized but not disbursed. To help remedy this slow disbursement of aid, the Rao Report recommended in 1964 that a larger proportion of aid should be non-project.[4] In the years 1963–4 India received considerable quantities of non-project assistance (apart from P.L. 480) for the first time. In the years 1965–6 about half the aid pledged was non-project, while for 1967 Consortium members have agreed to about $900 million (Rs. 6,800 million) of non-project aid.

However, the causes of slow disbursements are to be found on both sides. In India, slow disbursements may occur because of (*a*) inadequate project planning, i.e. faulty project preparation, programming and scheduling, (*b*) faults in complementary actions, e.g. failure of supplies of raw materials and components, and services like electricity and transport, and (*c*) failures in aggregate planning, e.g. non-availability of rupee resources, inadequate aggregate demand, wrong choice of top personnel and other wrong decisions. Even forms of aid which are avowedly the most useful, because they are not tied to projects, have been slowly disbursed. Thus 'Kipping loans' have, astonishingly, suffered from slow disbursements.

But the main reason for slow disbursement is found, the Rao Committee suggested, in the fact of project aid. Aid geared to the creation of capacity, it is said, is of little use and can be an obstacle if the main bottleneck is imports of raw materials and components, especially fertilizers and spare parts. The superiority of general-purpose aid over project, and even non-project but specific-purpose aid, has been increasingly recognized, and the change in the composition has contributed to speedier disbursements. The need for non-project aid grows as development progresses. A final reason for delays has been the terms of aid. The harder the terms, the more reluctant the borrower will be to draw quickly on a loan, because interest is charged from the date of drawing, not from the date of commitment. Thus the share of loans tends to be higher in the aid pipe-line than in total aid commitments.

However, more non-project aid and softening of terms, together with changes in the administrative machinery, especially in the vetting of import requirements, have produced in 1964 and 1965 a marked improvement in the rate of aid utilization. This is borne out by Table 4.

[4] Committee on the Utilization of External Assistance, *Report* (Min. of Finance, 1964).

4. THE IMPACT OF AID

There is a widespread impression that India receives large sums of aid. This is, of course, true in the sense that India is a large country, containing 30 per cent of the population of the under-developed world. But it is not true if the relevant measure, viz. aid per head, is

Table 4

UTILIZATION OF LOANS
(Rs. m.)

	Authorized and undisbursed (1)	*Used in following year (2)*	*2/1 per cent*
March 1961	6,571	2,296	34·9
1962	8,378	3,058	36·5
1963	11,292	3,918	34·7
1964	11,755	4,831	41·1
1965	11,886	4,991	42·0

Source: Reserve Bank of India, *Report on Currency and Finance 1965–6*, Part I, Table 2.

used. India received in 1961 \$1·5, in 1962 \$1·7, and in 1963 \$2·1 from O.E.C.D. countries and multilateral agencies, compared with Pakistan's massive doses: \$2·8 excluding Indus Waters Scheme, \$4·0 including it (some of this should, however, be credited to India) in 1962; \$4·2 excluding, \$4·9 including it (1963), and a further rise to about \$6·0 in 1964. Stepping up gross aid to \$10,000 million for the period 1966–70 would mean raising aid per head to \$4 a year, still considerably below the level of Pakistan and of many other aid recipients. Whatever aid criteria one wishes to choose, India should be given much higher priority than it receives now.[5] India is one of the poorest countries. Its development potential is high. It has an efficient administration, a high level of education and skills, and a reserve of potential entrepreneurship. Its plans are well conceived and it has applied stringent import controls and high levels of domestic taxation. There can be no doubt that it has a structural balance of payments problem and considerable absorptive capacity. It enjoys constitutional democracy and has been the victim of an attack by China. What India does will serve as an example to others. Whether one's criteria are cold war, the encouragement of democratic government, the promotion of self-help, good performance, the

[5] This is powerfully argued in I.M.D. Little and J.M. Clifford, *International Aid* (London, 1965), pp. 226, 231, 234.

relief of the needy, or the activation of development potential, India should qualify for massive aid. In fact it is grossly under-aided.

Both the Right and the Left have attacked India's reliance on foreign aid, which both tend to exaggerate. The Right argues that aid, by encouraging central planning and public prestige projects, discourages the growth of private savings and private initiative, frightens away foreign enterprise, discourages economy in the use of capital, and generally destroys the basis of decentralized decision-taking which, on this view, is the prerequisite of development. Aid thus is thought to perpetuate the system which makes aid necessary; some go further and say that it pauperizes the country, making it increasingly dependent on external assistance.

The Left attacks aid on the ground that, by supporting reactionary groups in power, it retards the introduction of the institutional and political reforms, particularly effective land reform, which are necessary for development. Aid, on this view, props up reform-resisting oligarchies and conservative and feudal social systems, and again perpetuates the system which makes it necessary.

These arguments, which fit in well with the general disenchantment with aid among donors, are difficult to quantify and to assess. We shall discuss the argument in the context of food aid below. In order to bring out the costs and benefits of aid, and also in order to present clear political choices, it might be possible to draw up two simultaneous plans: one with a somewhat smaller reliance on aid, the other with somewhat more aid and with possible concessions to the donors. The cost of aid in the widest sense, including policies adopted or sacrificed, would thus be brought out clearly.

Table 5 shows the uses to which aid has been allocated. It adds to the total resources available to the community. It may be used to raise consumption, private investment, or government expenditure. In this general case, the value of aid to India is equal to the value of these additions. But if it helps to break a bottleneck – foreign exchange, particular items of equipment, or particular skills – the value of aid to India exceeds the nominal value of aid given. It makes fuller utilization of capacities in other sectors of the economy possible. Against this, it is possible that an aid-financed project imposes a burden of recurrent or other contributory expenditure on the domestic economy, and that these resources could have been used more productively in other lines. In such conditions the value of aid to India falls short of its nominal value. In so far as aid is available in freely-spendable foreign exchange, its value is likely to exceed its nominal value. The more it is tied to projects and donor procurement, the less likely will this be.

Table 5

DISTRIBUTION OF FOREIGN LOANS/CREDITS BY PURPOSES
(Figures in brackets show percentage distribution)
(Rs. m.)

	Authorized				Utilized			
Loans/Credits	(*1*) *Up to end of 1st Plan*	(*2*) *During 2nd Plan*	(*3*) *During 3rd Plan*	*Total 1 to 3*	(*1*) *Up to end of 1st Plan*	(*2*) *During 2nd Plan*	(*3*) *During 3rd Plan*	*Total 1 to 3*
1. Railway Development	156 (6·9)	1,952 (15·1)	1,392 (6·1)	3,500 (9·2)	156 (12·3)	1,432 (20·1)	1,850 (10·1)	3,438 (12·8)
2. Power Projects	196 (8·6)	623 (4·8)	2,414 (10·5)	3,233 (8·5)	121 (9·6)	293 (4·1)	1,529 (8·3)	1,943 (7·2)
3. Iron and Steel Projects*	786 (34·7)	2,242 (17·4)	2,078 (9·1)	5,106 (13·4)	27 (2·1)	2,541 (35·6)	1,049 (5·7)	3,617 (13·5)
4. Ports and Development	— —	205 (1·6)	186 (0·8)	391 (1·0)	— —	68 (0·9)	180 (1·0)	248 (0·9)
5. Transport and Communication	— —	148 (1·2)	930 (4·1)	1,078 (2·9)	— —	90 (1·3)	759 (4·1)	849 (3·2)
6. Industrial Development	193 (8·5)	7,555 (58·7)	15,266 (66·7)	23,014 (60·5)	23 (1·8)	2,554 (35·8)	12,836 (69·6)	15,413 (57·5)
7. Agricultural Development	34 (1·5)	— —	621 (2·7)	655 (1·7)	34 (2·7)	— —	225 (1·2)	259 (1·0)
8. Wheat Loans	903 (39·8)	157 (1·2)	— —	1,060 (2·8)	903 (71·5)	157 (2·2)	— —	1,060 (3·9)
Total	2,268 (100·0)	12,882 (100·0)	22,887 (100·0)	38,037 (100·0)	1,264 (100·0)	7,135 (100·0)	18,428 (100·0)	26,827 (100·0)

* Includes Orissa Iron Ore Project.
Source: Reserve Bank of India, *Report on Currency and Finance 1965–6* (1966), Statement 83.

The conventional approach to analysing the impact of aid is to regard it as filling either of two gaps, depending upon which is larger. If growth is seen as a function of the ratio of investment to national income, aid is seen as filling the gap between target investment and domestic savings. Alternatively, if growth is regarded as constrained by foreign exchange, aid fills the gap between the foreign exchange required to achieve a given growth target, and the foreign exchange earned by visible and invisible exports plus private capital flows.

The weakness of the double gap approach is that it makes assumptions, sometimes justified in advanced economies, which are unwarranted for India. The savings gap approach assumes that the relationship between investment and additional output is fairly stable, that consumption makes no contribution to output, and that home and foreign savings are interchangeable. But in the diagnosis of India it is normal to assume that the dominant bottleneck is not savings, but foreign exchange. And we have certainly witnessed situations in which potential domestic savings have run to waste for lack of foreign exchange. Aid requirements therefore tend to be approached through the trade gap. This analysis assumes that growth of domestic production could be accelerated with more foreign exchange.

We see from Table 6 that the contribution of external finance to public plan outlay is large. However, the apparently greater dependence on external assistance in the Draft Fourth Plan is due to the rise in the rupee figure resulting from devaluation; in fact, if corrected for devaluation, the proportion of aid-financed public outlay is less in the Fourth than in the Third Plan. It may be that without aid India would have increased its already strong tax efforts even more, but it is impossible to dispute that the Second and Third Plans would have been smaller without aid.

Consider aid as a provider of foreign exchange, assuming that domestic savings are not the dominant constraint. The withdrawal of aid would then have necessitated a combination of four courses of action: non-development import retardation, development import substitution, export expansion, and a shift of plan outlay into areas with low foreign exchange requirements. Since the foreign exchange crisis of 1957–8 India has imposed the most stringent controls on imports of consumer goods. Table 7 shows that if foodgrains, 82 per cent of which consist of P.L. 480 imports, are excluded, the total value of consumer goods imports was lower in the Third Plan than in the First. Little foreign exchange can be gained by further restrictions of consumption imports. As for the second course, development-import substitution, raw materials and equipment are closely scruti-

Table 6

FINANCING OF PUBLIC OUTLAY
(Rs.m.)

Sources	*1st Plan*	*2nd Plan*	*3rd Plan*	*4th Plan*
1. Balance from Current Revenues	3,820	110	−4,730	33,450
2. Surpluses of Public Enterprises	1,150	1,670	6,960	13,450
3. Capital Receipts	6,860	14,390	21,390	38,800
4. Deficit Financing	3,330	9,540	11,510	—
5. Additional Taxation	2,550	10,520	26,600	27,300
6. Budgetary Receipts corresponding to External Assistance	1,890	10,490	24,550	47,000 (*a*)
7. Total Resources	19,600	46,720	86,280	160,000
Row 6/Row 7 per cent	9·6	22·5	28·5	29·4 (*b*)

(*a*) Post devaluation.
(*b*) This figure is not comparable with the previous figures because of devaluation (see text).

Source: Material and Financial Balances, pp. 117–18, Table F.R.2.

nized for possible indigenous replacement. In any case, import substitution of equipment requires, in the initial stages, larger, not smaller, imports. It is the strenuous attempt to set up domestic import-substituting capital goods industries which is responsible for the growth of raw material and capital imports.

There has been considerable unused capacity in Indian industry, largely as a result of inadequate imports of raw materials, compo-

Table 7

IMPORTS OF CONSUMER GOODS
(Rs. m.)

	1st Plan	*2nd Plan*	*3rd Plan*
Consumer Goods	8,878	10,742	12,786
Foodgrains	6,015	8,046	10,330
Non-foodgrains	2,863	2,696	2,456
P.L. 480	51	5,448	8,800
P.L. 480 as percentage of total foodgrains	1·8	68·0	85·0

Source: Fourth Five-year Plan, 1966, pp. 100–2.

nents and spare parts. A change in the composition of imports – a higher proportion of maintenance imports and a lower proportion of imports tied to new industrial capacity – would indeed lead to higher capacity utilization. But there is little scope for substituting domestic production for imports in such a way as to reduce import requirements substantially in the near future.

Export expansion, unaccompanied by an equivalent fall in unit prices of exports, is the third way of reducing dependence on aid. Indian exports stagnated during the First and Second Plans. They rose between 1960 and 1964–5, but seem to have run out of steam since. Traditional exports (tea, jute, cotton) run into limitations of demand, and non-traditional exports, though they showed impressive increases, are still a small proportion of the total. Exports of engineering goods, iron ore and steel, and chemicals are still less than 10 per cent of total exports. No doubt it is in the expansion of these exports that future earnings prospects lie, but foreign exchange will be needed in order to build up this export potential.

The fourth method of saving foreign exchange is to change the composition of plan outlay in the direction of economizing in foreign exchange. This means more for agriculture, less for industry. In the Third Plan public outlay in agriculture and irrigation was Rs. 14,600 million, exclusive of industries producing agricultural inputs such as fertilizers, and in medium and large industries Rs. 25,700 million. If aid reductions had forced a substantial switch of investment from industry to agriculture, some foreign exchange could have been saved, though limitations of absorptive capacity may have retarded growth. An increase in agricultural inputs such as fertilizers does require foreign exchange, directly if these are imported, and indirectly if domestic fertilizer plants are to be put up.

We conclude that added foreign exchange shortages would have led to even more severe cuts in the Second and Third Plans, even if domestic savings had been available. In addition, it is most unlikely that the Government of India could have raised enough resources to maintain the size of the Plans even if structural balance of payments problems had not constituted an obstacle. These considerations suggest that the Second and Third Plans would have been reduced by an amount greater than the aid provided, if aid had been reduced. Or, to put the same point the other way round, in spite of some waste in the preparation, execution and management of some projects, additional aid enables India to mobilize a multiple of the resources provided by aid.

. . . .

In spite of errors and some faulty management, there is no doubt that India could absorb substantially more aid than it receives now. But the solution is more complex than simply changing the composition of aid in the direction of more maintenance imports. The contrast between project- and non-project aid over-simplifies the real issues. Not all capacity which has been created in India is equally valuable from a development point of view, and to underwrite maintenance imports for all existing capacity may lead to fuller utilization of capacity that should not be more fully used and may encourage the creation of undesirable capacity. On the other hand, economic progress, the unequal degree of capacity under-utilization, and the fact that fuller utilization of the capital goods industries is possible only if new projects are started, imply that *some* new projects will have to be started, say some new fertilizer plants, while there is still under-utilization in less important sectors. It is then essential that these projects should be well selected, well prepared, and well executed. Donors should offer assistance in sector and project selection, execution, and planning, as well as raising the proportion of non-project aid. These measures would not only raise the productivity of aid directly, but would also lead to fuller utilization of existing capacity, thereby raising output indirectly. They would reduce the need for detailed physical controls, economize in scarce administrative talent, and thus contribute to higher productivity and better morale.

But all this is relevant largely for the urban industrial sector. The most serious constraint on development, apart from population growth, is the relative stagnation until recently in many rural areas.

Table 8

	Percentage of net domestic product at factor cost 1964–5	*Annual growth rates 1961–5*	*Weighted growth*
Agriculture	51	2·7	1·4
Industry	18	7·4 (assume 10)	1·3 (1·8)
Services	31	6·7	2·1
All sectors	100	4·8 (5·3)	4·8 (5·3)

Even a substantial speeding up of the already high industrial growth rate is bound to be halted unless food production is raised by much more than it has been in the past. Project the figures for 1961–5 into the future. Industrial output increased annually by 7·4 per cent, services by 6·7 per cent, and agricultural output by 2·7 per cent.[6]

[6] Calculated from *Fourth Draft Plan, 1966* pp. 62–3.

Weighting these growth rates by their respective shares in 1964–5 in net domestic product at factor cost, the total growth is 4·8 per cent, which is 0·8 per cent per annum less than the projected rate of growth 1964–5 to 1970–1 (see Table 8). Even if we assume that industrial output is raised by the planned 10 per cent per annum, the aggregate growth rate is raised, initially, to only 5·3 per cent. The lag of agricultural production constitutes a serious brake on the power of foreign aid to speed up development. Slow growth in agriculture limits essential supplies to industry, demand for mass-produced industrial products, and the savings ratio. Aid can, of course, also contribute to the growth of agricultural output and to rural development, particularly through higher fertilizer imports, but its efficacy there is more limited than in urban manufacturing industry. It can do relatively little to promote land reform or effective agricultural extension services on the spot. But more recently there have been promising signs that farmers, encouraged by high prices and responding to new techniques, have in some areas substantially increased production.

5. FOOD AID FROM AMERICA

Over half the aid India has received from the U.S. and slightly less than a third of the total aid it has utilized has been in the form of commodities. (Part of the non-project aid also takes the form of commodities.) A small amount of this was received under the U.S. Mutual Security Act (P.L. 665), but by far the greater part has come under the U.S. Agricultural Trade Development and Assistance Act (P.L. 480), particularly under Title I which authorizes the sale of U.S. agricultural commodities for foreign currencies. Between India's first P.L. 480 agreement with the U.S. in 1956 and the end of the Third Plan, the total sales proceeds of P.L. 480 imports amounted to Rs. 156,730 million. Four-fifths of these counterpart funds were lent or granted to India; 7 per cent were loaned to U.S. private enterprises,[7] the remaining funds (13 per cent) have been retained by the U.S. Government for its own use.

Though self-sufficiency in foodgrains received top priority in the Third Plan, imports of P.L. 480 foodgrains have increased markedly since 1961–2. And this rise is not solely the result of large imports in 1965–6 following the disastrous harvest; year by year throughout the Plan, cereals imports have increased. Table 9 shows that nearly all the increase in imports during the Third Plan can be accounted

[7] Under the Cooley Amendment, Cooley rupees have, according to A.I.D., attracted over fifty American investors to India.

for by larger quantities of P.L. 480 imports. Domestic production of foodgrains stagnated during the first three years of the Plan and fell severely in the fifth year, so that dependence on imported food has increased: in 1961 net imports of cereals were just over 5·2 per cent of net production; by 1963 this figure had risen to 7·8 per cent, and by 1964 to over 11 per cent.[8]

But the growing size of U.S. food shipments is entirely contrary to American aid philosophy. U.S. aid, perhaps more than that of other donors, is intended to promote self-reliance, not to undermine it. America has expressed its dissatisfaction with India. The most obvious expression of this dissatisfaction was President Johnson's four-month delay at the end of 1966 in sanctioning new P.L. 480 agreements with India, but another sign was the American stipulation in 1965 that India must pay in foreign currencies the whole cost of P.L. 480 freight, not just 50 per cent as previously. This has been followed by the U.S. Food for Freedom Act which is intended to move countries receiving American food aid from soft currency payments to a system of dollar payments on long terms, but the Act is unlikely to be applied in its full rigour to India for some time. The U.S. has in effect indicated to India its reluctance to continue food shipments at the present high levels. For one thing, the Americans feel that others should share the burden of feeding India. It is for this reason that the U.S. has been the major force in getting food and food-related aid co-ordinated through the World Bank Consortium. Also, U.S. Government wheat stocks have in recent years fallen dramatically, largely because of increased food aid, especially to India. This has led to the removal of area limits in order to stimulate U.S. grain production.

There is, however, a deeper reason for the American reluctance to continue large-scale commodity shipments to India. The Americans fear that dependence on P.L. 480 food will breed ever greater dependence. It is felt by some Indians as well as Americans that U.S. surplus food, available almost for the asking in years of good harvests as well as bad, has undermined India's determination to tackle its agricultural problem seriously. In particular, food management, and especially efforts to draw out the marketable surplus, may have suffered as a result of P.L. 480 aid. True, self-sufficiency in foodgrains received top priority in the Third Plan. But this was not achieved and has now been carried over to become a major target in the Fourth Plan. Though weather played its part in this failure, it is not yet clear that India has yet hit upon a combination of policies which will ensure a high and sustained rate of growth in

[8] Min. of Finance, *Economic Survey of India 1965–6* (1966), Table 1:4.

agriculture. India has cut the share of investment in agriculture and has not a sufficiently strong policy to get trained personnel into rural areas. Such policies will involve difficult and unpopular choices and changes, and the Indians may prefer to postpone making them as long as possible. Certainly such postponement will be easier the more India can rely upon the U.S. to bail it out of its worst consequences.

But U.S. commodity aid may have had a more direct impact on agricultural production via its effect on cultivator incentives. P.L. 480 funds have been a major source of aid to the public sector. It is estimated that during the Third Plan funds arising from P.L. 480 aid financed over 10 per cent of public developmental outlay. P.L. 480 aid accounted for 56 per cent of the external assistance to public outlay. Because of the dangers of too much deficit financing and of the unpopularity of higher taxes, the Indian Government

Table 9

(Rs. m.)

	1961–2	*1962–3*	*1963–4*	*1964–5*	*1965–6*
Total imports	11,071	11,356	12,229	13,490	13,490
P.L. 480 foodgrains	710	1,120	1,730	2,250	2,680
Net total imports	10,361	10,236	10,499	11,240	10,810

Source: Fourth Five-Year Plan, 1966, p. 102.

has had an interest in making P.L. 480 imports and sales as large as possible, to raise funds to finance its plans. Larger P.L. 480 sales exert a downward pressure on food prices, and thus reduce incentives for cultivators. They also divert limited sources of credit away from agriculture. A difficult choice has therefore faced the Indian Government: to acquire a non-inflationary source of finance for its Plans, or to provide incentives for agriculture. The critics argue that the Government has favoured the former too much.

There are two ways for the Government to control the net availability of cereals directly. It can vary P.L. 480 imports, or it can vary the level of its cereal stocks. Table 10 shows increases over the previous year of net production of cereals and of net availability, i.e. net production plus imports less additions to stocks. It will be seen that Government imports and stocks policy has in most years had a stabilizing effect on the supply of cereals. However, this stabilizing effect has been very slight; in 1958–9, for example, the Government did very little to offset the large increase in the supply of cereals following the excellent harvest. In Table 11, column 4 shows the contribution to net availability of imports of cereals and changes in stocks. The trend of imports less additions to stocks has clearly been upwards. Only in two years since 1956 – when the first P.L. 480 agreement was made with the U.S. – has this trend been halted: 1958–9 and 1960–1, both years of bumper harvests. But the fall in imports less stock additions in these two years has been very small. The pattern is now clear: in years when agricultural production has fallen or risen only slightly, imports less stock additions have increased; in years of good harvests, they have remained stable. In years of bad harvests, therefore, the Government has used imports and stocks to put downward pressure on cereal prices, but in good years it has not lowered imports and added to stocks to offset the downward pressure on prices exerted by domestic production, but has simply kept cereal imports less stock additions at their former levels.

Turning now to the actual prices of cereals, it can be seen from Table 11 that cereal prices rose from 1956 to 1958. Also the cultivators' terms of trade, i.e. the ratio of the wholesale price index of cereals to the general wholesale price index, improved. But in 1959 production was 8 million tons higher, while imports and stock withdrawals were still at the same level as in 1958 – the net result was a fall in cereal prices from 107 to 104, and in the cultivators' terms of trade from 95 to 90.

In 1960 net availability of cereals was just below that of 1959, since the small fall in net production was offset by a large increase in imports, most of which was used to build up Government stocks. The quantity of cereals available was not sufficient to push cereal

Table 10

PERCENTAGE CHANGES IN NET PRODUCTION AND NET AVAILABILITY

	1956–7	*1957–8*	*1958–9*	*1959–60*
Net production	+4·7	−6·3	+16·1	−0·9
Net availability	+4·0	−4·7	+14·8	−0·3

	1960–1	*1961–2*	*1962–3*	*1963–4*	*1964–5*
Net production	+6·7	+2·4	−5·6	+4·7	+8·3
Net availability	−6·3	+2·8	−4·7	+9·1	+5·7

Source: Ministry of Finance, *Economic Survey of India 1965–6* (1966).

prices down, but it was sufficient to prevent them from sharing in the general price rise; as a result the cultivators' terms of trade fell from 90 to 83. In 1961 net output increased by 6·7 per cent; imports and stock withdrawals fell only slightly; net availability increased by 6·3 per cent; cereal prices and cultivators' terms of trade again fell. There followed three years of stagnation in agriculture.

Table 11

	1 *Net production of cereals* (a)	*2* *Imports of cereals*	*3* *Change in Govt. stocks*	*4* *Imports plus stock reductions*	*5* *Net Availability of cereals*	*6* *Index No. of cereals prices* (b)	*7* *Cultivators' terms of trade*
1956	50·34	1·04	−0·60	1·64	52·34	96	91
1957	52·68	3·63	+0·86	2·77	55·45	101	93
1958	49·36	3·22	−0·27	3·49	52·85	107	95
1959	57·30	3·86	+0·49	3·37	60·67	104	90
1960	56·77	5·13	+1·40	3·73	60·50	104	83
1961	60·65	3·49	−0·17	3·66	64·31	102	82
1962	62·08	3·64	−0·36	4·00	66·08	106	83
1963	58·63*	4·55*	−0·02	4·57	63·20	116	86
1964	61·41*	6·26*	−1·26	7·52	68·93	139	91
1965	66·52*	7·45*	+1·12	6·33	72·85	148	—

* Provisional.
Cols. 1, 2, 3, 4, and 5 units: mill. tonnes.
(a) Refers to agricultural year July–June: 1956 figure refers to net production in 1955–6. Net production is 8·75 per cent of total production, 12·5 per cent being provided for feed, seed requirements, and wastage.
(b) Refers to financial year March to February: 1956 figure for example refers to 1956–7. The base year of the Index is 1952–3 (= 100), as for col. 7.
Sources: Economic Survey of India 1965–6. Reserve Bank of India, *Report on Currency and Finance 1965–6* (1966), Statements 12 and 13.

The evidence linking P.L. 480 imports and lower levels of cereal production is strong but circumstantial. There are a number of possible objections. Firstly, while P.L. 480 imports are mostly in the form of wheat, a high proportion of cereal consumption is in the form of rice. The two are not perfect substitutes. Secondly, the ratio of the wholesale price index of cereals to the general wholesale price index may be a poor indication of the actual terms of trade of agriculturalists.[9] Thirdly, though the agricultural stagnation of the early 60s came after large imports of P.L. 480 cereals, the weather and shortages of agricultural inputs were probably more important contributing factors. Fourthly, change in area cultivated is possibly a more accurate indication of producers' decisions than output. The impact of P.L. 480 on crop areas is less clear – in 1964, for example, the area under cereals was slightly higher than in 1961, and the area under wheat, the commodity most affected by P.L. 480, was only slightly lower. However, a recent econometric study of P.L. 480 in India by J. S. Mann lends support to the view that P.L. 480 has had a depressing effect on cereal prices and production.[10] In this study Mann estimates that an increase in *per capita* imports of cereals under P.L. 480 of one pound (219,995 metric tons with the estimated 1962 population of 485 million has resulted in a 0·54 per cent drop in wholesale cereal prices in the same year and a decline in output in the second year of about 0·5 pounds of cereals *per capita* (about 109,997 tons with the same population). Output tends to rise in later years so that the depressing impact on output is trimmed to about 0·3 pounds *per capita* in the long run. This study measures only the direct impact of P.L. 480 imports; the indirect impact via the effect of readily available food aid on Planners' attitudes to agriculture is not estimated.

The conclusion is not that ending. P.L. 480 imports is an urgent matter deserving a higher priority. Indeed, Mann uses his analysis to argue the opposite: that since P.L. 480 cereal imports are only partially offset by the decline in domestic supply, they can make a positive contribution to filling the food gap. The inescapable fact is that for the time being India simply cannot do without food from abroad. In the two years 1965–6 India will have received about 19 million tons of food aid, which is equal to the Draft Outline estimate for the whole Plan period. As late as 1975–6, minimum likely average import requirements for foodgrains will still be as high as 7 million metric tons per year.[11] This continuing need for foreign food is reflected in the special Consortium arrangements for co-ordinating food aid to India; they amount in essence to a method which enables the U.S. to share with other donors the task – one it considers far from finished – of feeding India. Given a still

[9] See in this connexion V.G. Mutalik-Desai, 'Terms of Trade and Food Surplus', *Indian J. Agric. Econ.*, Jan.–Mar. 1966 (Bombay).

[10] J.S. Mann, 'The Impact of P.L. 480 Imports', *J. of Farm Economics*, February 1967, Vol. 49, 1, Pt 1.

[11] U.S. Dept of Agriculture, *Supply of and Demand for Selected Agricultural Products in India, Projections to 1975–6*, E.R.S. For. 100.

sizeable flow of food aid to India over the next decade, the important lesson from past experience is the need to control the amount reaching the consumer, in particular to limit it when domestic harvests are good. In years of good harvests P.L. 480 cereals should be stockpiled.

. . . .

7
REPORT OF THE COMMITTEE ON UTILIZATION OF EXTERNAL ASSISTANCE*

ANALYSIS OF ASSISTANCE RECEIVED

A number of steps are involved in the negotiation and utilization of external assistance, and several different types of aid are made available. It will be useful to set out the various steps involved and the main types of external assistance.

The first step is a commitment or pledge of assistance, which constitutes an indication of the willingness in principle of a country or an institution to grant assistance of a specified amount. This is in the nature of an advance commitment which helps the recipient country to plan utilization over a corresponding period. In the case of countries and institutions which are members of the Aid India Club (India Consortium) the pledges of assistance are made after a review of the development of the Indian economy and the requirements of further assistance at Consortium meetings. The U.S.S.R. and other countries, which are not members of the Consortium, pledge assistance after bilateral discussions. The pledges of aid are subject to appropriate legislative action or other authorization by the lending country or institution and to the conclusion of bilateral loan agreements.

The next step is the authorization of aid, which is secured when a formal loan agreement has been concluded. In a number of instances, the conclusion of the loan agreement would take place after the detailed requirements of the projects to be financed from the assistance have been worked out. In other instances, such as in the case of loans to cover raw material or miscellaneous machinery requirements, the loan authorization may take place at an earlier stage.

Loans may be tied to projects or alternatively they may be available for non-project purposes. When loans are project-tied, they can be utilized only for the import of equipment for the specific identified project. It may be mentioned that loans from the International

* Excerpts from the Report published by the Ministry of Finance, 1964.

Development Association, while tied to projects, can also be drawn to cover expenditures incurred within India in rupees. Loans, which are not tied to projects, may be available to finance imports of components and raw materials, or in some few cases they may be granted to postpone debt repayments falling due. For example, the U.S. A.I.D. has given some loans for import of raw materials such as metals and fertilizers while West Germany has extended loans for refinancing debt repayments due on Rourkela.

There is another sense in which assistance may be tied. This relates to the permitted sources of supply of materials to be financed by the assistance. In the recent past, nearly all country assistance has been tied to purchase in the countries providing aid. The I.B.R.D. and I.D.A. loans, however, are not so tied.

Some countries (e.g. France, Belgium and Italy) extend medium-term credits on a 'supplier to importer basis'. This is because the institutional arrangements in these countries are such that suppliers' credits are easier to arrange than direct Government lending. The credit risk of the supplier is covered by the country concerned under a suitable export credit insurance scheme.

In the case of assistance to finance imports into India, the disbursements are related to the payments to the foreign suppliers with whom orders have been placed. The utilization is effected primarily by either of two methods – the letter of commitment procedure and the reimbursement procedure.

Letter of commitment procedure: The letter of commitment procedure is an undertaking by the lending country/institution to the banker of the suppliers that at the request of the borrower through a letter of credit, the banker is to make payments to the suppliers and that the amounts so paid will be reimbursed to the banker by the lending country/institution. This procedure is in vogue in respect of the credits made available by the International Bank for Reconstruction and Development (I.B.R.D. or World Bank) and some of the loans from the United States Agency for International Development (U.S. A.I.D.). A variation of the letter of commitment procedure is the 'Direct Payment' method under which payments to the suppliers are made directly out of the credit. This system is in operation in respect of U.K. and I.B.R.D. credits.

Reimbursement Procedure: Under this system payments to the suppliers are made initially through normal banking channels from free foreign exchange. After payments have been made the individual importers are required to supply to the borrower, who in this case is the Government of India, connected documents, e.g. receipted invoice, a certificate of origin of the goods, etc. These documents are later presented to the lender to claim reimbursement of the amount already paid to the suppliers. Under the reimbursement procedure, there is an initial outgo from the foreign exchange reserves of the importer's country, which is subsequently recouped from the loan account.

The reimbursement method is more popular among suppliers as they prefer payment through normal banking channels. This arrangement is also preferred by private importers in India as the procedures are simpler. This method is in vogue in respect of most of the Government to Government credits that India has received.

The loans from East European countries are repayable through the export of goods. The repayments are made to rupee accounts, which are utilized by these countries to purchase goods in India.

PRESENT PROCEDURES FOR NEGOTIATION OF ASSISTANCE

In this section the present procedures for the negotiation of assistance are described. We consider in the first place the negotiation of assistance with institutions and countries which are members of the Aid India Consortium sponsored by the World Bank. The Consortium holds periodic meetings to consider the quantum of assistance that can be made available. A meeting has before it detailed information regarding the overall economic progress of the Indian economy and the developments in important individual sectors. While till recently the memorandum describing economic trends has been prepared by the World Bank staff, the Government of India has prepared the memorandum for the March 1964 meeting and the I.B.R.D. has circulated this together with a brief covering note. The Consortium is also furnished at the same time with a list of the projects and programmes for which assistance is sought.

At the Consortium meeting, the progress of the Indian economy is reviewed, the country's aid requirements are assessed, and each country and institution pledges a certain quantum of assistance in principle. Sometimes it is necessary for the Consortium to meet initially for a general review of India's aid requirements and to meet again after a time interval for purposes of pledging assistance.

After aid has been pledged, the Government of India makes proposals to each country or institution with regard to the specific purposes for which its assistance should be utilized. In some cases, loan agreements can then be concluded specifying the terms and conditions of lending and the broad purposes for which the money can be utilized. Individual public sector authorities or private firms in India are thereafter authorized by the Indian Government to place orders within the framework of the inter-governmental agreement.

In certain other cases, such as with regard to assistance from the World Bank or loans to cover large project requirements from the U.S.A., there is no overall agreement. The lending authorities satisfy themselves in the first place regarding the broad economic soundness of the proposals put forward by the Indian Government and thereafter negotiate detailed loan agreements with the Indian project authorities concerned. Orders can be placed for equipment only after the detailed loan agreements have been concluded.

When assistance takes the form of suppliers' credits, the Indian importers and the suppliers abroad have to negotiate a sale contract. This has to be processed through the concerned financial intermediaries in the country providing assistance. It is necessary for the Indian importers to provide acceptable guarantees of payment to the foreign suppliers.

The procedure of negotiation of loan agreements can be time-consuming. We have examined the time taken to conclude loan agreements to implement the pledges given at various Consortium meetings. We find that most of the loan agreements to cover amounts pledged in August 1958 Consortium were signed between December 24, 1958 and January 6, 1959. There was a similar delay with regard to the pledges made at the Consortium conference of March 1959. In most instances, the loan agreements were signed between June and November 1960. The second U.S. Export Import Bank Loan Agreement for Rs. 23·81 crores for procurement of capital equipment for development programmes, and the German Credit Agreement of Rs. 11·71 crores for Rourkela refinancing were signed only in January 1961. Again, with regard to the commitments made at the Consortium conference of June 1961 there were a number of cases in which loan agreements were signed after a year or more. Examples are the I.B.R.D. credit of Rs. 14·29 crores for I.C.I.C.I., the I.D.A. credit of Rs. 9·52 crores for the Kothagudam Power Project, the U.S. A.I.D. credit of Rs. 7·62 crores for the Delhi Power Project, the A.I.D. non-project loan of Rs. 114·29 crores and the German credit of Rs. 47·62 crores for Rourkela expansion.

In the case of bilateral negotiations with non-Consortium sources, there are also a number of stages. For example, the U.S.S.R. had, even prior to the start of the Third Plan, pledged assistance in principle for a number of industrial projects. The tentative list of the projects to be financed is then discussed between the Governments. For each project, a preliminary feasibility report is usually drawn up. If this is satisfactory, an agreement is concluded for preparation of a detailed project report and working drawings. The agreement for supply of plant and machinery follows the acceptance of the detailed project report and there are separate agreements with regard to the deputation of foreign technicians and specialists and the training of Indian technicians. As at the end of December 1963, orders placed amounted to 64 per cent of the assistance pledged by the U.S.S.R. and other East European countries. Even allowing for the fact that East European assistance is being utilized largely for projects requiring a relatively longer period for study and construction such as the manufacture of heavy machinery, the ordering against assistance has been unduly slow. The actual drawal of funds earmarked for such projects must, of course, necessarily be slow as the manufacture and delivery of equipment will be spread over a number of years.

On the evidence available, there can be no doubt that the process of aid utilization requires to be speeded up at all stages.

CAUSES OF SLOW UTILIZATION

Our earlier analysis has shown that aid in non-project form can be utilized more rapidly than project aid. The availability of a greater share of aid in non-project form would thus speed up utilization.

Non-project assistance is required for the purchase of commodities of various kinds and particularly those required for developmental purposes. It is a mistake to identify the import of equipment with the use of foreign exchange for developmental purposes. Aid giving countries and institutions may prefer the project approach because it is assumed that the impact of project assistance is easier to assess. We, however, feel that, when the whole development effort is planned, as is the case with India, there is no difficulty in assessing the impact of non-project assistance.

A number of commodities like fertilizers, steel and non-ferrous metals are used directly for developmental purposes, even if they are not capital equipment. The importance of stepping up the supplies of fertilizers in order to secure larger agricultural outputs is obvious. The use of a larger proportion of external assistance to finance metals, components, etc. is also essential if the country is to be independent of assistance within a reasonable period of time. It is now generally accepted that while India must steadily increase export earnings, there must also be a rapid build up of production within the country of the industrial, power and transport equipment needed to sustain a higher rate of growth. During the last few years considerable capacity has been established for such production, but its use depends to a significant degree on the availability of imported components and raw materials. If, therefore, industrial capacity is to be effective, assistance in the next few years must be increasingly available for the import of these items.

The so-called non-project aid also covers equipment of small value needed for the setting up of small-scale units and for expansion and modernization both of large and small units. Aid used for this purpose is non-project only in the sense that detailed specific appraisal of each scheme by the lending authority is not feasible. From the economic point of view, however, it contributes as much directly to the expansion of industrial capacity as project aid proper. Yet another area that has to be covered by such non-project aid is the 'secondary' requirements of projects. For instance, while the project aid would cover only the actual cost of the plant and machinery, there would be ancillary import requirements of construction machinery and of materials like steel (the cost of which may be considerable) which are required for the civil construction works.

Non-project aid is also needed to cover external debt repayments arising from loans contracted in the past on an unduly short-term basis. While some assistance has been available for this purpose so far, the country has, by and large, to service external debt out of free foreign exchange resources as additional assistance has been tied to commmodity purchase, and particularly to capital equipment. Assistance would go further if it were available for debt refinancing, releasing free foreign exchange for the purchase of goods needed for the full utilization of the country's growing productive capacity.

There has, no doubt, been some increase in the last few years in the share of aid available for non-project purposes, and currently around 40 per cent of Consortium assistance is of this kind. A further increase in the share of non-project aid will speed up utilization, promote the efficient use of industrial capacity in the country and secure a larger quantum of import with a given amount of external assistance.

A considerable part of external assistance must, however, continue to be tied to projects. The rate of utilization of such assistance will depend on the speed and efficiency with which projects are implemented. We have, therefore, found it necessary to consider the arrangements for the preparation and implementation of projects, both in the public and private sectors. We have found that sufficient attention is not paid at the present time to the preparatory work needed prior to the decision to finally go ahead with the project. This inadequate planning has been a major cause of delay in aid utilization. Improvements in this field would perhaps make the most important contribution to speedier and more effective utilization of project assistance.

Once it has been decided to implement a project, the actual execution is also delayed for a number of reasons. These include afterthoughts with regard to the scope of the project, delays in land acquisition, frequent references to administrative Ministries and to the Finance Ministry, inadequate planning by the project authorities, and time-consuming screening of import applications from the view-point of indigenous availability.

Private sector projects are delayed partly for the same reasons as the projects in the public sector. The industrial licensing procedures are, however, more specific to this sector. While the interim recommendations of another Committee, which have been accepted recently by Government, should help to eliminate many of the delays, we have also made certain recommendations in order to speed up aid utilization by private sector projects.

The use of non-project assistance is also delayed as a result of faulty allocation and licensing procedures, and we have devoted some attention to this matter.

The aid-giving countries and institutions can help to promote speedier utilization through amendments in their policies and procedures. We have referred above to the need for a larger share of assistance to be made available in non-project form. The reduction in the time lag between the pledging of assistance and the conclusion of loan agreements would be of great value. A number of procedural changes have also been suggested.

Finally, we have pointed out that the overall review of foreign exchange budgeting procedures can result in prompter and more effective use of assistance. At the present time the budgeting is done only six months ahead, with the result that effective forward planning by public sector authorities or private industrial units is rendered difficult. There is also inadequate co-ordination between the use of external assistance and of free foreign exchange. Better planning in this respect would help to speed up utilization.

STEPS TO IMPROVE AID UTILIZATION IN THE PUBLIC SECTOR

We shall now examine the steps that can be taken to speed up the use of assistance earmarked for public sector projects. As we have pointed out earlier, what is required is, in fact, better preparation of projects and more efficient implementation generally; speedier utilization of aid will be a by-product of such an increase in the efficiency of execution of projects.

We have been impressed by the fact that the projects included in lists put forward to the Consortium are often not ready for immediate implementation in the event of funds being made available. In fact, there is a dearth of well-conceived projects for which all the necessary preparations have been made for the placing of orders as soon as foreign exchange becomes available. A thorough review of the arrangements at present in vogue for project preparation appears to be essential.

There is an important middle ground between the overall national mapping of resources on the one hand and detailed work on individual projects on the other, which middle ground is today comparatively neglected. Organizations such as Geological Survey of India carry out surveys of the overall national resources of different types of minerals. Similarly, continuing studies are undertaken on a general basis of meteorological conditions, forest resources, soil characteristics, etc. There is not, however, enough detailed study of mineral availabilities, soil conditions, forest resource availabilities, etc., in specific areas from the specific viewpoint of the establishment of individual industries. For example, the expansion of the cement industry is being delayed because there has not been an adequate study from the viewpoint of commercial exploitation of limestone availabilities. Similarly, in spite of the big expansion envisaged in aluminium production, the bauxite resources have not been studied in sufficient detail. It is only when a decision, in principle, has more or less been taken to establish an individual industrial unit in a certain location that studies in depth are made of material availabilities, water resources, etc. This naturally results in considerable delay in implementation. We are of the view that considerably greater attention must be paid to industry-oriented geological, meteorological, mineral, soil, water and forest resource studies, which necessarily will mean, in many cases also, area-oriented studies in depth. We recommend that assistance be sought from the U.N. Special Fund and the World Bank for these surveys. The results of these surveys should be available for both the public and the private sectors and thus enable them to get a better view of the development programmes they can undertake.

Another essential step prior to the preparation of a detailed project report is the preparation of an economic and technical feasibility study. It is only if a large number of feasibility studies are available that the most promising opportunities can be identified and detailed project reports commissioned. It is on the basis of feasibility studies that rational decisions can be taken as to the most worth while among alternative investment possibilities. We would emphasize that the feasibility report should not merely be technological in character but should fully explore the economic aspects, taking due account of the possibilities of economizing on the use of scarce resources such as foreign exchange. No project should be proposed for aid unless a feasibility report has been completed. These reports must be of a high standard so that they are accepted by the institutions and countries providing assistance as justification for the acceptance of the projects in principle. The planning organizations in the public sector undertakings and in certain technical agencies of government such as National Industrial Development Corporation have recently been strengthened and are better equipped than before to undertake such feasibility studies. There should be further strengthening of the concerned agencies, and a sufficient number of feasibility studies should be prepared in order that the most promising among them may be chosen as a basis for project report preparation.

The preparation of a detailed project report is the next stage. There has been a natural tendency to defer the preparation of such reports until assistance for the project has been promised or at any rate until the probable source of assistance has been located. The reason advanced to justify the postponement of preparation of project reports to this late stage is that the appropriate agency to be chosen for preparation of the report may depend on the source of finance. The instructions to the agency preparing the report may also depend on the type of aid, since most of the 'country' aid is tied to that source of supply; for example, the project report would need to be based on the use of American equipment and processes if American financing is sought. Again, the East European countries have normally wished to prepare the project reports for projects to be financed by them. We consider, however, that in spite of these difficulties it is desirable for Government to commission project reports for the important projects likely to be put forward for external financing, in advance of the identification of the source of aid. Even if further studies need to be done after earmarking of assistance from a particular source, considerable time will have been saved as a result of the preparation of the project report before asking for assistance. We recommend, therefore, that detailed project reports should be undertaken in every case, either through consultancy firms or departmentally, in advance of the final earmarking of assistance for the project. It would be desirable to draw up panels of firms which should be Indian as far as possible but may also include foreign firms for preparation of project reports in each major field, such as power, steel and heavy industries. The World Bank, the U.N.T.A.B. (United Nations Technical Assistance Board), etc. can assist Government in selecting suitable firms for inclusion in the panels. We recommend further that the aid-giving countries should be requested to agree to finance the preparation of project reports involving substantial foreign exchange expenditure, without necessarily committing themselves to financing the projects themselves.

Once a project report has been prepared and approved and assistance has been secured, it is important that the scope of the project should not be altered. We have found that changes at a later stage in the scope of projects are an important cause of delays in implementation. The preparation and scrutiny of adequate feasibility reports prior to the project report preparation stage would operate to remove a major reason for change in the scope of projects at a later stage. Thus, financial clearance was given for the ophthalmic glass project with Russian collaboration only recently, though the credit provision was made in 1957 under the 500 million roubles credit negotiated in 1956. There were some delays initially because the question of whether foreign collaboration was most necessary was raised. Later, however, after the preparation of the project report, doubts arose as to the extent of the market and the profitability of production. These are matters which should have been settled at an earlier stage. There are other instances in which the capacity to be established has been increased after the detailed project report has been prepared, because of revision of estimates of requirements; the Gorakhpur Fertilizer Project, the Namrup Fertilizer Project, and the Durgapur Special Steels Project provide examples. Another example of a project which has been badly delayed as a result of change in the scope of the project at a late stage is the Salandi Irrigation Scheme sanctioned against an I.D.A. credit of dollars 8 million; the agreement was signed in November 1961 and became effective in January 1962.

Another cause of delay has been with regard to the acquisition of land. The present legal position is such that land acquisition procedures tend to be very protracted. We are aware that the selection and acquisition of land for industrial units has often been done inefficiently and haphazardly in the past and that, therefore, there is considerable public feeling that the Government's authority to acquire land should be circumscribed. There have been instances in which land has been acquired and a very considerable time has elapsed before it has been put to industrial use. The payment of compensation to and rehabilitation of agriculturists whose land has been acquired has often been tardy and inefficient. The site chosen has sometimes been changed after acquisition of land. Certainly, there should be careful selection of land before acquisition, and it should be taken over only at the stage when construction work can be started. The implementation of industrial projects and use of assistance should not, however, be held up because of lengthy procedures for acquisition of land. We recommend that Government review the legal position and take whatever steps are necessary to speed up land acquisition. The legislation should, of course, have adequate safeguards against abuse of the powers.

As a result of lack of proper advance planning of industrial projects, there is not always proper estimation of the overall cost at the outset. We should like to stress the importance of preparation of reasonably accurate overall financial estimates. To avoid delays in execution, suitable time-table should also be prepared at the start, against which progress can be measured. If the project authorities make proper preparations through adequate advance planning, the frequent reference to the administrative Ministry and the Finance Ministry can be done away with. The project should then be given complete freedom within the overall amount to place orders, subject to there being no material change in the scope of the work.

Action on the above lines should result in both prompter use of external assistance and in reducing the rupee investment on projects in the public sector.

PROCEDURES FOR DISBURSEMENT OF PROJECT AID

We consider now the various procedures for ordering and import of equipment and the drawal of foreign assistance. We discuss in particular the procedures for screening applications from the viewpoint of indigenous availability, and the financial checks exercised by the administrative Ministry and the Finance Ministry with regard to imports by public sector projects.

The scrutiny of import applications is undertaken primarily by the Directorate General of Technical Development, though for certain items other technical agencies of Government may be concerned. Broadly, the procedure is that the detailed lists of goods are submitted along with the import application to the D.G.T.D. The officers of the D.G.T.D. go through the lists to see whether any of the items can be secured from indigenous manufacturers. They may ask the project authority to try firms who are making some of the items sought to be imported. If the project authority can produce evidence to show that the indigenous manufacturers cannot supply the items, or that the delivery dates are undoubtedly prolonged, the import may be allowed. The officers of the D.G.T.D. also check to see that the overall value of the import proposed is reasonable having regard to the list of goods.

It has been represented to us that this system results in considerable delays. When the list of goods is long, a number of officers in the D.G.T.D. will be concerned with the scrutiny and considerable time may be taken. When the capacity available in the country for the manufacture of an item is inadequate to meet all demands, and imports must be permitted to some extent, the process of referring every applicant to the indigenous manufacturers and permitting import only to those who are turned down wastes time. The deletion of minor items from complete plants may not result in any appreciable foreign exchange saving, particularly if the import content of the indigenous production is taken into account. The quality of the indigenous product may not always be satisfactory, and there may be difficulties in securing guarantees from the foreign suppliers of the main equipment if the use of some items of indigenous equipment is insisted on. Most important of all, it has been pointed out that in many lines the delivery periods of indigenous manufacturers are very prolonged, and that therefore the use of expensive imported equipment may be delayed because of the lack of balancing equipment to be procured in India. An extreme case came to our notice where, in the case of a dairy development scheme aided by U.N.I.C.E.F. (United Nations International Children Emergency Fund), a cheese plant was not allowed to be imported as some components of a cheese plant were made in India. In the end, we are told, Government had to purchase the whole cheese plant and lost the opportunity of getting it free from the aiding agency.

Officers of the Department of Technical Development have explained to us that much is being done to minimize the inconvenience to projects as a result of the detailed scrutiny of the lists of goods. The deletion of doubtful items is not insisted on, if they do not constitute more than, say, 5 per cent of the total cost of the imported equipment. Periodic meetings of officers are held at which pending applications are considered and finally disposed of. The indigenous manufacturers are asked to supply monthly reports of production, and outstanding orders, and the Department can ascertain from these reports the up-to-date supply position of each item. Delivery dates are stated to be taken into account when considering whether import should be allowed. A list of indigenous manufacturers with names, addresses and detailed items produced has been published and is kept up to date so that the project authority can fully explore indigenous sources before applying for import. The detailed screening for indigenous availability is stated to be essential if full use is to be made of the manufacturing capacity in the country and waste of foreign exchange is to be avoided; project authorities often prefer imports purely on grounds of somewhat lower cost, even though fully satisfactory indigenous products are available for prompt delivery. The detailed screening has been simplified in the case of some industries by prescribing monetary ceiling for standard plants; for example, today foreign exchange to the extent of Rs. 45 lakhs is allowed for each cement plant of 100 tons per day capacity. It is expected that in two to three years the figure of Rs. 45 lakhs can be very substantially reduced, when items such as heavy castings are indigenously available. Meanwhile, within the monetary ceilings, each importer of a standard plant in the cement, paper, sugar or superphosphate industries has flexibility with regard to the items to be imported and bought indigenously respectively.

We are fully convinced that the screening by the D.G.T.D. has resulted in promoting desirable growth of Indian industry, particularly in the field of machinery manufacture. There cannot be any question of wasting foreign exchange by permitting imports of items that are indigenously available on an economic basis in order to cater to any irrational preferences of project authorities for imported supplies or to eliminate the inconvenience of combining indigenous and imported supplies. Nevertheless, we feel that certain further amendments should be made in the procedures in force at present in order to secure prompter utilization of assistance. We consider that the changes that we have recommended are not likely to result in any significant import of items that are indigenously available. The most effective safeguard against unnecessary import is the limited allotment of total foreign exchange made available to each project in the public or the private sector, whether for capital equipment or for components and raw materials. It is in the interest of the project itself, therefore, to do its utmost to locate indigenous sources of supply in order to use the available foreign exchange in the most effective manner.

As has been mentioned above, the practice has already been introduced of setting monetary limits for the import of standard plants in certain industries such as cement, sugar and superphosphates. Each unit has the flexibility to decide which items to import and which to secure indigenously, within the monetary ceiling. As a result, the most effective use can be made of indigenous capacity, while minimizing the delay in the setting up of plants. We recommend that this procedure be extended to as many industries as possible. There need not be any detailed scrutiny of items, provided that the monetary ceilings are adhered to and subject of course to the exclusion of banned items.

POLICIES AND PROCEDURES OF AID-GIVING COUNTRIES

A major contribution that can be made by the aid-giving countries and institutions to prompter utilization will be through an increase in the share of non-project assistance. We have argued earlier that a larger quantum of non-project assistance would, given the present stage of development of the Indian economy, be of considerable value, apart from securing quicker utilization. An allied point is that project assistance can legitimately be defined more liberally to cover components and balancing plants required to be imported to manufacture complete plants in India, and the initial stock of components of machinery manufacturing industries whose equipment is financed by aid.

We have referred also earlier to the considerable delay between the pledging of assistance and the conclusion of loan agreements. We have suggested that delays for which India is responsible can be reduced if the preparation of projects is carried further before assistance is requested. The countries and institutions providing assistance can help by making a selection in principle of projects and programmes as part of the Consortium exercise. Alternatively, the process of selection could be completed within a specified period of say two months after a Consortium meeting. Even if the formal conclusion of loan agreements takes somewhat longer, it could be agreed that orders for equipment should be placed immediately after acceptance in principle, and that payments made after that date would be eligible for reimbursements.

We have suggested above that panels of firms should be drawn up for the preparation of project reports in different fields, and that the aid-giving countries and institutions should agree to finance project reports even if the projects themselves are not later picked up for finance. It would help if the aid-giving countries and institutions agree to accept project reports prepared by firms on the panel without insisting that a firm nominated by the aid-giving agency should prepare a project report.

The earmarking of the entire foreign exchange cost of a project at the start is a major cause for apparent delay in utilization. The partial financing technique provides one solution to this difficulty. Under partial financing arrangements, the lending country or institution ear-marks in the first instance only part of the foreign exchange needed for the project. This amount would cover the payments in, say, the first year of the implementation of the project. In each subsequent period, funds would be earmarked against the further assistance that may be made available, broadly to cover the payments in that period. As a result, the funds allocated in a year can be more or less fully utilized in that year without being carried forward to cover payments in later years against orders already placed. The difficulty with the partial financing technique is that, if sufficient funds are not allotted by the aid-giving country or institution in later periods, or if there is no agreement on the use of funds that may be earmarked to cover these payments, there may be no alternative but to use free foreign exchange. Partial financing can, therefore, only be acceptable if there is a clear understanding that payments falling due will be a first charge on such assistance as may be made available by the particular country or institution. Also, it would be wise to limit the application of this technique to projects of high priority. Within these limitations it can play a useful part in speeding up utilization by reducing the amount of assistance which is in the pipe-line.

The bulk of project aid will, in the present circumstances, continue to be tied to projects in the country providing assistance. In practice, most projects require small amounts of equipment from third countries, and location of suitable means of financing of such requirements has taken time and has resulted in delay in the implementation of projects. To give an example, the Foundry Forge Project at Ranchi has required some import of equipment outside Eastern Europe and the financing arrangements have taken time to complete. It would be of considerable assistance if at least 10 per cent of the aid made available for a project is permitted to be utilized in third countries.

The World Bank and the I.D.A. require that orders should be awarded to the lowest tenderer, and they do not permit the grant of preference to indigenous suppliers. Under Indian conditions, there are a number of instances in which Indian suppliers charge somewhat higher prices in terms of rupees but require less foreign exchange for undertaking an order. The World Bank and the I.D.A. should be asked to relax, in appropriate cases, the requirement that only the lowest tender should be accepted, in order to enable fuller use to be made of the industrial capacity available in India and to facilitate the conserving of foreign exchange resources.

The American authorities require that the use of American assistance should be based on tenders confined to American firms. In cases in which global tenders were invited in the first instance, re-tendering in the U.S.A. has become necessary when it has been decided to use American assistance. The American authorities should be requested to accept the results of global tenders, if a reasonable number of American firms have participated. The order would, of course, be awarded to the lowest among the American tenderers.

In a number of instances, there are minimum value restrictions on ordering against external assistance. We appreciate the desire of aid-giving countries and institutions to keep paper work to a minimum. Nevertheless, the minimum value conditions operate unfairly against the smaller units. At least in so far as requirements of the small industry are concerned, those giving aid should endeavour to remove the restrictions.

8
AID THROUGH TRADE: CASE STUDY OF INDIA*

by Dharam Narain
Professor, Institute of Economic Growth, Delhi

1. INTRODUCTION

All through the three Five-Year Plans, India's efforts at the planned development of its economy have tended to increase its import requirements much faster than its export earnings. This has resulted in a continuing strain on the balance of payments. Since the late 1950s, India has experienced a particularly acute and chronic shortage of foreign exchange and has increasingly relied upon the inflow of foreign aid to close its balance of payments gap. The inflow of external loan assistance, however, has created problems of its own: the cost of credit-financed imports has often been significantly higher than of those purchased through its foreign exchange earnings; and the debt service has imposed on India a burden which over the years has become truly onerous.

The problems India has faced have not been entirely unique to it: these have been shared, in a greater or lesser degree, by many other developing countries. And it is against this background that some developed countries, notably socialist countries, have sought to help developing countries by providing them with new trade outlets. The mechanism through which such trade is effected is twofold:

(*a*) bilateral trade and payments arrangements, including long-term export contracts and industrial branch agreements based on partial division of labour between the countries concerned;
(*b*) repayment of loans in mutually agreed products of debtor countries or in the currency of debtor countries.

The object of this paper is to attempt an analysis of the Indian experience in respect of the working of this twofold mechanism.

Although India has trade agreements with some thirty countries,

* U.N.C.T.A.D. *Report*, T.D./B.C./C., 3/57 (mimeo, 1968), Chs. 1–3 only.

the really important amongst these have been the trade and payments agreements it has concluded with the socialist countries of Eastern Europe. As will be seen from Table 1, the expansion of India's trade with the socialist countries, within the framework of these agreements, has indeed been remarkable.

This trade has enabled India to import plant and equipment, industrial raw materials and components, all vital to its development, in exchange for its staple commodities such as tea, coffee and tobacco, crude materials such as iron ore and traditional manufactures such as jute goods.

Table 1

MAIN CHANGES IN THE DIRECTION OF INDIA'S FOREIGN TRADE, 1951–65

Annual average (millions of Rupees)

Item	*First Plan 1951–5*	*Second Plan 1956–60*	*Third Plan 1961–5*	*Change between 1951–5 and 1961–5*
Exports to:*				
Socialist countries	50·8	357·1	1,132·9	1,082·1
Rest of the world	6,007·8	5,735·1	6,483·9	476·1
Total:	6,058·6	6,092·2	7,616·8	1,558·2
Imports from:				
Socialist countries	56·7	361·6	1,256·0	1,199·3
Rest of the world	7,177·3	9,402·9	11,193·2	4,015·9
Total:	7,234·0	9,764·5	12,449·2	5,215·2

* Including re-exports.

Source: Director General of Commercial Intelligence and Statistics, Government of India, Calcutta.

The expansion of this trade, however, has occurred alongside an increase in the volume of loan assistance India has received from the socialist countries of Eastern Europe. Part of the imports from these countries has been financed by such loan assistance and the rest by Indian exports. The fact that total exports were stagnant during most of the 1950s imparts great significance to this rapid increase in Indian exports to the socialist countries.

Ostensibly, the element of aid in the trade and payments arrangements India presently has with the socialist countries of Eastern Europe consists in the fact that, faced as the country is with an acute shortage of free foreign exchange, it is allowed to pay for its imports in inconvertible rupees. This implies that to the extent that it is able to meet its growing import requirements from these sources, the expansion of exports to them tends to be automatic. And what is true of the arrangements for the payments for its imports is also true of the debt-service payments India makes to these countries. But, even though the increase in exports to socialist countries has been very impressive, the real element of aid depends upon how far these exports have been truly additional rather than at the expense of exports to free currency areas. For only to the extent that the increase in exports has been a net increase can it be said to have enlarged India's overall capacity to obtain non-aid financed imports from abroad and improved the country's debt servicing capacity. But to the extent that it represents a mere diversion of exports from free-currency areas, apart from not increasing net exports, the loss of free-currency earnings caused by such a diversion might even have reduced the capacity to buy requirements in the cheapest markets overseas.

It is, therefore, pertinent to enquire how far this rapid increase in India's exports to socialist countries has displaced its exports to free-currency areas. Such displacement may or may not accompany a physical diversion to third countries of the goods initially purchased by socialist countries from India. But when it does, the consequence for India could be doubly serious. Such physical diversion carries with it the risk of these goods being sold at a discount in other markets, thus dislocating India's normal trade with its traditional markets, besides involving the country in an immediate loss of the free foreign exchange that such diversion entails.

Section 2 is, therefore, devoted to an examination of the issue of 'additionality' in respect of India's exports to socialist countries. It has to be borne in mind that the cost of diversion of India's exports from free-currency areas to socialist countries, to the extent such diversion has occurred, as well as the gain to India from the increase in its exports to socialist countries, even in the measure that it constitutes a net addition to India's exports to the rest of the world, depends upon the terms of trade, i.e. the prices at which India has been able to sell her goods to the socialist countries and the prices at which it has had to buy from them. Consequently, Section 3 will be devoted to a comparison of each set of prices in respect of both the socialist and other countries. . . .

2. 'ADDITIONALITY' IN RESPECT OF INDIA'S EXPORTS TO SOCIALIST COUNTRIES OF EASTERN EUROPE

Ideally, an analysis of the extent of diversion from free-currency areas involved in India's exports to socialist countries calls for a comparison between what her exports to free-currency areas have been and what they would have been in the absence of exports to socialist countries. Such a comparison, being hypothetical, would be hazardous. One could seek guidance from trends in the past, when India did not export to socialist countries. But except in those cases where there is a reasonable assurance that the factors underlying these trends have not changed over time, a mere mechanical extension of these trends to a later period is clearly unwarranted. And an effort to adjust these trends for the changed circumstances involves a quantification of the effect of those changes which, even as an approximation, is far from easy. Furthermore, to attempt it for each commodity is a stupendous task in terms of the time that would be required. Lastly, even minimum guidance from the past is not available for commodities which have entered into the 'export basket' only recently. Of necessity, therefore, what is attempted in this study is more modest: to ascertain, as far as possible, whether India's exports to socialist countries have displaced actual exports to other countries and in the process throw light, in so far as is feasible, on the adverse effect they might have exercised on India's potential exports.

An examination of the behaviour of India's exports of commodities which possess a significant weight in her exports to socialist countries shows these commodities as falling into two categories: those in respect of which an increase in the volume of exports to socialist countries has been associated with an increase in India's exports to the rest of the world and others in respect of which increased exports to socialist countries have been accompanied by a decline in exports to other countries. The latter category can be further subdivided: one component consisting of commodities the exports of which to the rest of the world show a continuing decline over the entire period considered here (1952/3–1965/6) and the other component consisting of those commodities the decline in whose exports is confined to the 1960s. . . .

Table 2 summarizes the behaviour over time of exports of commodities falling into the first of the three categories. The period under study has been divided into three parts. The first period shown covers the four years ending 1955–6, when exports to socialist countries were negligible or nil, the second period comprises the four years ending 1960 and the third period refers to the quinquennium ending 1965–6.[1] For brevity, these will be referred to as periods one, two and three.

From amongst the commodities belonging to the first category, an increase in India's exports of oilcakes, cashew kernels and iron ore to the socialist countries has gone hand in hand with an increase in the value as well as the volume of their exports to other countries. In terms of volume, India's exports of coffee, mica and footwear have also increased to both sets of countries, though in terms of value, the exports of mica and coffee to other countries suffered a set-back in the third compared with the first two periods, while those of footwear suffered a set-back in the second period. Since increased purchases by the socialist countries could exercise only an upward and not a downward effect on prices, the decline in unit values, implicit in a decrease in the total value of exports accompanying a rise in their volume, must be the result of factors other than India's exports to socialist countries, except in the event of their reselling Indian goods at a discount in other markets. In the case of mica at least, this last possibility is easily ruled out by the fact that the decline in the total value of mica exports to other countries in the third period compared to what it was in the second has been found to be the result of a change in the composition of the mica 'export basket.' With the possible exception of coffee, it has thus been possible to conclude that India's exports of these commodities (i.e. commodities included in category one) to socialist countries have not displaced her actual exports of these commodities to other countries. In fact, an examination of the prospects of exports of natural mica and iron ore from India, for the period under reference, supports, on the qualitative plane at least, the inference that India's trade with socialist countries has not displaced even its potential exports of these commodities to other countries.

Table 3 summarizes the behaviour of exports of commodities in respect of which an increase in India's exports to socialist countries has been associated with a decline in the volume of exports to the rest of the world in the 1960s. The decline in India's exports of tea to the rest of the world was produced in the main by a twofold phenomenon: stagnation of total imports of tea into the United Kingdom in the third compared with the second period and a continuing loss, over the period considered here, of India's share in this market. Neither of these factors, however, has been found, in any important

[1] Since the data are not readily available on a uniform basis, the statistics for some years are in terms of calendar years while for others they are in terms of fiscal years.

Table 2

EXPORTS OF SELECTED ITEMS FROM INDIA

	Annual average (Thousand tons)			Annual average (Million rupees)		
	1952–3 to 1955–6	*1957 to 1960*	*1961–2 to 1965–6*	*1952–3 to 1955–6*	*1957 to 1960*	*1961–2 to 1965–6*
Oilcakes and meal						
Socialist countries	—	34·8	390·4	—	13·1	150·1
Others	54·3	291·8	483·2	17·2	99·9	166·3
Cashew kernels						
Socialist countries	—	4·7	12·8	—	20·4	59·2
Others	30·3	34·3	36·9	119·0	139·0	171·4
Iron ore						
Socialist countries	311·5	789·3	1,844·2	14·3	39·8	84·2
Others	817·3	1,231·8	8,418·0	35·7	90·2	288·7
Coffee						
Socialist countries	—	4·1	14·0	—	19·2	58·5
Others	4·5	10·8	12·2	30·0	50·5	44·1
Mica*						
Socialist countries	1·1	13·2	27·8	2·3	11·7	28·8
Others	172·9	225·7	305·4	78·0	84·3	73·3
Footwear†						
Socialist countries	—	0·5	0·8	—	12·4	16·1
Others	4·1	4·1	6·0	17·5	15·0	20·3

* Quantity in hundreds of tons.
† Quantity in million pairs.
Source: Director General of Commercial Intelligence and Statistics (D.G.C.I. and S.).

Table 3

EXPORTS OF SELECTED ITEMS FROM INDIA

	Annual average			*Annual average*		
	1953–3 to 1955–6	*1957 to 1960*	*1961–2 to 1965–6*	*1952–3 to 1955–6*	*1957 to 1960*	*1961–2 to 1965–6*
	(Thousand tons)			(Million rupees)		
Tea						
Socialist countries	—	10·8	20·4	—	80·3	136·5
Others	198·8	199·3	188·8	1,091·7	1,183·0	1,092·4
Jute manufactures						
Socialist countries	—	20·0	105·0	0·1	29·6	191·8
Others	816·4	822·0	788·4	1,212·0	1,102·2	1,421·7
Tobacco (unmanufactured)						
Socialist countries	0·5	3·9	28·2	0·6	6·4	64·6
Others	32·2	38·7	32·4	113·9	140·4	129·6
Groundnuts						
Socialist countries	—	1·1	11·6	—	9·0	12·6
Others	17·2	17·4	14·7	18·1	15·6	14·9
Castor oil						
Socialist countries	—	6·9	15·6	—	11·2	24·1
Others	30·9	32·6	8·5	46·1	50·1	12·4

Source: D.G.C.I. and S.

measure, to be related to India's increased exports of tea to socialist countries.

The decline in India's exports of jute manufactures has been the result of the vigorous competition offered by Pakistan. Significantly enough the decline in India's exports of jute manufactures has been confined to sacking, a category of jute goods on which Pakistan's production and exports have concentrated. Having regard to the vigour of competition from Pakistan, and India's reluctance to react aggressively to its export subsidy, it appears doubtful if India would have been able to capture additional demand for packing materials even if she had not stepped up her exports to socialist countries. The latter do not, therefore, seem to have displaced even India's potential exports to other countries.

Since the bulk of India's exports of tobacco consists of Virginia flue-cured tobacco in which its main competitors are the United States and Southern Rhodesia, part of the explanation of the decline in India's exports of tobacco lies in the larger United States exports under the concessional schemes and part of it lies in the reduced off-take of Indian tobacco by the United Kingdom, the latter having been the result of the United Kingdom's agreement with Rhodesian producers to take increased quantities of Rhodesian tobacco. The first factor is unrelated to India's increased exports of tobacco to socialist countries. But the possibility that the increased imports of Rhodesian tobacco by the United Kingdom were partly a result of inadequate supplies from India as a consequence of increased off-take of Indian tobacco by socialist countries cannot be ruled out. Available evidence, however, does seem to suggest that the displacement, if any, of India's exports of tobacco to other countries caused by its exports to socialist countries may not have been large.

Amongst oilseeds and oils, India exports mostly groundnuts and castor oil to socialist countries.

The decline in the value of India's exports of groundnuts to the rest of the world in the second compared with the first period was the result of the depressed level of the world prices of groundnuts in 1958 and 1959 brought about by the jump in the volume of world exports of groundnuts in these two years. And a decline in the value as well as in the volume of India's exports of groundnuts to countries other than those of the socialist group in the third period compared to the second was the result of government policy of not permitting the export of more than limited quantities, in view of the upward pressure on the domestic prices of seeds and oils experienced since the latter half of 1963 and accentuated by the poor crop of 1965–6. That the tightening of the controls reduced the exports both to the socialist and other countries makes it clear that it was not a case of displacement of the actual exports to the latter by those to the former set of countries.

The decline in India's exports of castor oil to other countries, confined to the third period, was the result of sagging world prices consequent upon larger Brazilian production and exports of castor oil, which, considered in relation to domestic prices in India, reduced the attractiveness of exports to these markets.

The third category comprises goat-skins, manganese ore, wool (raw), lac and pepper in respect of which India's average annual exports to the rest of the world have registered a continuing decline over the entire period considered here (1952/3–1965/6) (Table 4).

The decline in India's exports of manganese ore has been intimately linked to the ground India lost to Brazil in the United States market and this has been the result of a desire on the part of the United States to find a closer and more secure source of supply.

The explanation of the decline in India's exports of lac lies in the cost advantages Thailand has acquired over India which has enabled it to offer effective competition to India.

In the absence of data on the cost of production of black pepper for countries, principally Sarawak and Indonesia, which offered price competition to India, it is not possible to say how far this adverse shift in India's competitive position reflects the cost advantage acquired by its competitors. It could well be that the purchases of Indian black pepper by socialist countries pushed up its relative price to the detriment of India's exports of this commodity to other countries. In the case of wool (raw) and goat-skins also the possibility that exports to socialist countries have led to a reduction in India's exports to other countries cannot be ruled out.

To sum up, while the commodities covered in the foregoing analysis account for 85–90 per cent of India's exports to socialist countries in the 1960s, the share of the last four commodities – black pepper, raw wool, goat-skins, and unmanufactured tobacco, in respect to which exports to socialist countries could have displaced India's exports to the rest of the world – has ranged from about 14 to 20 per cent. Even though the quantification of actual displacement has not been possible, the figures do seem to suggest that something like 70 per cent, at least, of India's exports to socialist countries have not been at the expense of its exports to other markets.

India's exports to socialist countries of Eastern Europe would not represent a genuine addition to her total exports if these countries were to resell part of their imports from India to other countries. In discussing the issue of physical diversion to third markets of the

Table 4

EXPORTS OF SELECTED ITEMS FROM INDIA

	Annual average			Annual average		
	1952–3 to 1955–6	*1957 to 1960*	*1961–2 to 1965–6*	*1952–3 to 1955–6*	*1957 to 1960*	*1961–2 to 1965–6*
	(Hundred tons)			(Million rupees)		
Goat skins						
Socialist countries	12·3	57·1	78·4	8·5	49·3	58·2
Others	90·8	61·0	37·6	48·1	33·9	25·4
Wool (raw)						
Socialist countries	—	32·9	53·9	—	20·4	33·5
Others	138·5	130·4	60·6	81·6	78·1	35·1
Lac						
Socialist countries	27·5	15·5	31·2	2·9	4·0	8·1
Others	285·8	253·3	153·8	88·1	59·7	36·3
Pepper						
Socialist countries	15·8	64·8	91·2	8·8	20·0	34·3
Others	126·8	95·5	119·2	92·8	31·3	42·6
Manganese Ore*						
Socialist countries	—	45·8	138·2	—	7·3	17·0
Others	1,259·3	1,169·5	989·2	174·0	178·3	85·6

* Quantity in thousand tons.

Source: D.C.G.I. and S.

goods purchased by the socialist countries in India, it is necessary to distinguish between two kinds of phenomena. One consists of the possible re-export of the goods socialist countries purchase from India and the other refers to the direct shunting of such goods to third markets without bringing them into the import–export statistics.

Although the available statistics impose a great many limitations on the examination of these phenomena, the evidence does not suggest any large-scale diversion to free currency areas of the goods socialist countries have purchased in India. The maximum re-exports, of jute manufactures and oilcakes – in respect of which significant re-exports are possible – do not account for more than 3·5 per cent of India's total exports to socialist countries in the 1960s. To say this is not to suggest that socialist countries have not participated in switch trade. There are specific instances of their having shipped Indian goods to third markets; moreover, complaints regarding such re-sale, forbidden by the Trade Agreements, have tended to multiply in recent years. All that is being suggested is, and that is the overall conclusion of this section, that so far as available evidence goes, India's exports to socialist countries until now appear to have been largely (perhaps to the extent of two-thirds or more) a net addition to its exports to countries other than socialist countries. How far a softer outlet for India's exports provided by the socialist countries has weakened the pressures in India to export more to other countries is anybody's guess. It seems most unlikely that with all the pressures that the absence of this outlet may have generated, India would have been able to add a major fraction of Rs. 1,500 million – representing the average annual increase in the values of its exports to socialist countries since the early 1950s – to its export earnings from the rest of the world over and above what it had already achieved.

3. COMPARATIVE PRICES OF INDIA'S EXPORTS TO, AND IMPORTS FROM, SOCIALIST COUNTRIES OF EASTERN EUROPE AND OTHER COUNTRIES

The only comprehensive data available for a comparison between the prices which India has realized for her exports to socialist countries and for those to other countries consist of unit values derivable from the total values and quantities of individual items of export to various countries. But differences in unit values of exports to various destinations may reflect both differences in the quality of a product exported to different countries as also differences in prices of products of a uniform quality. And the fact that the two kinds of differences are inter-mixed in unknown proportions vitiates comparability of the unit values pertaining to different destinations. Since quality differences could not be explicitly allowed for, a decision was taken to reduce their incidence by not using the unit values pertaining to broad commodity categories, but considering instead the unit values, derived from the data available for each specific item within a commodity category. For example, where data were separately available for different grades and descriptions of a commodity, these have been used. Although this procedure reduces the incidence of quality differences, it provides no assurance that they have been eliminated. Hence, such commodities as mica and tobacco, for example (where quality differences were large and appeared to persist even after the data were examined in detail) were kept out of the picture. But since even in the case of other commodities it could not be assumed that quality differences had been eliminated, the assumption has been made that such differences pertaining to different commodities and different destinations are likely to cancel each other out, at least partially, if an aggregation is attempted. Therefore the unit values have been worked out for the socialist countries as one group and the remaining countries as another. Furthermore, although unit values are worked out for each specific item, the ratios of the unit values of each item pertaining to the two sets of countries are combined for each year into an overall index.[2] This has been prompted by the caution that too much should not be made of ratios pertaining to any specific item; instead, the overall picture should be taken to be a more reliable, though admittedly a very rough, indicator of the differences in the prices India has realized for its exports from the two sets of countries.

The weights used for combining specific commodity-ratios into an overall index for each year, are the percentage shares of specific items in the total value of the export of these items to socialist countries. Since the composition of the 'basket of exports' to socialist countries which is considered here and which forms the basis of the weighting patterns adopted, has changed over time, the

[2] The items covered by the indices of unit values of India's exports to socialist and other countries are the following: (1) defatted groundnut meal, (2) castor oil, (3) cashew kernels, (4) iron ore and concentrates, (5) black tea, (6) goat-skins – dry salted, (7) goat-skins – pickled, (8) lac – shellac, (9) jute hessian bags – new, (10) jute sacking bags – new, (11) jute corn sacks, (12) tarpaulins of jute, (13) jute hessian cloth, (14) sheep or lamb wool greasy back washed, (15) pepper, (16) coffee – unroasted Arabica cherry, (17) coffee – unroasted Arabica plantation A, (18) coffee – unroasted Arabica plantation B, (19) coffee – unroasted Robusta, (20) coffee – unroasted others excluding Arabica cherry and Robusta.

Table 5

RATIOS OF UNIT VALUES OF EXPORTS TO SOCIALIST COUNTRIES OF EASTERN EUROPE AND REST OF THE WORLD

1957	120 (80)*
1958	113 (81)
1959	112 (76)
1960–1	110 (80)
1961–2	108 (78)
1962–3	107 (72)
1963–4	104 (68)
1964–5	114 (70)
1965–6	107 (72)

* The figures in brackets are percentage shares of the selected items in India's total exports to socialist countries of Eastern Europe.

comparison between the prices realized from the two sets of countries should be made separately for each year.[3] The indices presented in Table 5 show how the overall unit value of the 'basket of exports' to socialist countries compares with the unit value of the same 'basket', equated to 100, if it had been exported to other countries.[4]

According to knowledgeable business circles, prices paid by some of the socialist countries for India's internationally traded commodities have been 5 to 10 per cent higher than those prevailing in the rest of the world. This qualitative evidence appears to be consistent with the results obtained by a comparison of unit values of India's exports to the two sets of countries, at any rate for the 1960s.

On the import side, the statistical difficulties mentioned above are even greater. India's imports are much more diversified than her exports. Plant and machinery have a large weight[5] in the 'basket' of India's imports from socialist countries and items of machinery imported from different sources are subject to so many differences of design, specifications and performance that a comparison is far from easy. Therefore a different treatment has been accorded to the

[3] Since the data are not readily available on a uniform basis, the statistics for some years are in terms of calendar years while for others in terms of fiscal years.

[4] It needs to be mentioned that to the extent that a larger export of these items to the rest of the world would have resulted in a lowering of the unit values India realized for them, the indices presented here understate the extent of price advantage India has derived from her exports to socialist countries.

[5] These accounted, on the average, for about 57 per cent of India's total imports from socialist countries in the 1960s.

plant and equipment component of the 'import basket' from that given to the rest, consisting of industrial raw materials and intermediate goods.

As regards imports of industrial raw materials and intermediates, use has been made of import unit values but focused, by and large, on such items as could be considered broadly homogeneous;[6] and

[6] The items covered by the indices of unit values of India's imports from socialist and other countries are the following:

A. *Copper:* (1) Copper unwrought ingots billets, etc.
(2) Copper wire bars (Electrolyte)
B. *Zinc:* (1) Zinc or zinc spelter unwrought ingot cakes, etc.
C. *Aluminium:* (1) Aluminium ingots
(2) Aluminium bars and rods
(3) Aluminium hand drawn aluminium conductor
D. *Paper:* (1) Glassine paper
(2) White newsprint W.D. pulp 70 per cent and over
(3) Glazed newsprint
E. Petroleum and petroleum products: (1) Kerosene superior
(2) H.S. Diesel
(3) Furnace oil
(4) Base oil
(5) Kerosene inferior
(6) Montax wax
F. Organic chemicals: (1) Butyl alcohol, (2) Carbolic acid (commercial), (3) Beta napthol, (4) Camphor synthetic, (5) Formic acid, (6) Dimethyl aniline, (7) Sodium naphthionate, (8) Salicylic acid, (9) Urea containing 45 per cent nitrogen, (10) Oxalic acid, (11) D.D.T., (12) Pentaery thritol, (13) Rongalite.
G. *Inorganic chemicals:* (1) Light sodium carbonate or soda ash, (2) Ammonium bicarbonate, (3) Ammonium nitrate, (4) Berium chloride, (5) Sodium hydrosulphite, (6) Sodium nitrite, (7) Potassium carbonate, (8) Potassium ferrocyanide, (9) Solid sodium hydroxide or caustic soda, (10) Sodium cyanide, (11) Titanium dixoide, (12) Barium carbonate excluding natural, (13) Potassium cyanide, (14) Sodium ferrocyanide, (14) Barium nitrate.
H. *Iron and steel:* (1) Ferro phosphorus, (2) Blooms billets and slab of iron or steel, (3) Bars of steel excluding alloy and cast n.e.s., (4) Universal black sheets plains uncoated, (5) Universal plates over ⅛ in. not galvanized tinned and uncoated, (6) Universal sheets up to ⅛ in. not galvanized tinned and uncoated, (7) Universal plates and sheets uncoated not galvanized or tinned n.e.s., (8) Steel tubes and fittings welded or drawn galvanized over 6 in. diameter, (9) Spring steel unfabricated, (10) Universal plate shipbuilding not galvanized or tinned or coated, (11) Tubes of steel galvanized up to 6 in. diameter, (12) Galvanized plain plates, sheets coated, (13) Stainless steel sheets coated, (14) Dynamo and motor universal steel sheets, (15) Pig iron including cast, (16) Wire rod of high carbon alloy steel, (17) Universal heavy plate sheets above 4·75 mm. thick of Lloyds quality, (18) Universal heavy plate sheets above 4·75 mm. thick of boiler quality, (19) Plates sheets below 3 mm. thick uncoated of deep drawing quality, (20) Galvanized sheets plain corrugated below 3 mm. thick, (21) Galvanized sheets corrugated, coated and below 3 mm. thick, (22) Galvanized iron steel wire except wire rod, (23) Seamless tubes and pipes iron or steel except cast iron welded.

even in the case of these, where differences in respect of quality and specifications were suspected to be significant, use has been made of alternative sets of price data. The index for this category of imports has been prepared on the same basis as has been adopted for exports: the ratios of the unit values or prices of each item pertaining to the two sets of countries are combined for each year into an overall index, the weights used for combining them being the percentage shares of specific items in the total value of the import of these items from the socialist countries. But while the basis adopted for the preparation of this index is the same as that for exports, a wider coverage has been sacrificed to ensure a rough comparability between the prices of imports obtained from different sources. Since the weighting pattern adopted has changed over time, as in the case of exports, the comparison between the prices paid to the two sets of countries should be made separately for each year.

The indices presented in Table 6[7] are to be interpreted in the same way as those for exports: they show how the overall unit values of the 'basket of imports' of industrial raw materials and intermediate products from socialist countries compares with the unit value of the same 'basket', equated to 100, if it had been imported from other countries.

For machinery, quotations supplied by manufacturers in various countries have been used and have been confined to items for which the specifications from different sources were identical. In view of the

Table 6

RATIOS OF UNIT VALUES OF IMPORTS OF SELECTED INDUSTRIAL RAW MATERIALS AND INTERMEDIATE PRODUCTS FROM SOCIALIST COUNTRIES AND REST OF THE WORLD

1961–2	92·4 (17·8)*
1962–3	92·1 (32·6)
1963–4	88·7 (36·8)
1964–5	93·2 (42·2)
1965–6	101·1 (46·9)

* The figures in brackets are percentage shares of the selected items in India's total imports of industrial raw materials and intermediate products from socialist countries of Eastern Europe.

[7] The indices pertain to fiscal years.

difficulty of finding items of this type, it was possible to make such a comparison for only ten items.

Since the coverage on the import side is very limited and the specifications available for different items of machinery considered here may be considered inadequate, the conclusion that can be drawn from the data examined here can be no more than highly tentative. On the whole, it shows that the prices of India's imports from socialist countries have been lower than of similar imports from other countries. This, however, is not wholly in conformity with the opinion of knowledgeable business circles. According to these, the prices of machinery supplied by the socialist countries are generally higher, in some cases up to 25 per cent higher than international prices. It may be that having regard to the difficulties of making comparison between the prices of machines from different sources, the evidence examined has been too inadequate to reveal the true picture. Alternatively, it could be that the statement referred to above applies to credit-financed imports of machinery from socialist countries. If the latter is the case, which is quite likely, one cannot ignore the fact that prices of credit-financed imports from other countries too may be higher than of those purchased with free currency earnings.[8] Pending a very much more thorough investigation than it has been possible to carry out, all that can be done is to make a tentative conclusion that the evidence examined suggests that the Indian terms of trade with socialist countries have, on balance, probably not been less favourable to India than its terms of trade with other countries, and may possibly have been more favourable.

4. SUMMARY

The available evidence indicates that the bulk of India's rapidly expanding exports to socialist countries have constituted a net addition to India's export earnings. With the exception of a few commodities, these exports have not been at the cost of India's exports to the rest of the world. Although there are instances of re-export of Indian goods by the socialist countries, this does not seem to have taken place on a large scale.

An analysis of comparative prices of India's exports to, and imports from, the socialist countries of Eastern Europe on the one

[8] '. . . estimates vary, but suggest that India might normally be paying anything between 6 and 15 per cent, sometimes as much as 20–30 per cent, above ruling prices for aid-supported imports'. (Michael Kidron, *Foreign Investment in India*, p. 122.)

hand and from the rest of the world on the other leads to a tentative conclusion that India's terms of trade with the socialist countries have, on balance, probably been not less favourable to India than her terms of trade with other countries, and may have been more favourable.

India's trade with the socialist countries of Eastern Europe takes place within the framework of bilateral trade and payments arrangements and since 1959 bilateral settlement in inconvertible rupees has been the rule. It appears that this financial mechanism has promoted a balanced growth of trade between India and the socialist countries.*

India's imports from the socialist countries of Eastern Europe have been financed partly by loans extended by the latter countries. These loans have typically carried an interest rate of 2·5 per cent per annum and have a repayment period of twelve years. Debt service charges are repaid through exports of Indian goods, largely of traditional types, to socialist countries. This mechanism for repayment of debt has helped to alleviate India's debt service problem. However, relatively little has yet been done to promote imports by socialist countries of products manufactured by enterprises built with their assistance.

There are substantial possibilities for further expansion of trade between India and the socialist countries of Eastern Europe. However, a fuller utilization of the available potential will require parallel action both on the part of India and of the socialist countries. India would need to expand exportable supplies of the items in strong demand from the socialist countries. Socialist countries would have to be prepared to diversify greatly their purchases in India particularly by including manufactures and semi-manufactures on a growing scale.

* [The discussion of the problems summarized in the following sections is omitted from this extract – Ed.]

9
FOREIGN COLLABORATION IN INDIAN INDUSTRY*

FOREIGN INVESTMENT THROUGH SUBSIDIARIES

Foreign companies operate abroad generally through two main forms of organization, viz. the branch and the subsidiary. The *branch* acts for the parent company which is incorporated abroad; it has no local capital (except working capital borrowed from banks) and the management functions are exercised by the direct appointees from headquarters. At end-March 1965 branches of foreign companies accounted for about Rs. 269 crores out of a total of Rs. 613 crores of direct foreign investment; plantations, petroleum and services accounted for 90 per cent of aggregate branch investment. The balance of Rs. 344 crores of direct foreign investment was accounted for by subsidiaries and other foreign controlled companies.[1] This Survey *excludes* branches since its purpose is to study companies incorporated in India with specific reference to foreign *technical* collaboration. Branches do not, in the nature of things, have formal technical collaboration arrangements with their parent organizations, and branch investment predominates in sectors where the possibilities of technical collaboration are limited.

In the *subsidiary* the unit is incorporated in India but the majority control (more than 50 per cent) is by a single foreign company. In practice, the extent of foreign control in subsidiaries ranges anywhere between the 51 per cent minimum and the 100 per cent wholly foreign owned. The subsidiaries account for a substantial part of the growth of foreign investment in India and in recent years their

* Excerpts from the report published by the Reverse Bank of India in 1969. (Part of a section dealing with general features of subdiaries has been excluded – Ed.)

[1] India's International Investment Position 1963–4 and 1964–5. *Reverse Bank of India Bulletin*, January 1967.

investments have, by and large, been in technologically intensive sectors of industry. Hence, the subsidiary is generally in the *avant garde* for the transmission of technology to developing countries. It typifies foreign investment which has, by adjusting itself to the changing needs of local enterprise and resources, become a *joint venture* while maintaining its foreign identity and affiliation to its parent. A subsidiary, even though wholly foreign owned, is generally well integrated into the domestic economy and uses local personnel to a larger extent than a branch......

COVERAGE OF COMPANIES

The Survey covered 224 subsidiaries of which 121 were public limited and 103 private limited companies. Of these, 92 subsidiaries had formal technical collaboration agreements. While about three-fifths of the public limited subsidiaries had formal technical collaboration arrangements, only about one-fifth of the private limited subsidiaries had such formal arrangements (Table 1).

Table 1

NUMBER OF COMPANIES AND AGREEMENTS COVERED

Companies/Agreements	*Public Ltd.*	*Private Ltd.*	*Total*
Number of Companies covered	121	103	224
Of which			
Number of Companies with technical collaboration	71	21	92
Number of Agreements	115	29	144

Nearly three-fifths (or 130) of the 224 subsidiaries were incorporated by end-1947 and these were mainly in services, chemicals, metals and light consumer industries; of these 130 companies, only 32 companies had formal technical collaboration arrangements (Tables 2 and 3). Only 35 subsidiaries were incorporated during 1948–55, of which 13 companies had formal technical collaboration arrangements. Over one-half of the 59 companies incorporated during 1956–64 were in machinery and machine tools and chemicals; of these 59 companies, 47 companies had technical collaboration. The subsidiaries with technical collaboration arrangements reflected the shift over time to the technologically intensive industries. Over one-half of the 92 companies with technical collaboration were incorporated during 1956–64. Nearly 70 per cent of the 92 companies with technical collaboration were in chemicals, machinery and machine tools, electrical goods and transport equipment. While less than one-fourth of the companies incorporated prior to end-1947 entered into technical collaboration arrangements, the corresponding proportions for companies incorporated during 1948–55 and 1956–64 were one-third and about four-fifths respectively; this emphasizes the increasing importance of technical collaboration arrangements.

Table 2

INDUSTRYWISE DISTRIBUTION OF COMPANIES BY DATE OF INCORPORATION

Industry	*Number of companies* Up to end-1947	*1948–55*	*1956–64*	*Total*
I. Plantations Mining and Petroleum	7	4	—	11
II. Manufacturing	69	22	54	145
Foods, Beverages and Tobacco	6	1	2	9
Textile Products	4	—	—	4
Transport Equipment	3	3	4	10
Machinery and Machine Tools	4	4	16	24
Metals and Metal Products	9	1	7	17
Electrical Goods and Machinery	6	2	5	13
Chemicals and Allied Products	29	9	16	54
(*i*) Basic Industrial	3	2	4	9
(*ii*) Medicines and Pharmaceuticals	10	4	6	20
(*iii*) Others	16	3	6	25
Miscellaneous	8	2	4	14
III. Services	54	9	5	68
Total (I+II+III)	130	35	59	224

Well over four-fifths of public limited subsidiaries were in manufacturing while the corresponding proportion for private limited subsidiaries was 44 per cent. About one-half of the private limited subsidiaries were in the services sector. Between 1960–1 and 1963–4 the number of subsidiaries increased from 201 to 224, the increase being mainly in transport equipment, machinery and machine tools and chemicals.

A sizewise distribution of subsidiaries revealed some interesting features. There were 18 subsidiaries with total capital employed of over Rs. 10 crores each and these large companies accounted for well over half of the total capital employed by subsidiaries (Table 4). Companies with total capital employed of Rs. 1 crore or less each accounted for over one-half of the total number of subsidiaries; these small subsidiaries were evenly distributed among public limited

Table 3

INDUSTRYWISE DISTRIBUTION OF COMPANIES WITH TECHNICAL COLLABORATION BY DATE OF INCORPORATION

Industry	*Number of companies* Up to end-1947	1948–55	1956–64	Total	*Total number of agreements*
I. Plantations, Mining and Petroleum	1	1	—	2	6
II. Manufacturing	28	12	44	84	132
Foods, Beverages and Tobacco	1	—	2	3	3
Transport Equipment	1	3	4	8	8
Machinery and Machine Tools	3	1	14	18	27
Metals and Metal Products	3	1	5	9	26
Electrical Goods and Machinery	6	1	5	12	19
Chemicals and Allied Products	9	5	11	25	39
(*i*) Basic Industrial	2	1	3	6	13
(*ii*) Medicines and Pharmaceuticals	5	2	6	13	19
(*iii*) Others	2	2	2	6	7
Miscellaneous	5	1	3	9	10
III. Services	3	—	3	6	6
Total (*I+II+III*)	32	13	47	92	144

and private limited companies. The total capital employed of the public limited subsidiaries was thrice that of the private limited subsidiaries. In 1963–4 the ratio of net worth to total capital employed was a little less than 50 per cent for public limited subsidiaries and 37 per cent for private limited subsidiaries. Within the public limited subsidiaries the smaller companies had a lower ratio than the larger companies.

Table 4

TOTAL CAPITAL EMPLOYED AND TOTAL NET WORTH BY SIZE OF COMPANY (1963–4)

(Rs. crores)

Size of company (Total capital employed)	*Public Ltd.* No. of companies (*1*)	Total capital employed (*2*)	Total net worth (*3*)	(*3*) as percentage of (*2*) (*4*)	*Private Ltd.* No. of companies (*1*)	Total capital employed (*2*)	Total net worth (*3*)	(*3*) as percentage of (*2*) (*4*)	*Total* No. of companies (*1*)	Total capital employed (*2*)	Total net worth (*3*)	(*3*) as percentage of (*2*) (*4*)
1. Up to Rs. 25 lakhs	26	3·3	1·0	30·3	38	3·3	1·3	39·4	64	6·6	2·3	34·8
2. Over Rs. 25 lakhs and up to Rs. 1 crore	36	20·2	8·6	42·6	25	15·5	5·0	32·3	61	35·7	13·6	38·1
3. Over Rs. 1 crore and up to Rs. 5 crores	32	84·7	40·4	47·7	33	63·3	19·7	31·1	65	148·0	60·1	40·6
4. Over Rs. 5 crores and up to Rs. 10 crores	14	94·8	47·9	50·5	2	14·4	6·4	44·4	16	109·2	54·3	49·7
5. Over Rs. 10 crores	13	254·1	128·2	50·5	5	59·1	25·1	42·5	18	313·2	153·3	48·9
Total	121	457·1	226·1	49·5	103	155·6	57·5	36·9	224	612·7	283·6	46·3

FINANCIAL PARTICIPATION

This section examines the financial participation in subsidiaries through equity, direct loan arrangements and their profitability.

(*i*) *The Foreign Share of Paid-up Capital*

Over one-half of the 224 subsidiaries were wholly foreign owned; of the wholly foreign owned subsidiaries, nearly three-fourths were incorporated by end-1947. In more recent years there has been a perceptible tendency towards setting up subsidiaries with some Indian participation and a little over two-thirds of the subsidiaries incorporated during 1956–64 had less than 74 per cent foreign participation (Table 5), which is in consonance with government policy of

Table 5

DISTRIBUTION OF FOREIGN EQUITY CAPITAL BY DATE OF COMPANY INCORPORATION

Percentage of Foreign equity to total equity capital	*Number of companies*				
	Up to end-1947	*1948–55*	*1956–60*	*1961–4*	*Total*
50·1–73·9	33	10	27	13	83
74 –79·9	4	—	2	1	7
80 –89·9	7	1	6	—	14
90 –99·9	3	—	1	2	6
100	83	24	6	1	114
Total Number of Companies	130	35	42	17	224

enabling the Indian partner to have a say in changes in the articles of incorporation.

The foreign share of paid-up capital of subsidiaries consists, almost exclusively, of equity capital. The share of foreign equity in total equity capital in 1963–4 for public limited companies was a little over 75 per cent while that for private limited companies was around 99 per cent (Table 6). The extent of foreign equity capital in all subsidiaries taken together increased from Rs. 98·5 crores in 1960–1 to Rs. 127·7 crores in 1963–4, though as a proportion of the total, the share of such capital declined from 82·1 per cent to 78·5 per cent. Of the total foreign equity capital of Rs. 127·7 crores in subsidiaries in 1963–4, public limited companies accounted for about

83 per cent. Manufacturing accounted for three-fourths of total foreign equity capital in subsidiaries. The degree of foreign control varied from 100 per cent in plantations and mining, textiles and stationery and office equipment to less than 70 per cent in transport equipment, machinery and machine tools, metals and metal products and rubber goods (Table 7). The operation of wholly-owned subsidiaries was mainly concentrated in plantation, extractive and service sectors; in the manufacturing sector they were prominent in textiles and medicines and pharmaceuticals.

Table 6

ORDINARY SHARES: FOREIGN AND TOTAL

(Rs. crores)

Equity capital	*1960–1*	*1961–2*	*1962–3*	*1963–4*
Public Ltd.				
Total	100·7	116·4	128·6	140·9
Foreign	79·9	90·2	98·4	106·3
Percentage of Foreign to Total	79·4	77·5	76·5	75·4
Private Ltd.				
Total	19·3	21·2	21·3	21·7
Foreign	18·6	20·8	21·0	21·4
Percentage of Foreign to Total	96·1	98·0	98·5	99·0
All Companies				
Total	120·0	137·6	149·9	162·6
Foreign	98·5	111·0	119·4	127·7
Percentage of Foreign to Total	82·1	80·6	79·6	78·5

The U.K. accounted for 70–75 per cent of total foreign equity capital in subsidiaries while the U.S. accounted for a little less than 13 per cent. Between 1960–1 and 1963–4 the extent of foreign control (i.e. the ratio of foreign equity capital to total equity capital) decreased from 84 per cent to 81 per cent in the case of the U.K., and from 88 per cent to 84 per cent in the case of the U.S.; the extent of foreign control was lowest for Swedish controlled companies which declined marginally over the period from 55 per cent to 54 per cent (Table 8). As the largest foreign investor, the U.K. was predominant in practically all lines of manufacturing. The U.K.'s share of foreign paid-up capital in different sectors of industry in 1963–4 ranged from 100 per cent in textile products, 95 per cent in foods, beverages and tobacco and 79 per cent in transport equipment to 68 per cent in chemicals, 64 per cent in metals and 58 per cent in electrical goods to 44 per cent in machinery and machine tools and

Table 7

INDUSTRYWISE DISTRIBUTION OF ORDINARY SHARES HELD ABROAD

(Rs. crores)

Industry	1960–1 Total (1)	1960–1 Foreign (2)	1960–1 (2) as percentage of (1) (3)	1961–2 Total (1)	1961–2 Foreign (2)	1961–2 (2) as percentage of (1) (3)	1962–3 Total (1)	1962–3 Foreign (2)	1962–3 (2) as percentage of (1) (3)	1963–4 Total (1)	1963–4 Foreign (2)	1963–4 (2) as percentage of (1) (3)
I. *Plantations and Mining*	2·3	2·3	100·0	2·3	2·3	100·0	2·3	2·3	100·0	2·3	2·3	100·0
II. *Petroleum*	21·7	21·3	98·2	22·4	22·0	98·2	22·4	22·0	98·2	22·4	22·0	98·2
III. *Manufacturing*	87·3	68·5	78·5	103·9	79·7	76·7	116·2	88·1	75·8	128·9	96·3	74·7
Foods, Beverages and Tobacco	17·4	15·8	90·7	18·0	16·2	90·0	18·2	16·4	90·1	18·5	16·6	89·7
Textile Products	2·3	2·3	100·0	2·3	2·3	100·0	2·3	2·3	100·0	2·3	2·3	100·0
Transport Equipment	4·6	2·9	63·0	9·0	5·4	60·0	10·9	6·7	61·5	12·6	7·7	61·1
Machinery and Machine Tools	2·1	1·7	81·0	2·5	1·8	72·0	7·4	4·9	66·2	7·8	5·3	67·9
Metals and Metal Products	12·1	8·0	66·1	13·0	8·7	66·9	13·7	9·1	66·4	20·0	13·1	65·5
Electrical Goods and Machinery	9·0	6·5	72·2	9·8	7·2	73·5	10·4	7·4	71·2	10·7	7·7	72·0
Chemicals and Allied Products	28·2	22·3	79·1	32·1	25·3	78·8	36·1	28·5	78·9	39·8	30·7	77·1
(*i*) Basic Industrial	8·9	6·0	67·4	10·0	6·8	68·0	10·1	6·9	68·3	12·7	8·4	66·1
(*ii*) Medicines and Pharmaceuticals	7·0	6·2	88·5	9·2	8·3	90·2	10·4	9·0	86·5	11·1	9·4	84·7
(*iii*) Others	12·3	10·1	82·1	12·9	10·2	79·1	15·6	12·6	80·8	16·0	12·9	80·6
Stationery and Office Equipment	2·8	2·8	100·0	2·8	2·8	100·0	2·8	2·8	100·0	2·8	2·8	100·0
Rubber Goods	5·3	3·3	62·3	10·4	6·6	63·5	10·4	6·6	63·5	10·4	6·6	63·5
Miscellaneous	3·5	2·9	82·9	4·0	3·4	85·0	4·0	3·4	85·0	4·0	3·5	87·5
IV. Services	8·7	6·4	73·6	9·0	7·0	77·8	9·0	7·0	77·7	9·0	7·1	78·9
Total (I+II+III+IV)	120·0	98·5	82·1	137·6	111·0	80·6	149·9	119·4	79·6	162·6	127·7	78·5

Table 8

COUNTRYWISE DISTRIBUTION OF ORDINARY SHARES HELD ABROAD

(Rs. crores)

Equity Capital	*U.K.*	*U.S.A.*	*Switzer-land*	*Sweden*	*Canada*	*France*	*West Germany*	*Others*	*Total*
1960–1									
Total	88·8	14·0	2·8	3·1	4·1	—	1·9	5·3	120·0
Foreign	74·9	12·4	2·5	1·7	2·6	—	1·1	3·3	98·5
Percentage of Foreign to Total	84·3	88·5	89·3	54·8	63·4	—	57·9	62·3	82·1
1961–2									
Total	99·3	16·5	6·3	3·7	4·1	—	2·4	5·3	137·6
Foreign	81·8	14·5	4·0	2·0	2·6	—	1·4	4·7	111·0
Percentage of Foreign to Total	82·4	87·8	63·5	54·1	63·4	—	58·3	88·7	80·6
1962–3									
Total	101·3	18·8	6·3	7·9	4·0	3·6	3·0	5·0	149·9
Foreign	84·0	15·8	4·7	4·2	2·6	2·5	1·7	3·9	119·4
Percentage of Foreign to Total	82·9	84·0	74·6	53·2	65·1	69·4	56·7	78·0	79·6
1963–4									
Total	110·7	19·4	6·4	8·0	6·1	3·9	2·9	5·2	162·6
Foreign	90·0	16·3	4·8	4·3	4·0	2·6	1·7	4·0	127·7
Percentage of Foreign to Total	81·3	84·0	75·0	53·8	65·6	66·7	58·6	76·9	78·5

36 per cent in rubber goods. The share of the U.S. investments ranged from 40 per cent in rubber goods, 34 per cent in stationery and office equipment, 26 per cent in electrical goods to 10 per cent in chemicals and 2 per cent in metals. West Germany was an important investor in transport equipment, Sweden in machinery and machine tools. Canada in metals and metal products and Switzerland in rubber goods.

(*ii*) *Profitability of Subsidiaries*

This section examines profitability of the subsidiaries; first the gross profits are assessed against the total capital employed and then the actual dividend remittances are matched with the foreign net worth of these companies. The net dividend remittance and its relation to foreign net worth is an indicator of the immediate investment income liability of the host country in terms of foreign exchange as well as the immediate cash receipt of the investing country. By definition, the ratio of dividend remittance to foreign net worth is low since the dividend remittance is net of reinvestment and the tax deduction on dividends.

(*a*) *Gross Profits:* During 1960–1 to 1963–4, the gross profits to total capital employed of subsidiaries ranged between 14 per cent and 15 per cent for public limited companies and between 15 per cent and 19 per cent for private limited companies (Table 9). The ratio of gross

Table 9

GROSS PROFITS AS PERCENTAGE OF TOTAL CAPITAL EMPLOYED

(Percentages)

Year	*Public Ltd.*	*Private Ltd.*	*Total*
1960–1	15·3	15·3	15·3
1961–2	14·3	17·4	15·1
1962–3	14·3	18·2	15·3
1963–4	15·2	19·5	16·3

profits to total capital employed was the highest in manufacturing and the lowest in services; further, in manufacturing in 1963–4, the ratio was over 20 per cent in the case of textiles, medicines and pharmaceuticals and stationery and office equipment. The ratio of gross profits to total capital employed in the case of private limited companies in 1963–4 was over 30 per cent in the case of foods, beverages and tobacco, machinery and machine tools and medicines and pharmaceuticals.

The 1963–4 ratio of gross profits to total capital employed of subsidiaries of 16·3 per cent is higher than the profit rate of 1,654 public and private limited companies covered by the Reserve Bank company finance studies which was only 10·1 per cent. The ratio for public limited subsidiaries of 15·2 per cent in 1963–4 was higher than the ratio of 10·6 per cent for the 1,333 public limited companies. The ratio for private limited subsidiaries for 1963–4 was 19·5 per cent as compared with 12·5 per cent ratio for the 501 private limited companies covered by the company finance studies. (Table 11.)

Table 10

GROSS PROFITS AS PERCENTAGE OF TOTAL CAPITAL EMPLOYED —INDUSTRYWISE

(Percentages)

Industry	*1960–1*	*1961–2*	*1962–3*	*1963–4*
I. Plantations and Mining	12·7	13·6	15·3	13·7
II. Petroleum	13·5	14·0	14·3	14·1
III. Manufacturing	17·0	16·2	16·4	17·9
Foods, Beverages and Tobacco	16·2	15·3	17·6	17·1
Textile Products	12·0	13·9	16·7	22·2
Transport Equipment	18·4	16·7	15·1	17·9
Machinery and Machine Tools	17·3	21·6	12·9	18·1
Metals and Metal Products	12·8	10·5	11·5	15·9
Electrical Goods and Machinery	14·2	13·3	16·3	17·9
Chemicals and Allied Products	20·4	18·2	19·2	19·7
(*i*) Basic Industrial	15·8	12·5	13·4	13·0
(*ii*) Medicines and Pharmaceuticals	24·0	22·9	22·8	25·4
(*iii*) Others	20·4	18·2	20·1	19·4
Stationery and Office Equipment	18·3	18·6	15·3	20·6
Rubber Goods	14·4	18·0	14·0	12·8
Miscellaneous	19·0	22·0	24·7	24·5
IV. Services	8·9	9·3	8·1	7·9
Total (*I*+*II*+*III*+*IV*)	15·3	15·1	15·3	16·3

Nearly 10 per cent of the subsidiaries were set up during 1961–4. Moreover, the newer sectors of investment, viz., machinery and machine tools, metals, transport equipment, electrical goods and chemicals also attained rates of return close to the average which points to a general conclusion that the newer subsidiaries yielded profits in a reasonably short period.

Table 11

GROSS PROFITS AS PERCENTAGE OF TOTAL CAPITAL EMPLOYED (COMPANY FINANCES DATA)
(Percentages)

Company group	*1963–4*	*1964–5*
1. 291 Foreign Controlled Rupee Companies	13·8	14·3
2. 1,333 Public Limited Companies	10·6	10·3
3. 501 Private Limited Companies	12·5	12·0
4. 1,654 Public and Private Limited Companies*	10·1	9·5

* Excluding 180 foreign controlled rupee companies.
Source: 'Finances of Branches of Foreign Companies and Foreign Controlled Rupee Companies, 1964–5', *Reserve Bank of India Bulletin*, July 1967.

(*b*) *Dividend Remittances:* Dividend remittances by subsidiaries usually form the major direct foreign exchange cost to the host country and also provide an important criterion of the gain to the investing country. The dividend remittances were, therefore, classified by industry, country and type of company and an attempt was made to derive rates of dividend remittance on foreign net worth for a period of four years, 1960–1 to 1963–4, which would serve as a benchmark for subsequent evaluation of the profitability of these companies. Since remittance data were of considerable relevance to this study, *estimates* were prepared for 1964–5 to 1966–7 on the basis of company returns.

Table 12

DIVIDEND REMITTANCES ABROAD
(Rs. lakhs)

Year	*Public Ltd.*	*Private Ltd.*	*Total*
1960–1	720	312	1032
1961–2	916	362	1278
1962–3	1054	560	1614
1963–4	973	342	1315
1964–5*	1193	431	1624
1965–6*	1118	404	1522
1966–7*	1190	434	1624

* Estimates

Table 13

INDUSTRYWISE DIVIDEND REMITTANCES ABROAD

(Rs. lakhs)

	Actuals				*Estimates*		
	1960–1	*1961–2*	*1962–3*	*1963–4*	*1964–5*	*1965–6*	*1966–7*
I. Plantations and Mining	17	25	27	36	45	38	38
II. Petroleum	2,10	2,98	2,93	3,52	4,17	3,08	3,08
III. Manufacturing	7,64	8,98	12,12	8,69	11,00	11,11	12,11
Foods, Beverages and Tobacco	1,04	1,21	1,35	1,08	1,19	1,36	1,45
Textile Products	2	2	28	33	3	25	25
Transport Equipment	22	42	47	48	58	67	74
Machinery and Machine Tools	12	14	26	28	55	40	43
Metals and Metal Products	64	80	99	97	1,31	1,44	1,41
Electrical Goods and Machinery	69	88	79	47	74	77	88
Chemicals and Allied Products	3,05	3,94	5,62	3,64	4,56	4,54	4,88
(*i*) Basic Industrial	19	47	99	67	83	89	97
(*ii*) Medicines and Pharmaceuticals	1,02	1,25	1,92	1,61	1,94	1,75	1,94
(*iii*) Others	1,84	2,22	2,71	1,36	1,79	1,90	1,97
Rubber Goods	1,15	72	1,19	1,10	1,06	87	1,25
Miscellaneous	71	85	1,17	34	98	81	82
IV. Services	41	57	82	58	62	65	67
Total (*I+II+III+IV*)	10,32	12,78	16,14	13,15	16,24	15,22	16,24

Dividend remittances abroad by subsidiaries rose from Rs. 1,032 lakhs in 1960–1 to Rs. 1,614 lakhs in 1962–3 but declined to Rs. 1,315 lakhs in 1963–4. Estimates indicated that dividend remittances during 1966–7 were marginally higher than in 1962–3 (Table 12). Dividend remittances by subsidiaries in the petroleum industry ranged between a low of Rs. 210 lakhs and a high of Rs. 417 lakhs, while those in chemicals ranged between Rs. 305 lakhs and Rs. 562 lakhs. The sharp rise in remittances in 1962–3 and the decline in 1963–4 was, to a large extent, on account of a few chemical companies (Table 13). Country-wise, the dividend remittances were predominantly accounted for by the U.K. subsidiaries ranging between Rs. 757 lakhs and Rs. 1,185 lakhs, and the U.S. subsidiaries ranging between Rs. 191 lakhs and Rs. 273 lakhs (Table 14).

Table 14

COUNTRYWISE DIVIDEND REMITTANCES ABROAD

(Rs. lakhs)

Country	*1960–1*	*1961–2*	*1962–3*	*1963–4*	*1964–5*	*1965–6*	*1966–7*
U.K.	7,57	9,21	11,55	9,37	11,24	11,10	11,85
U.S.A.	2,08	2,41	2,42	2,56	2,73	1,91	2,07
Others	67	1,16	2,17	1,22	2,27	2,21	2,32
Total	10,32	12,78	16,14	13,15	16,24	15,22	16,24

The ratios of dividend remittances to foreign net worth during 1960–1 to 1963–4 were uniformly higher for private limited companies than for public limited companies (Table 15). This is a reflection not so much of the efficiency of the private limited companies as their characteristic of operating with a lower base of owned funds than public limited subsidiaries. Country-wise, the ratio of dividend remittances to foreign net worth ranged between 5·7 per cent and 7·8 per cent for the U.K. subsidiaries, between 5·5 per cent and 6·5

Table 15

DIVIDEND REMITTANCE AS PERCENTAGE OF FOREIGN NET WORTH

(Percentages)

Type of company	*1960–1*	*1961–2*	*1962–3*	*1963–4*
Public Ltd.	4·9	5·7	6·1	5·3
Private Ltd.	7·9	7·8	11·4	6·1
Total	5·6	6·2	7·3	5·4

per cent for the U.S. subsidiaries and between 3·4 per cent and 7·2 per cent for subsidiaries of 'other' countries (Table 16). The year to year remittances to the larger investing countries, viz. the U.K. and the U.S., varied less than those to the other smaller investing countries. The sharp changes in remittances to 'other' countries were due to the bunching of dividend remittances in 1962–3 and 1964–5 by a few chemical companies, while the subsequent high level in 1965–6 and 1966–7 was due to the coming to fruition of some projects. Industry-wise the rate of dividend remittance was *below the average* for plantations and mining, foods, beverages and tobacco,

Table 16

DIVIDEND REMITTANCE AS PERCENTAGE OF FOREIGN NET WORTH—COUNTRYWISE

(Percentages)

Country	*1960–1*	*1961–2*	*1962–3*	*1963–4*
U.K.	5·7	6·6	7·8	6·0
U.S.A.	6·5	5·9	5·6	5·5
Others	3·5	4·4	7·2	3·4
Total	5·6	6·2	7·3	5·4

transport equipment, machinery and machine tools, metals and metal products and services and *above the average* for electrical goods and machinery, chemicals and rubber (Table 17). The industries where the rates of dividend remittance were below average were either nascent industries or industries where reinvestment of earnings was high or sectors like services, where trading companies were less active than hitherto. The rate of dividend remittance on foreign net worth for all subsidiaries ranged between 5·4 per cent to 7·3 per cent. The dividends ratios of subsidiaries were somewhat higher than the rates of other Indian companies (Table 18).

There is no direct relationship between the ratio of gross profits to total capital employed and the ratio of dividend remittance to foreign net worth, since depending on the capital structure and reinvestment policies a given ratio of gross profits to total capital employed can yield a higher or lower ratio of dividend remittance to foreign net worth.

The 1963–4 remittances have been analysed further by size of company and dividend remittance range (Table 19). Of the 224 companies, 77 companies did not remit any dividends while 117 companies remitted up to 10 per cent and 30 companies over 10 per

Table 17

DIVIDEND REMITTANCE AS PERCENTAGE OF FOREIGN NET WORTH—INDUSTRYWISE

(Percentages)

Industry	*1960–1*	*1961–2*	*1962–3*	*1963–4*
I. Plantations and Mining	2·5	3·3	3·8	4·5
II. Petroleum	4·7	6·4	6·0	7·0
III. Manufacturing	6·3	6·4	7·9	5·1
Foods, Beverages and Tobacco	3·9	4·4	4·8	3·7
Textile Products	0·9	0·8	9·9	9·8
Transport Equipment	3·9	4·8	4·5	3·9
Machinery and Machine Tools	3·9	4·1	3·8	3·8
Metals and Metal Products	4·3	4·8	5·5	4·5
Electrical Goods and Machinery	8·1	9·0	7·7	4·2
Chemicals and Allied Products	7·8	9·2	11·7	6·7
(*i*) Basic Industrial	2·0	4·8	9·1	5·1
(*ii*) Medicines and Pharmaceuticals	9·5	9·5	11·4	8·5
(*iii*) Others	9·7	11·2	13·4	6·1
Rubber Goods	9·9	4·1	7·3	6·7
Miscellaneous	7·2	7·7	10·1	2·4
IV. Services	3·6	4·5	6·2	4·3
Total (I+II+III+IV)	5·6	6·2	7·3	5·4

Table 18

DIVIDEND AS PERCENTAGE OF NET WORTH (COMPANY FINANCES DATA)

(Percentages)

Company group	*1963–4*	*1964 5*
1. 291 Foreign Controlled Rupee Companies	6·7	6·8
2. 1,333 Public Limited Companies	5·8	5·6
3. 501 Private Limited Companies	5·4	5·3
4. 1,654 Public and Private Limited Companies*	5·4	5·2

* Excluding 180 foreign controlled rupee companies.

Source: 'Finances of Branches of Foreign Companies and Foreign Controlled Rupee Companies, 1964–5', *Reserve Bank of India Bulletin*, July 1967.

cent; only 13 companies remitted over 15 per cent. The *nil* remittances by 77 companies were due to (*i*) nascent investment in the case of 23 companies which were incorporated after 1961 and (*ii*) the existence of a number of dormant companies under services; in addition the conversion of private limited companies into public limited units is generally associated with a substantial expansion or diversification of investment and activities (e.g. the shift of trading companies into manufacturing which is in a sense akin to nascent investment). The companies with *nil* remittances as well as the companies with remittances over 10 per cent were small units. The remittances of over 15 per cent were mainly by units with a total capital employed of Rs. 1 crore or less each.

Table 19

DIVIDEND REMITTANCE AS PERCENTAGE OF FOREIGN NET WORTH BY SIZE OF COMPANY (1963–4)

Size of Company (Total capital Employed)	*Number of Companies*					
	Nil	*Up to 5 per cent*	*5·1 to 10 per cent*	*10·1 to 15 per cent*	*Over 15 per cent*	*Total*
Up to Rs. 25 lakhs	37	8	7	6	6	64
Over Rs. 25 lakhs and up to Rs. 1 crore	16	16	19	6	4	61
Over Rs. 1 crore and up to Rs. 5 crores	19	22	20	3	1	65
Over Rs. 5 crores and up to Rs. 10 crores	3	7	4	—	2	16
Over Rs. 10 crores	2	9	5	2	—	18
Total	77	62	55	17	13	224

(*iii*) *Foreign Currency Loans*

To the extent that subsidiaries resort to outside funds, their borrowings, in the main, are derived from local funds, and direct borrowings from parents or affiliates are small. This Survey covered only *direct* loan arrangements since the purpose was to analyse loans obtained by the subsidiaries themselves; thus, arrangements under which the government or other institutions undertook the foreign exchange liabilities were excluded.

The outstanding of net direct loans obtained by the subsidiaries in foreign currency increased from Rs. 717 lakhs in 1960–1 to Rs. 1,148 lakhs in 1963–4. Reflecting the increased outstandings, during the same period repayments increased from Rs. 17 lakhs to Rs. 171 lakhs, while interest payments increased from Rs. 14 lakhs to Rs. 32 lakhs (Table 20). Of the net loans outstanding in March 1964, over three-fourths were accounted for by public limited companies. The

U.K. subsidiaries accounted for 80 per cent of the net outstandings of all subsidiaries. Industrywise, chemicals accounted for over 40 per cent, metals for 16 per cent and transport equipment for 14 per cent (Table 21). Interest remittances increased gradually from Rs. 14 lakhs in 1960–1 to an estimated Rs. 70 lakhs in 1966–7, the public limited companies accounting for the bulk of payments (Table 22). Payments to the U.K. were a little less than three-fourths of the total. The interest remittances in relation to net loan outstandings suggested a low average rate of interest (Table 23). This

Table 20

FOREIGN CURRENCY LOANS*

(Rs. lakhs)

Items	*1960–1*	*1961–2*	*1962–3*	*1963–4*
1. Amount utilized during the year	2,34	1,59	2,98	2,82
2. Net amount outstanding	7,17	7,87	10,37	11,48
3. Principal repaid during the year	17	89	48	1,71
4. Interest remitted during the year	14	23	30	32

* Directly obtained by the companies.

Table 21

INDUSTRYWISE FOREIGN CURRENCY LOANS – NET OUTSTANDINGS

(Rs. lakhs)

Industry	*1960–1*	*1961–2*	*1962–3*	*1963–4*
I. Plantations, Mining and Petroleum	—	45	45	45
II. Manuafacturing	5,53	6,10	8,57	9,47
Foods, Beverages and Tobacco	—	—	—	1
Transport Equipment	70	97	1,26	1,58
Machinery and Machine Tools	21	9	9	15
Metals and Metal Products	87	1,11	2,75	1,77
Electrical Goods and Machinery	58	48	48	70
Chemicals and Allied Products	2,93	3,32	3,92	4,76
(*i*) Basic Industrial	1,07	1,16	1,92	2,34
(*ii*) Medicines and Pharmaceuticals	1,86	2,06	1,87	2,13
(*iii*) Others	—	10	13	29
Miscellaneous	24	13	7	50
III. Services	1,64	1,32	1,35	1,56
Total (I+II+III)	7,17	7,87	10,37	11,48

Table 22

INTEREST REMITTANCES ON FOREIGN LOANS

(Rs. lakhs)

	Actuals				*Estimates*		
Type of company	*1960–1*	*1961–2*	*1962–3*	*1963–4*	*1964–5*	*1965–6*	*1966–7*
Public Ltd.	10	18	22	26	37	53	63
Private Ltd.	4	5	8	6	8	6	7
Total	14	23	30	32	45	59	70

Table 23

INTEREST REMITTANCES ON FOREIGN LOANS—INDUSTRYWISE

(Rs. lakhs)

	Actuals				*Estimates*		
Industry	*1960–1*	*1961–2*	*1962–3*	*1963–4*	*1964–5*	*1965–6*	*1966–7*
I. Plantations, Mining and Petroleum	—	—	—	—	—	—	—
II. Manufacturing	12	21	28	30	43	59	68
Foods, Beverages and Tobacco	—	—	—	—	—	—	—
Transport Equipment	1	3	5	7	10	11	11
Machinery and Machine Tools	—	—	—	—	—	—	—
Metals and Metal Products	1	3	5	10	14	16	23
Electrical Goods and Machinery	3	3	2	2	4	4	6
Chemicals and Allied Products	7	11	14	11	15	19	17
(*i*) Basic Industrial	3	5	5	4	8	9	9
(*ii*) Medicines and Pharmaceuticals	4	6	9	7	7	7	8
(*iii*) Others	—	—	—	—	—	3	—
Miscellaneous	—	1	2	—	—	9	11
III. Services	2	2	2	2	2	—	2
Total (I+II+III)	14	23	30	32	45	59	70

was explained by two factors. First, some of the loans obtained from the parent organizations were interest free. Secondly, interest payments over a certain rate were subject to tax; hence interest remittance rates appeared low when juxtaposed with the net loans outstanding.

TRENDS IN PRODUCTION AND FOREIGN TRADE

Over the period 1960–1 to 1966–7 the value of production (at net ex-factory sale price) of subsidiaries increased from Rs. 381 crores to an estimated Rs. 789 crores, i.e. an increase of 107 per cent. Public limited companies accounted for about three-fourths of total production (Table 24). Petroleum, chemicals, metals and metal products, rubber goods and transport equipment accounted for about 70 per cent of total production of subsidiaries; this was in contrast with branches which, apart from petroleum, were almost exclusively concentrated in plantations, mining and services.

Table 24

VALUE OF TOTAL PRODUCTION (AT NET EX-FACTORY SALE PRICE)

(Rs. crores)

Year	*Public Ltd.*	*Private Ltd.*	*Total*
1960–1	274·4	106·9	381·3
1961–2	315·4	118·1	433·5
1962–3	354·4	128·5	482·9
1963–4	403·8	146·5	550·3
1964–5*	471·2	162·2	633·4
1965–6*	531·2	178·3	709·5
1966–7*	594·5	194·3	788·8

* Estimates

Between 1960–1 and 1966–7, the increase in production of subsidiaries was sizeable in a number of industries such as chemicals, metals and metal products, transport equipment, machinery and machine tools, electrical goods and machinery and rubber goods.

Some indication of the importance of subsidiaries in Indian industry can be obtained by comparing the total capital employed by subsidiaries on March 31, 1964, as compared with that of the 1,333 selected joint stock public limited companies of the Reserve Bank of India company finances studies. The industry classification of the company finances studies and the Foreign Collaboration Survey were not strictly comparable; this required a reclassification of the company finances studies data. The public limited subsidiaries were compared with the 1,333 companies. The overall ratio of the total capital employed by public limited subsidiaries to that by the

1,333 companies was only 13 per cent, though the ratio was substantially higher at 83 per cent for rubber goods, 58 per cent for medicines and pharmaceuticals, 49 per cent in the broad group of chemicals and allied products, 48 per cent in petroleum, 28 per cent in electrical goods and 20 per cent in foods, beverages and tobacco (Table 25). The private limited subsidiaries were also important particularly in certain industries like rubber goods, medicines and pharmaceuticals and electrical goods.

The imports of subsidiaries (excluding those financed by foreign equity or loan capital) increased from Rs. 99 crores in 1960–1 to an

Table 25

TOTAL CAPITAL EMPLOYED IN 1963–4—SUBSIDIARIES AND THE 1,333 PUBLIC LIMITED COMPANIES

(Rs. lakhs)

Industry	*Public Ltd. subsidiaries* (*1*)	*Private Ltd. subsidiaries* (2)	*1,333 selected Public Ltd. Cos.** (*3*)	(*1*) *as percentage of* (*3*) (*4*)
Plantations	—	17,04	67,88	—
Mining	42	—	71,95	0·5
Petroleum	86,04	64	1,78,99	48·0
Foods, Beverages and Tobacco	43,35	2,05	2,20,46	19·7
Textile Products	—	5,53	8,34,52	—
Transport Equipment	30,57	5,69	2,10,52	14·5
Machinery and Machine Tools	11,59	8,12	1,42,76	8·1
Metals and Metal Products	63,37	5,49	4,77,91	13·3
Electrical Goods and Machinery	33,38	13,42	1,19,59	27·9
Chemicals and Allied Products	1,13,38	37,97	2,29,77	49·3
Of which				
Medicines and Pharmaceuticals	29,75	21,16	50,89	58·4
Rubber Goods	35,66	12,31	43,21	82·5
Miscellaneous	16,36	10,82	4,87,52	3·4
Services	23,00	36,39	4,05,57	5·7
Total	4,57,12	1,55,47	34,90,55	13·1

* *Source:* 'Finances of Indian Joint Stock Companies, 1965–6', *Reserve Bank of India Bulletin*, December 1967.

estimated Rs. 122 crores in 1966–7 (Table 26). Excluding petroleum, imports of subsidiaries rose from Rs. 57 crores in 1960–1 to an estimated Rs. 72 crores in 1966–7. The bulk of imports by subsidiaries (88 per cent) was accounted for by raw materials. Industry-wise, two-fifths of total imports were accounted for by petroleum while metals, chemicals, transport equipment and rubber were the other important industries which relied on imports. Imports of the services sector were very small and this was explained by the decline in the role of trading companies.

Table 26

VALUE OF IMPORTS AND EXPORTS

(Rs. crores)

Year	*Value of imports*†	*Value of exports*
1960–1	98·7	25·4
1961–2	97·1	29·8
1962–3	95·1	29·6
1963–4	100·9	29·8
1964–5*	104·0	33·8
1965–6*	114·0	33·3
1966–7*	121·8	36·8

* Estimates.

† Excluding imports financed by foreign equity capital and loans directly obtained by the companies.

Exports of subsidiaries rose gradually from Rs. 25 crores in 1960–1 to an estimated Rs. 37 crores in 1966–7. In the sphere of exports, private limited companies were predominant and accounted for two-thirds of total exports by subsidiaries; this was mainly due to the plantation sector which accounted for one-half of the exports by all subsidiaries. Exports of newer manufactures other than chemicals accounted for a small portion of total exports, though such exports showed gradual improvement. In 1966–7 the engineering, metals, chemicals and rubber goods exports of subsidiaries aggregated over Rs. 9 crores.

The industries in which post-Independence subsidiary investment was channelled were those where import substitution was important. In the initial stages these subsidiaries required sizeable imports of plant, machinery and raw materials. With increasing investment by

Table 27

FOREIGN TRADE AS PERCENTAGE OF TOTAL PRODUCTION

(Percentages)

Industry	*Exports as percentage of total production*				*Imports* as percentage of total production*			
	1960–1	*1961–2*	*1962–3*	*1963–4*	*1960–1*	*1961–2*	*1962–3*	*1963–4*
I. Plantations and Mining	53·6	53·0	52·7	39·3	0·3	0·3	—	0·6
II. Petroleum	2·5	5·0	2·7	3·0	64·0	63·3	58·1	60·1
III. Manufacturing	1·9	1·9	2·0	2·4	18·6	15·2	13·3	11·3
Foods, Beverages and Tobacco	—	0·3	0·2	0·2	2·0	1·0	2·1	0·8
Textile Products	22·2	18·8	14·0	13·4	8·9	8·3	5·3	7·5
Transport Equipment	—	—	0·4	0·3	30·2	24·2	17·5	15·1
Machinery and Machine Tools	—	—	—	—	47·1	38·1	30·0	33·6
Metals and Metal Products	0·9	1·1	1·1	0·6	16·6	15·6	11·4	8·5
Electrical Goods and Machinery	1·3	2·4	1·4	1·7	32·2	25·6	16·8	14·5
Chemicals and Allied Products	1·9	2·0	2·2	3·9	14·1	10·0	9·6	7·6
(*i*) Basic Industrial	1·0	0·6	0·5	0·5	14·1	9·9	12·3	8·1
(*ii*) Medicines and Pharmaceuticals	1·2	1·0	1·2	0·8	24·6	16·5	14·8	9·6
(*iii*) Others	2·3	2·8	3·1	6·1	10·4	7·5	6·8	6·5
Rubber Goods	0·4	0·6	1·1	1·4	36·2	29·7	28·2	23·8
Miscellaneous	7·8	6·8	7·5	5·9	16·4	12·9	10·9	12·8
IV. Services†	62·8	72·3	77·3	73·1	100·0	104·3	109·1	101·9
Total (*I+II+III+IV*)	6·7	6·9	6·1	5·4	25·9	22·4	19·7	18·3

* Excluding imports financed by foreign equity capital and loans directly obtained by the companies.

† The ratios of foreign trade to production for the services sector are of very limited significance, since the high ratios merely reflected the fact that the services sector had a number of trading companies while production was only a more recent activity.

subsidiaries in these industries, the level of imports was higher than that of exports since the contribution of subsidiaries to exports was in spheres where fresh investment was very low, e.g. plantation and mining.

Exports as a percentage of total production for all the subsidiaries declined from 6·7 per cent in 1960–1 to 5·4 per cent in 1963–4; similarly the ratio of imports to total output declined from 25·9 per cent in 1960–1 to 18·3 per cent in 1963–4. The main industry group responsible for a decline in the overall export ratio was plantations and mining in respect of which production increased from Rs. 29·1 crores to Rs. 34·1 crores while exports declined from Rs. 15·6 crores to Rs. 13·4 crores causing the percentage of exports to output to decline from 53·6 in 1960–1 to 39·3 in 1963–4. For petroleum and manufacturing the export ratios increased over the period. Exports of the manufacturing group increased from Rs. 5·5 crores in 1960–1 to Rs. 10·3 crores in 1963–4 and the ratio of exports to total output rose from 1·9 per cent to 2·4 per cent over the period. In the manufacturing sector exports of chemicals and allied products increased almost three-fold and the export ratio rose from 1·9 per cent in 1960–1 to 3·9 per cent in 1963–4. Except for marginal cases like rubber goods and electrical goods and machinery, export ratios declined for most of the sub-sectors of the manufacturing sector. (Table 27.)

While there was a small decline in the ratio of imports to total production of the petroleum industry from 64 per cent in 1960–1 to 60 per cent in 1963–4 there was a steep decline in the import ratio of the manufacturing sector from 18·6 per cent to 11·3 per cent with the absolute volume of imports also declining from Rs. 52·5 crores to Rs. 49 crores. Import ratios declined for all the sub-groups of the manufacturing sector. For transport equipment while production increased by threefold the import ratio declined over the period from 30·2 per cent to 15·1 per cent. The import ratio for chemicals and allied products declined from 14·1 per cent to 7·6 per cent; for medicines and pharmaceuticals the decline was steeper from 24·6 per cent to 9·6 per cent.

10
INDUSTRIAL LICENSING*

by Jagdish Bhagwati

Professor of Economics, Massachusetts Institute of Technology

and Padma Desai

Research Associate, Russian Research Centre, Harvard University

The Industries (Development and Regulation) Act of 1951, following closely upon the Industrial Policy Resolution of 1948, provided the framework for the licensing and regulation of industrial investments (and related questions such as pricing and distribution controls) in the country during the period of the three Five-Year Plans and thereafter. As the Minister of Industry and Supply correctly observed, when introducing the Bill to the Select Committee of Parliament on April 6, 1949:

> '. . . the object of this Bill is to create a suitable legislative framework by virtue of which the industrial policy can be implemented. This Bill, I would say, constitutes a landmark in the industrial legislation of India. It marks the beginning of a planning for the industrial development of this country.'[1]

This was indeed the case: but the precise form that this regulation and planning was to take was to be deficient and, from the viewpoint of both economic efficiency and the very objectives it aimed at, almost a contradiction of what rational governmental intervention would imply. . . . .

1. OBJECTIVES AND INSTRUMENTS OF INDUSTRIAL LICENSING

Among the principcal objectives which the Industrial Policy Resolution listed, and which the Industries Act, 1951, was designed to implement, were:

* In J.N. Bhagwati and P. Desai, *India: Planning for Industrialization – Industrialization and Trade Policies since 1951* (O.E.C.D., Oxford, 1970). (Small parts of this chapter, number 13 in the book, have been excluded. They deal mainly with elaboration of points made elsewhere in the chapter – Ed.)

[1] Quoted in the *Ninth Report of the Estimates Committee* (1967–8).

(1) the development and regulation of industrial investments and production according to Plan priorities and targets;

(2) the protection and encouragement of 'small' industries;

(3) the prevention of concentration of ownership of industries; and

(4) balanced economic development of the different regions in the country, so as to reduce disparities in levels of development.[2]

In order to pursue these objectives, the Industries Act conferred powers upon the Government, which included (i) all existing undertakings in the 'scheduled' industries had to be registered with the Government, and (ii) no 'new' industrial undertaking could be established, nor any 'substantial extention' effected to existing plants, without the prior procurement of a licence from the Central Government.[3] Although the initial list of scheduled industries covered only forty-two major industries, with the gaps left therein 'more by accident than design',[4] this was eventually expanded to include an additional twenty-eight industries in 1956; the schedule, as obtaining at the time of June 1966 devaluation, being nearly complete.

Although the detailed procedures occasionally varied through the period of our study, the principal organizational features were relatively constant and can be briefly described. In essence, with a few exceptions, the applications for industrial licences were cleared by an (Inter-Ministerial) Licensing Committee, set up in September 1952 to operate within the framework of the 1951 Industries Act.[5]

[2] *Ninth Report of the Estimates Committee*, pp. 11–12.

[3] There were also powers for regulating the supply, distribution, and prices of the products of the Scheduled Industries. And in 1953, extensive powers were conferred on the Government to order an investigation of any scheduled unit or industry on suspicion that output had been reduced or price had been increased or quality had deteriorated without 'justification', and thereafter to take over its management if necessary.

[4] *Ninth Report of the Estimates Committee*, p. 20.

[5] The exceptions were relatively unimportant.

'To obviate the necessity of all cases coming up to the Licensing Committee, some delegations have been made by the Committee to the administrative ministries. The following categories of applications are generally disposed of without reference to the Licensing Committee subject to the State Government or Governments concerned having no objection and provided the schemes are found satisfactory after technical scrutiny:

(*a*) Where it is necessary to regularize the manufacturing activities of existing industrial undertakings;

(*b*) Where a change of location within one State or from one State to another is proposed;

(*c*) Where the production of new articles is proposed and such production

The applications were generally placed before the Licensing Committee for approval only when they had already been recommended by the administrative Ministry within whose general jurisdiction the specific, applicant industry would lie. Where such recommendation was withheld, the application went to the Rejection Committee, to be reconsidered for grant or rejection of the licence. The final decision on the issuance of the licence was taken, on the advice of these Committees, at the level of the Minister for Industrial Development.

A Directorate General of Technical Development (D.G.T.D.) was set up with the task (among others) of examining from a technical angle the applications under the Industries Act for establishing new units or undertaking substantial expansion. The Estimates Committee (1967–8) has described the functions of the D.G.T.D. in this connection:

> 'The D.G.T.D. makes a techno-economic appreciation of the applications for industrial licensing, indicating *inter alia:*
>
> '(*a*) if there is need for more capacity for the item(s) of production proposed in the application, also keeping in view import substitution and export possibilities;
>
> '(*b*) if the scheme of manufacture is technically sound;
>
> '(*c*) whether the capacity asked for by the entrepreneur is commensurate with the capital goods to be installed, taking into consideration the capital goods which the party may already possess;
>
> '(*d*) whether the scheme as submitted or as further modified in the light of discussion with D.G.T.D. will ensure reaching the maximum possible indigenous content within a reasonable time;
>
> '(*e*) whether the plant to be installed and/or method of manufacture to be adopted is modern and economic;
>
> '(*f*) whether the location lends it to economic viability and disposal of affluents.'
>
> 'Based on the aforesaid basic considerations D.G.T.D. recommends to the Licensing Committee either acceptance or rejection of the application.'[6]

---

does not involve installations of any additional machinery or the use of imported raw material;

(*d*) Applications in respect of items which have been put on the rejection list. These are ordinarily rejected without submission to Licensing Committee.'

Ninth Report of the Estimates Committee, pp. 137–8.

[6] *Ninth Report of the Estimates Committee*, pp. 200–1.

Quite apart from the industrial Licensing Committee, there were numerous other physical controls to be cleared by the prospective investor. The C.G. (capital goods) licence had to be procured from the C.G. Licensing Committee which cleared allocations of import licences for the purpose: a procedure which could not be obviated if imports of capital goods were necessary. Furthermore, if there was foreign collaboration involved, the (inter-Ministerial) Foreign Agreements Committee got into the picture and its consent to the terms of the collaboration had to be secured as well. In many cases, where the local finance had to be procured from a State financial institution, such as the Industrial Finance Corporation (I.F.C.), the scrutinies exercised by these committees were repeated afresh.

II. ECONOMIC EFFICIENCY OF THE LICENSING SYSTEM FROM THE VIEWPOINT OF INDUSTRIAL PLANNING

. . . .

Absence of criteria

The licensing system was supposed to operate within the framework of targets which had been worked out by other agencies such as the Planning Commission. Its function was therefore to ensure that, within this framework, the actual choice of plants, technologies, locations etc., was carried out in a manner which would ensure social, as distinct from private, profitability. If this were not the case, and private entrepreneurs could be expected to ensure social advantage as well, then suitable fiscal incentives and taxes designed to keep industrial investments within the defined targets would be an efficient and adequate policy and detailed licensing of literally thousands of applications for licences would be a highly wasteful procedure. Thus the important questions are: (*a*) what criteria were defined to deal with the applications; and (*b*) were they systematically deployed in practice? If our answers to these questions are negative, the situation through the three Plans appears to have been one in which not only were the targets themselves fixed without any systematic attention to costs and benefits, but even the methods by which economic choices relating to their fulfilment were made were defective and could not be described as constituting 'rational' intervention.

(*1*) *Operation of Licensing Committee*

That the Licensing Committee operated essentially in an *ad hoc* manner, without explicit statement and weighting of different objectives and without explicit publication of any criteria in terms of which applicants could assess their chances of getting licences with reasonable firmness and hence plan more soundly, has long been known. Detailed *official* analyses of the licensing procedures and policies, which have recently been made, have only underlined this conclusion:

. . . .

'3.7. Asked during evidence whether any general principles had been laid down for issuing licences for establishing new undertakings or substantial expansion of existing undertakings, the representative of the Ministry of Industrial Development and Company Affairs informed the Committee that "*Not in the sense of laying down principles.* But the things are well-known, that the unit should be economical and so on and it is the normal principle that we prefer expansion of the existing unit to setting up a new one as it is less costly."

'3.8. Asked further whether any general principles have been formulated by Government on the advice of the Sub-Committee of the Central Advisory Council, as provided in Rule 18* of the Registration and Licensing of Industrial Undertakings Rules, 1952, the Secretary of the Ministry stated that "*I don't think they have laid down any principles.* This Council meets, there is an exchange of information and matters are discussed." . . .

'3.11. The Committee are concerned to note that since the inception of the licensing system under the Industries (Development and Regulation) Act, 1951, no general principles/guidelines have been laid down which are followed for the consideration of applications for grant of an industrial licence for establishing a new undertaking/expansion of existing undertaking under the Act although the Rules specifically provide for it. It is obvious that in the absence of such principles/guidelines, the merits of each application are apt to be judged on an *ad hoc* basis.[7]

'*In the absence of well ordered priorities* and flexibility of inter-related programmes at various levels of performance, *there has been a tendency to rely upon various ad hoc criteria.* One of these has been

* Rule 18 of the Registration and Licensing of Industrial Undertakings Rules 1952 lays down that 'A Sub-Committee of the Central Advisory Council shall be constituted which will review all licences issued, varied, amended or revoked from time to time and advise the Government on the general principles to be followed in the issue of licenses for establishing new undertakings or substantial expansion of the existing undertakings.'

[7] *Ninth Report of the Estimates Committee*, pp. 135–6 [italics have been inserted by the authors in paragraphs 3.7 and 3.8].

the policy of licensing projects, the foreign exchange costs of which on capital and/or maintenance account are covered by available credits and/or foreign collaboration and/or export obligations. It can be said in defence of this policy that there has been no resulting distortion of planning or industrial development because the projects so approved are, in nearly all cases, included in the plan. That does not, however, answer the basic argument that this is a reversal or inversion of what is implied in planning. A project must first of all be intrinsically feasible and occupy a high place in the list of priorities before it can be considered for the allotment of scarce resources, especially foreign exchange. Just because a project is, or can be made, amenable to availability of foreign exchange should not qualify it for approval.'[8]

. . . .

The absence of explicit *economic* criteria as also the weighting of different objectives, in the grant or rejection of industrial licences was matched, through the period, by the generally poor quality of the 'techno-economic' examination of proposed industrial investments which the D.G.T.D. was supposed to carry out in each case. There is no evidence of any studies having been carried out by the D.G.T.D. of the optimal size, time-phasing, and location of industrial units, for example, in order to guide the Licensing Committee in its deliberations.[9] A detailed examination of the working of the D.G.T.D. by an American firm of consultants was to confirm what many observers and applicants for licensing already knew: that few systematic criteria, if any, existed in the D.G.T.D.'s decision-making process and that the D.G.T.D. was occasionally demanding duplicate information which, in any case, was not scrutinized for inconsistencies and often remained on a company basis and few data existed on an aggregated product basis as would be the case if only techno-economic decisions were being taken in a systematic and informed manner.[10]

[8] Hazari, *Report of Committee on Industrial Licensing, 1969*. Pp. 19–20 [italics have been inserted by the authors.]

[9] This was pointed out by Bhagwati, 'Economics of Scale, Distribution of Industry and Programming', *Economic Weekly*, September 1, 1962. Attempts at discovering whether the D.G.T.D. had any such studies for the aluminium industry, in which Bhagwati was interested, revealed the absence at the time of even comprehension of such problems, leave aside their systematic resolution. Later work by T.N. Srinivasan and Alan Manne, at the Indian Statistical Institute, was to develop techniques for such analysis: Alan Manne (ed.), *Investments for Capacity Expansion.*

[10] Cf. *Ninth Report of the Estimates Committee*, pp. 216–18.

Not merely was the D.G.T.D. unable to evolve any traditions of 'techno-economic' work which would improve the efficiency of industrial planning and regulation,[11] and gear its informational system to such work, but even its *purely* technical work, devoid of any economic considerations, was of dubious quality, at best. The reports of both the Management Consultants from the United States and the local Mathur Team on the D.G.T.D.'s working, as also the examination of R.K. Hazari who reported on industrial planning to the Planning Commission, have agreed on the need to improve the technical strength of the D.G.T.D. and to prevent the organization from becoming technically obsolete. It is dubious how far such an organization, staffed generally with engineers whose technical qualifications and practical experience were limited (and commensurate only with the generally unattractive salaries they got, in relation to the private sectors' pay scales), whose desks were loaded with an average of nearly two thousand fresh applications for 'technical advice' every year, and whose informational system was ill-organized for taking decisions in the light of explicit criteria, could operate efficiently. In view of these limitations, one wonders if the D.G.T.D. could take even the purely technological decisions

[11] The economic quality of the D.G.T.D.'s work can be judged also from the following quote from the *Ninth Report of the Estimates Committee*, p. 207:

'The Director General of Technical Development has issued instructions (on December 29, 1965) that:

(*a*) The concept of indigenous content should be basically revised. The general object should be to start 100 per cent or near 100 per cent indigenous content, at least in the engineering industries.

(*b*) So far as the existing approvals are concerned, steps should be taken to improve upon the phased programmes earlier approved with a view to reaching 100 per cent indigenous content as early as practicable.

(*c*) So far as foreign collaborations are concerned, if a collaboration in a particular field has already been approved, fresh collaborations in the same field should be discouraged and the possibility of persuading the undertaking which has already come into existence, to part with their know-how to new-comers, on the basis of some payments, should be explored.

4.14 The representative of D.G.T.D. has informed the Committee during evidence that 'A much higher indigenous content is being insisted on in regard to all new licences. It may not be practicable in every industry to achieve 100 per cent indigenous content, but we are definitely insisting on a much higher percentage of indigenous content when new licences are being issued.' He added that 'The earlier units which were required to achieve an indigenous content of say 80 per cent, are now being pressurized to achieve a higher percentage themselves.'

Factors such as *indirect* import demands or the possibility of any particular process being uneconomic or the possiblity of there being *better* know-how available than what has been obtained in the past are matters which do not seem to have bothered the D.G.T.D. at all.

which might, in *some* sense, contribute improvements in the growth of industrial capacities justifying the bureaucratic apparatus and the delays which we shortly describe. An impartial analysis of the reasons stated and the methods of analysis used by the D.G.T.D. in declaring specific applications as technically or techno-economically unsound would be revealing: unfortunately, only an officially constituted body would be allowed to have access to the relevant files.

(*2*) *Inadequate and ill-organized information*

We have already referred briefly to the inefficient information system obtaining in the D.G.T.D. concerning industrial (and A.U.) licensing. The American Management Consultants showed that:

> '(i) The quality of data received by the D.G.T.D. is neither consistent nor is it audited.
>
> '(ii) The D.G.T.D.'s current information processing system is related to, but not fully compatible with, the information needs of industry and other government agencies. Many common needs exist which are not now satisfied by common data . . .
>
> '(iii) The D.G.T.D. most often request data from companies that is very similar to data already received. Moreover, the D.G.T.D. is not presently in a position to supply industry with desired statistical or reference data.
>
> '(iv) The data storage is by company and little data exists on a total product basis. . . .
>
> '(vi) Reliance is placed on manual checking and transferring of data to ledgers and on mental computations. These techniques are slow, are a source of inaccuracy, and are inappropriate to the large volume of data to be handled. Development Officers, as a result, seldom have all the data they desire available when making an allocation decision.'[12]

Further, the Mathur Study Team and other analysts have examined the 'G' return, which is required to be submitted by the licensee twice annually so that the D.G.T.D. and other interested authorities keep track of progress in implementation – a matter of admitted importance if industrial planning is seriously taken and is extended to ensuring that implementation of licensed capacities proceeds on plan and if new capacities are to be licensed on the basis of reliable information on the progress in installation of earlier-licensed capacities. This has shown that: (i) the D.G.T.D.

[12] *Ninth Report of the Estimates Committee*, pp. 216–17.

did not maintain this information with any degree of accuracy, with the G-returns coming in irregularly and sometimes with excessive delays if at all; (ii) the returns, in any case, received only *routine* and junior-level treatment in the vast majority of cases; and (iii) the copies of the return required to be sent to several other authorities such as the Planning Commission were merely filed and represented unfructuous work on the part of the licensee.[13] That mere licensing of capacities, within some margin of the targets where available, was enough to practice and there was no need to have a systematic analysis of the follow-through, to examine whether the targets (which were presumably taken very seriously, as we have argued) would be fulfilled *and* whether any remedial action would be necessary (in the shape, for example, of facilitating finance availability, prodding the State Governments involved, entry of the public sector if necessary), seems to have been the prevailing philosophy. The apparatus of 'returns' about the progress of the licensee was, in effect, a conspicuous substitute for actual analysis, evaluation, and rethinking of policies in the light of the progress of licensees in different industries.

(3) Sequential choice among applicants

So far we have discussed the absence of criteria and informed judgments on the question of rejecting or granting a *single* application for an industrial licence. However, we may well ask whether efficient industrial planning should not also be designed to choose, from among alternative applications for fulfilling a certain target, those which are socially most advantageous.

The procedure used by the Licensing Committee in general was to proceed on a first-come-first-served basis, reflecting to some extent the philosophy of 'fairness' in allocating a scarce resource (i.e. a profitable, industrial licence) that was also to characterize many other allocational decisions by the Indian bureaucracy.[14] This practice, combined with overall ceilings in many cases where targets were laid down, further resulted in several other inefficiencies such as the foreclosing of capacity by better-organized and better-informed industrial houses who could often put up the applications more quickly than others.

The effective elimination of efficient choice among different applicants that this procedure of licensing implied has been noted

[13] *Ninth Report of the Estimates Committee*, pp. 218–22.

[14] See, for example, our extensive discussion of such practices in import allocations in Ch. 17. Evidence supporting the 'first-come-first-served' rule is found in the *Ninth Report of the Estimates Committee*, p. 152.

by several economists and committees.[15] The latest official discussion of this question, contained in the Report on Industrial Licensing by the Estimates Committee (1967–8) is revealing and may be quoted at length:

'3.63. The Committee desired to know the views of Government regarding a suggestion made by a leading industrialist of the country that "it is not un-common that the application for expanding the existing plan facility or installing a new capacity has been granted to entrepreneur A, while an application from entrepreneur B for a similar licence has been rejected on the grounds that sufficient capacity has already been allowed though the investment cost and foreign exchange cost per annual tonne output of the project put up by the entrepreneur B is about one-third or one-fourth the cost per annual tonne of the project of entrepreneur A, merely because entrepreneur A applied for the licence earlier than the entrepreneur B. A more practical approach to this problem would be to invite from prospective entrepreneurs fairly firm statements regarding the current and capital cost per ton of the major products they wish to manufacture either anew or in the process of fresh expansion. The Government could then select that scheme which would, other things being equal, have the highest rate of return in terms of capital employed consistent with the lowest price chargeable to the consumer and the lowest foreign exchange content."

'3.64. The Secretary of the Ministry of Industrial Development and Company Affairs stated that "This is an important suggestion. I would like to consider it before offering any views. It is an interesting suggestion which, I think, will have to be considered carefully."

'3.65. In a written note subsequently furnished to the Committee the position has been explained by the Ministry of Industrial Development and Company Affairs as under:

'. . . The possibility of introducing a procedure of inviting applications in specified fields and considering them together periodically with a view to giving preference to entrepreneurs who require the minimum foreign exchange etc. was examined by the Industries Development Procedures Committee. The conclusion was that such a procedure is likely to present serious practical difficulties. This was likely to result in bunching of licences instead of their

[15] Cf. Bhagwati, 'Economies of Scale, Distribution of Industry and Programming', *Economic Weekly*, *op. cit.;* and the Report of the [Mathur] Study Team on D.G.T.D., *op. cit.*

being spread appropriately throughout the Plan period and would result in delays or failures to utilize available foreign loans and credits to the overall detriment of the interests of the country. The Committee, therefore, recommended that there need be no change in the present procedure. Though the Government have accepted the recommendation, further thought is being given to this matter.'[16]

Among the interesting aspects of this interchange between the Estimates Committee and the Ministry in overall charge of licensing procedures is the relative degree of surprise with which the proposal for simultaneous, as distinct from sequential, licensing fo competing applications was received by the Ministry, as late as 1966.[17] Also, the reasons cited for the rejection of a revised procedure, aimed at introducing considerations of choice, appear to have been hastily drawn up: for example, while licences may have been bunched under this procedure, there was massive evidence of their bunching, in any case, under the existing procedures;[18] indeed the proposal made for simultaneous licensing at repeated intervals might have made it necessary for the licensing authorities to give more systematic thought to phasing than was evident through the period. Furthermore, it is equally likely that some form of simultaneous consideration of industrial licensing applications would have been an inducement to the licensing bodies to evolve *some* systematic criteria and compelled the D.G.T.D. to undertake supporting analysis. The sequential licensing procedures were, in fact, part of the general apathy to notions of efficient industrial planning and regulation.

(4) Delays

The two Swaminathan Committees, reporting in 1964 and 1966, as also the Mathur Study Team's Report on the D.G.T.D., revealed

[16] *Ibid.*, pp. 152–4.

[17] We hasten to add that the notion that simultaneous consideration should result in choice of projects with 'minimum foreign exchange content' is of course absurd as it ignores *indirect* imports and also implicitly puts an infinite price on foreign exchange.

[18] Cf. R.K. Hazari, *op. cit.*, p. 18:

'Licences are normally or, in most cases, issued for a capacity 10 to 25 per cent above the target for the end-Plan year and that, too, mostly around the beginning of a Plan period. An excessive—although quantitatively unverifiable . . . pressure is thus exerted on the available foreign exchange and possible collaborators and also on domestic suppliers. This leads to bottlenecks and delays, apart from adversely affecting the terms of negotiations with foreign and domestic suppliers and creditors.'

Also see the *Ninth Report of the Estimates Committee*, pp. 162–4.

several inefficiencies in the administrative procedures, leading to delays without any corresponding *quid pro quo*. The lapse of time in acquiring information in order to take informed decisions on licensing applications would have a social justification (assuming, of course, that the criteria used were sensible and social and private profitabilities diverged so as to necessitate rational intervention). But where the delays are attributable to inefficient procedures and inadequate appreciation of the opportunity cost of time and the necessity to implement programmes on schedule, they represent a net loss to society.

The first Swaminathan Committee found, for example, that the requirement under Rule 15 of the Registration and Licensing Undertakings Rule (1952) that the applications must be decided upon in three months, had been flouted in most cases, and without justification: 'during the course of case studies it has been noticed that undue delays have often taken place *in the process of mere physical distribution of applications*.'[19] The revised procedures suggested by this Committee were sought to be implemented and disposals of applications were expected to take five weeks: however, the subsequent investigation of the 1965 Mathur Study Team on the D.G.T.D. showed that, on the basis of 122 case studies, six months was still the *average* time taken for case disposal. The Estimates Committee, reporting in 1967, was still to find the procedures dilatory and was constrained to comment:

> 'While the Committee note that as a result of the implementation of the recommendations of the Industries Development Procedures Committee the time taken in the processing of applications for industrial licensing has come down from over 6 months, i.e. 180 days to nearly 145 days; they, however, consider that even the period of 145 days is still on the high side. The Committee cannot but strongly urge that constant endeavours should be made to bring down the period at least to the level of the time table (70 days in the case of more simple cases and abut 100 days in others) suggested by the Study Team on D.G.T.D. as a result of their case study. They have a feeling that if the records are kept properly up to date and the movement of the applications is closely watched, it should not be difficult to achieve the desired results.'[20]

These delays were characteristic of the entire bureaucratic regime involved in industrial licensing. With respect to the Foreign Agree-

[19] Cf. 'Speeding up Industrial Licensing', *Economic Weekly*, January 18, 1964 [italics have been inserted].

[20] *Ninth Report*, p. 172.

ments Committee, for example, the situation was equally dismal. Thus, the Estimates Committee (1967–8) again observed:

'. . . Government have furnished the following break-up of the time taken up to 6 months, between 6 months and one year and more than one year in deciding applications for foreign collaboration during the last 2 years:

	1965	*1966*
1. Total number of applications for foreign collaboration decided during the years 1965 and 1966	264	226
2. No. of applications out of (1) above which were decided within 6 months	153	138
3. No. of applications out of (1) above which were decided between 6 months and one year	79	51
4. No. of applications out of (1) above which were decided after more than a year	32	37

'. . . The Committee regret to note that there is considerable delay in finalizing applications for foreign collaborations. As many as 42 per cent applications in 1965 and 39 per cent in 1966 remained undecided after 6 months of their receipt. Out of these over 12 per cent in 1965 and over 16 per cent in 1966 were decided after more than a year. It would appear that strict watch is not being kept over the time taken in the disposal of these applications.[21]

For capital goods import licensing, for which separate clearance again had to be obtained from the C.G.C. (the Capital Goods Committee), Hazari has noted that:

'As of January 1964 (for which the latest data are available), 751 applications for foreign exchange equivalent to Rs. 231 crores (pre-devaluation) were pending with C.G.C. for more than one year. Applications received in 1961 and earlier, i.e. pending for more than two years, were 182, and these indented foreign exchange of Rs. 173 crores.'[22]

(5) *Administrative exemptions and restrictions without economic rationale*

. . . .

The licensing system, we may note, distinguished between three basic categories: applicants for: (i) new undertakings; (ii) substantial expansion; and (iii) manufacture of new articles.

[21] *Ibid.*, pp. 240–1.
[22] Hazari, *op. cit.*, p. 33, para. 41.1.

In addition to applications for setting up new plants, Section 13(*d*) of the Industries Act also laid down that no 'substantial expansion' could be undertaken by any licensed or registered industrial undertaking without prior procurement of a licence. Similarly, Section 11-A of the same Act had even laid down the condition that the manufacture of a 'new article', not specified in the initial licence, also required a fresh authorization and licence.

In practice, the 'substantial expansion' restriction was not merely ambiguous because entrepreneurs were unsure what the bureaucrats would consider to be substantial rather than insubstantial increment in productive capacity,[23] but there were also several instances where improvements in *productivity*, arising from greater efficiency, would not be 'legitimated' by the authorities. The difficulty arose because, in view of the general practice of allocating A.U. import licences *pro rata* to capacity – the authorities were suspicious of any claims that productivity had increased thanks to improvements in organization etc. But this also meant that better methods of capital utilization (e.g. through increased shifts or better management practices) were, in practice, difficult to adopt without much fuss and were occasionally frustrated.[24] A possible way to minimize such inefficiencies would have been to define substantial expansion in terms of *investments* rather than output: but clearly no thought was given to the matter.

In this connection, it is also worth noting a more novel criticism directed at the licensing bodies' general failure to approve of an

[23] *Ninth Report of the Estimates Committee*, p. 189:

During the course of evidence in October 1966, the Secretary of Ministry of Industrial Development and Company Affairs confirmed that 'the Industries Act does not define positively what is substantial expansion. It does not really lay down in terms of percentage'. About the percentage he stated that 'up to 10 per cent we do not really treat as in any way substantial, because if expansion of production takes place up to about 10 per cent, we recognize it automatically'. When asked to state after how many years the increase of 10 per cent was allowed, he stated that 'There was no fixed period but if the same entrepreneur comes' along every alternate year for a 10 per cent increase that will be taken note of.'

[24] Yet another effect of these occasional refusals to 'recognize' improved productive capacities was a tendency typically to understate the capacity figures which the D.G.T.D. compiled regularly for publication. These estimates, in any case, were notoriously bad, with no attempts made to define capacity systematically and with most of the estimates given on the basis of a single-shift only. Again, the 'techo-economic' inexpertise of the D.G.T.D., as revealed by their competence in dealing with the question of capacity estimation and evaluation of reasons for underutilization, was dismal. Cf. Bhagwati, 'Economics of Scale, Distribution of Industry and Programming', *Economic Weekly*, September 1, 1962.

industrial licence envisaging and approving expansion in different stages over a long period of time:

> 'It has been represented to the Committee by a leading industrialist that "Where expansion involves more than one stage, the practice of the Government has been to sanction only the first stage expansion without any assurance or guarantee that the subsequent expansion would follow automatically. The routes to two different stages of expansion, for technical reasons, cannot be identical though fundamentally the process is the same and unless the Government accord the company a letter of intent for entire expansion from first stage to last, it would be uneconomic to order out the equipment required for the expansion schemes in two different distinct stages." It has been suggested that "Where the expansion involves more than one stage, a letter of intent or licence should be issued for the entire expansion programme so that the industrial unit can take appropriate action to implement the entire expansion programme in an integrated and co-ordinated manner."
>
> '3.160. Expressing his views on the above suggestion, the Secretary of the Ministry of Industrial Development and Company Affairs stated during evidence that "This has to be very carefully considered in each case because otherwise a man may book a lot of capacity and create monopoly. We have to consider each case on merits and also consider what is the nature of the industry and the position of the industrialist."
>
> '3.161. It is well recognized that goods can be produced more economically by expansion of the existing units rather than by setting up new undertakings. Keeping in view the public demand for the supply of goods at competitive prices, the Committee suggest that Government should earnestly consider the suggestion that the expansion programme submitted by established units, may be expeditiously considered and where found acceptable, letters of intent covering the entire expansion programme may be issued provided this does not encourage and create monopolies. Import licences for implementing the expansion programme may be regulated keeping in view the stage of expansion and the availability of foreign exchange.'[25]

The Ministry's raising of the standard difficulty about monopoly creation, in this instance as in others, is clearly unconvincing and a convenient substitute for revising a licensing procedure which

[25] *Ninth Report of the Estimates Committee*, pp. 190–1.

was not worked out with reference to considerations of economic efficiency.

The *severe* restrictions on manufacture of 'new articles' had little economic rationale either. Although the diversification of production was to be permitted, with many restrictions including a ceiling of 25 per cent of the capacity, in 1965–6, the full-scale restrictions on diversification were to continue through practically the entire period of the three Plans. Since hardly any targets were specified at the level of detailed *products*, the restriction imposed was excessive even in relation to the stated objectives of planning; and relaxation permitting automatic diversification of output, within broader limits, would have been compatible with such objectives. In any case, for industries where *no* targets were specified, the possible diversification, in response to market forces, could have been allowed within yet *wider* limits.[26] The technological possibilities of product diversification, from the type of plant being sanctioned, could have also been readily considered, with the aid of the D.G.T.D. in such cases and, if necessary, certain products ruled out to begin with. Again, therefore, we have here an example of licensing procedures devised without reference to clear notions of efficient, industrial planning.

III. LOCATIONAL POLICY

We now examine the efficiency with which the licensing and regulation system managed to achieve the objectives of balanced development and prevention of concentration in the ownership of industrial wealth.

On locational policy, the Industries Act (1951), the Industrial Policy Resolutions and the Five-Year Plan documents have been equally articulate in stressing the need for balanced development. Any policy relating to industrial planning in a federal country such as India would, in any case, have had to come to terms with the needs of regional claims. In fact, the Licensing Committee's operation was continually sought to be influenced by the States which wished to attract industrial investments within their borders. Thus, the Estimates Committee (1967–8) records that:

[26] Note that our criticisms so far have been based on the limiting assumption that the targeting system was desirable and the targets should be fulfilled. Our preference for a system with indicative planning in most industries, with a few priority areas regulated in depth, would lead to still stronger criticism of such restrictions as the one on diversification.

'It has been stated by the official representative of the Ministry that "Quite a number of States keep on representing that their areas have not received adequate share of licences. I have not got the figures of the number of representations, but it is a fact that from time to time, Chief Ministers of States and Industries Ministers of States do write to us pointing out that their States, in their opinion, have not received a fair share of the licences. As my colleague explained, we have no compulsive means of attracting people to particular areas. We consider the applications as we receive them and provided the location in a particular area is not too uneconomic, other things being reasonably equal, we do give preference to the more underdeveloped areas."

'2.46. In reply to another question, the representative of the Planning Commission has informed the Committee during evidence that besides the economic and technological considerations "there may be other elements like regional considerations which may have to be introduced in the consideration of particular projects. But for major projects and for projects in the export industries particularly, the economic and technological considerations are considered paramount." '[27]

As the foregoing quote also underlines, the intervention by the States was not exactly unsuccessful and, except when there were major or, of late 'export-intensive' projects, the remaining applications could be influenced by political pulls and pressures. The considerable proliferation of *uneconomic-scale* plants which attended the progress of industrialization in the country during the three Plans has been generally admitted to be a consequence of these pressures, with the Licensing Committee preferring, *de facto*, to satisfy as many claimant states as possible.[28]

In effect, the situation was similar to that obtaining at the international level, where the eagerness to industrialize has led many less developed countries (L.D.C.s) to industrialize behind high tariff walls, and quantitative restrictions, prompting economists to advocate greater, *mutual* reduction in barriers to trade expansion enabling exploitation of economies of scale and specialization, *consistent with each L.D.C. attaining the same degree of industrialization.*[29]

[27] *Ninth Report*, paras. 2.45 and 2.46.

[28] In this policy, they were also assisted by their reference to the fear that monopoly power may follow if there were a fewer number of units in an industry. We return to this contention, exposing its fallacy, when we turn to the discussion of monopoly power and concentration.

[29] Cf. C.A. Cooper and B. Massell, 'Toward a General Theory of Customs

The failure of the Indian Planners to work out the space-dimension of their industrial targets, on the basis of economic efficiency constrained by state targets of overall industrial investments designed to assure the States that they would get some minimum industrialization, in effect left the field almost entirely to political pressures. With no State assured of ultimately (at the end of the Plan) getting some minimum largess, there was a scramble for most industrial licences, thus creating a great political pressure for dividing up each target among as many States as possible; with the Licensing Committee, aided in turn by no clues to optimal size, location, and phasing of expansion of plants by its 'techno-economic' counsel (the D.G.T.D.), these political pulls often ruled the day.[30]

The failure was thus again of industrial *planning*. Clearly, the level of real income that could be attained, subject to the political constraint that each State should have some pre-defined share of industrial investments, would be less than if there were no such constraints. But industrial planning in India failed to reduce the cost of such a constrained system to its minimum and, in fact, operated with a consistent bias in favour of plants being reduced to uneconomic scale most of the time.[31]

IV. CONCENTRATION AND MONOPOLY POWER

The success of the licensing and regulation system in checking the concentration of industrial ownership and in promoting a competi-

---

Unions for Developing Countries', *Journal of Political Economy*, October 1965; and J. Bhagwati, 'Trade Liberalization Among L.D.C.'s, Trade Theory and Gatt Rules' in J.N. Wolfe (ed.), *Value, Capital and Growth: Essays in Honour of J.R. Hicks*.

[30] Cf. the *Ninth Report of the Estimates Committee*, p. 195, quoting an eminent industrialist's evidence:

[The] Government were proposing to have two units of an industry in U.P. in the public sector. Then pressure came from Madhya Pradesh. They said: You must have something for us also. Out state is also backward. The result was that the Government yielded and decided to have one Unit in U.P. and another in M.P. This is purely because of regional consideration. This should not be the criterion for putting up an industry or industrial unit. Factors such as land, water, power and transport facilities must be taken into consideration before we finally decide on the location. To further elaborate this, I would point out to you that Government has been thinking of putting up steel plants in Salem and Andhra Pradesh. Tell me from raw-materials point of view or even power whether these two sites are suitable?

[31] Cf. Bhagwati, 'Economies of Scale . . . ', *Economic Weekly*, September 1962, *op. cit.* Also see Hazari's 1967 Report on *Industrial Planning and Licensing Policy*, *op. cit.*, pp. 24–5.

tive system was no greater and, paradoxically, the system is almost certain to have even worked in the contrary direction in many respects.

(i) As many observers, including the Monopolies Inquiry Commission (1965), have noted, the bigger business houses could utilize the licensing-plus-targeting system to the detriment of smaller rivals.[32] They could put in for licences more readily, since they were better informed and organized, and thus jump ahead of others in the queue – a matter of some importance, as we have seen, in a *sequential* licensing system. Furthermore, they could get their successful applications moving more quickly towards implementation and hence suffer a smaller risk of the licence-revocation practised by the licensing authorities: the market mechanism would not have made the smaller rivals quicker but it would have permitted them entry.[33] Moreover, the implicit acceptance of the availability of foreign collaboration and finance as a criterion for preferring an application, which Hazari had recorded, also put the smaller entrepreneur at a disadvantage in relation to bigger rivals with more international contacts.

(ii) More important, it appears likely from the available evidence that the bigger houses realized that they could corner a considerable amount of targeted capacity by putting in multiple and early applications for the *same* industry, and thus develop a fairly dominant place in the industries where this tactic worked.[34] Hazari, who has investigated this possibility at length, is inclined even to argue that the intention behind multiple applications was to 'foreclose capacity', the intention to implement the successful licence applications being sometimes not even serious, as in the case of some

[32] The percentage of licences issued to those applied for, works out at 71·6 per cent for big business and 65·1 per cent for the rest' according to the *Ninth Report*, p. 173, quoting the Monopolies Inquity Commission. This, of course, is only indicative rather than decisive.

[33] The following quote from the Monopolies Inquiry Commission, in the *Ninth Report*, p. 176, is of interest:

> Much more, we think, can be done, to make it easy for the comparatively smaller entrepreneur to get industrial and import licences without undue expenses and wasteful delay. Many of the leading industrialists, we understand, have found it necessary to maintain expensive establishments in the capital for facilitating the obtaining of licences. Those who cannot afford the expenses of running such establishments which include sometimes, it seems, large amounts required to employ high paid 'contactmen' and to give lavish parties, are at a disadvantage.

[34] Hazari has produced a considerable amount of evidence in support of his thesis that several industrial houses put in, often successfully, multiple applications for a single industry in a single Plan period. See Table 16, in *op. cit.*, which is particularly exhaustive on the house of Birlas.

Birla trading concerns which secured licences but had practically no assets, could not pursue them and ended up seeking their transfer or resale.

These arguments are obviously not decisive. Just as Adam Smith pointed to the possibility of collusion among independent producers, the reverse possibility of different Birla concerns, part of a huge and diffused empire, being competitive in seeking expansion – particularly when *reinvestment* of profits in expansion was restricted by licensing and other outlets were therefore necessary – is not entirely implausible. Furthermore, in view of the political pressures for regional balances that we have already described, it is possible that, rather than submit one application for a large plant in a single location, the business houses found it shrewder to submit more applications for smaller plants in *different* states. Hazari's contention thus bears more careful investigation; nonetheless, it is quite suggestive.

(iii) Much more pertinent, however, is the criticism that the entire attempt at controlling the growth of industrial houses in different industries by industrial licensing was likely to be ineffective as there were no provisions for preventing acquisition of existing undertakings by the industrial house.[35]

A belated awareness of this fundamental critique of the industrial policy, given its objective of reducing concentration, is evident in the statement of the Minister of Industrial Development and Company Affairs in the Rajya Sabha (the Upper House) on May 31, 1967:

> 'it is possible that today the Licensing Committee may give a licence to "A" who may have nothing to do with Birla, or Tata or any other company, but after that "A" has implemented all the requirements of that licence or has set up a particular industry, what is there to prevent Birla or Tata from purchasing that industry? Therefore in many of the cases when you find that the companies multiply, it may not be because of the defect in the licensing system or because of any illegality committed by our officers in giving licences but because of *this inherent defect in our system* and because of our

[35] Cf. J. Bhagwati and T.N. Srinivasan, 'Licensing and Control of Industry', paper submitted to the *Prime Minister's Conference for Young Industrialists*, March 1966: 'Under the existing system, since there is no effective control on resale of enterprises once they are licensed, it is not clear how the first objective [of reduction in concentration of ownership] is served by investment licensing. Even if there is resale control or anti-merger regulations, there is nothing to to prevent an entrepreneurial group getting licences through *benami* [i.e. use of different names] transactions. The same objectives could be more efficiently, though perhaps less dramatically, served by more positive action through easier access to credit and "know-how" to potential newcomers.'

inability to control such kind of lapses on the part of those who are getting licences, who are not able to carry on and then ultimately they are purchased by other big persons. These are matters which we have to take into consideration.'[36]

(iv) Finally, Bhagwati has pointed to another fundamental defect of the licensing-plus-targeting system, combined with strict Q.R.s on competing imports and non-transferability between firms of A.U. import licences for raw materials and components: namely, its elimination of the possibility of competition in any meaningful sense of the term:

'The first major point that occurs to an economist, when discussing the question of monopoly and competition in the Indian economy, is that a very large segment of the economy . . . works under monopolistic conditions. The creation of new capacity in the organized industrial sector is strictly controlled at various levels. Capital issues control, licensing and the permission to import machinery are the principal points at which the *entry* into an industry is controlled by the government. This is the concomitant of a system under which the government works with a set of *targets*. The net effect of this system is to make the entry of new competitors impossible – as the government will not allow creation of more capacity than current, estimated demand. It thus rules out the elimination of inefficient current producers by efficient, *new entrants*. It *also* rules out the possibility of the more efficient, *current* units expanding and eliminating the inefficient, current units: expansion by current units is as much subject to control within targets as expansion through new firms. (This elimination of competition is applicable even to the *utilization* of existing capacity. Materials and exchange are frequently allocated on a *pro rata* basis rather than to efficient producers.) If, then, competition from efficient rivals at home is ruled out by our economic planners, what about foreign competition? Here again, competition has no chance! The use of import quotas rules out the possibility of competition from abroad. We are thus in an economic situation where the possibility of competition from potential entry, by domestic or foreign rivals is minimized.'[37]

[36] Quoted in the *Ninth Report of the Estimates Committee*, p. 172 [italics have been inserted by the authors].

[37] Bhagwati, 'Monopoly in Public Enterprise', *The Working of the Public Sector* (Proceedings of the Third All-India Seminar on Public Enterprise at Hyderabad, 1963), *op. cit.*, pp. 91–2. Also see Bhagwati, *Economic Weekly*, September 1962, *op. cit.*

This picture is clearly overdrawn for emphasis. And Bhagwati was careful to note that exceptions would arise in industries where small-scale entry was easy and viable and where capacity creation based on the targets happened to exceed the actual demand – a fairly uncommon situation in Indian industries until 1966. But basically the picture was correct.

Thus, not merely was the licensing-targeting system, with related policies, responsible for creating monopolies over much of the industrial scene but also the attempts at breaking up plants into a larger number of uneconomic plants to increase the number of 'competitors' ignored the important economic insight that it is the possibility of *entry* that makes a situation competitive and not just increasing the number of units (especially in a framework which itself fostered a monopolistic environment).

. . . .

11
REPORT OF THE COMMITTEE ON STEEL CONTROL*

1. AN APPRAISAL OF THE STEEL CONTROL SYSTEM

The present system of control over steel operates mainly at four points:

(*a*) regulation of demand for different categories of steel;
(*b*) framing of the production programmes of the main producers and re-rollers of steel;
(*c*) determination of prices for the different categories of steel; and
(*d*) nomination of wholesale and retail agencies for distribution.

In the last few years, as a result of improvements in supply, control has been relaxed over several categories of steel, The distinction between 'relaxed' and 'unrelaxed' categories of steel turns, however, only on the method and extent of control sought to be exercised over demand. In the case of the 'unrelaxed' categories (at the moment, only sheets) control over demand takes the form of fixation of quotas for each consumer (or group of consumers) by various sponsoring authorities recognized for the purpose; no consumer can place orders for amounts in excess of the allotted quota. In the case of the 'relaxed' categories, on the other hand, there are no sponsoring authorities and also no quantitative limits to the demand that can be registered (though, when considered necessary, cuts in demand are made at a later stage by a process described as 'screening'). There is no difference between 'relaxed' and 'unrelaxed' categories in regard to the control of production programmes, agencies of distribution and control over prices.

* Excerpts from the Report Published by the Ministry of Steel, 1964. [See also the review of the Report on Steel Control by A.K. Bagchi in the *Indian Economic Review*, Vol. 1, No. 1, April 1966—Ed.]

The Role of the Iron and Steel Controller

The administration of the control system is centralized in the office of the Iron and Steel Controller. All indents for steel, whether of the 'relaxed' or 'unrelaxed' category, have to be routed through this office; all priorities (fixed by the Ministry of Steel and Heavy Industries) are administered by the Controller, the rolling programmes of all the producers have to be approved by him; and his office has to be notified of all deliveries of steel by producers.

Some of the important decisions which affect steel distribution are however, taken by other agencies outside the office of the Iron and Steel Controller. Thus,

(*a*) the prices allowed to producers for the 'base sections' of each category of steel (i.e. 'retention' prices) are fixed by the Ministry of Steel and Heavy Industries on the recommendations of the Tariff Commission.[1]

(*b*) the ceiling on imports of steel is set each half-year by the Ministry of Finance through foreign exchange allocations.

(*c*) the bulk allocation of the total estimated supply of the 'unrelaxed' categories, as between the various sponsoring authorities, is done by the Ministry of Steel, and the fixation of individual quotas is then left to the respective sponsoring authorities.

Essentially the function of the Iron and Steel Controller is to ensure that the rolling programmes of the producers achieve the maximum utilization of plant capacity and, at the same time, conform as closely as possible, given the technical constraints, to the pattern of demand for steel; and more particularly, that the producers give due priority to the requirements considered important from the national point of view. To prevent accumulation of backlogs on the order books of the producers, and the resulting delays in delivery of steel, the Controller is also expected to cut demands to the extent required by suitable administrative measures. Further, the Controller is expected to enforce the statutory price control.

For forming a view on this control system, it is necessary to consider (*a*) how far the Iron and Steel Controller succeeds in carrying out his responsibilities effectively and (*b*) to what extent the existing arrangements, including those which fall outside the direct responsibility of the Iron and Steel Controller, are necessary and adequate for achieving the objectives of control.

As indicated above, in the case of the 'unrelaxed' categories,

[1] Prices of other sections in each category are fixed by the Iron and Steel Controller through the determination of 'extras'.

the matching of demand with likely availabilities is done through the grant of individual consumer quotas by various sponsoring authorities within the bulk allocations made to them by the Ministry of Steel; no further cuts need be made, therefore, within the office of the Iron and Steel Controller. No cuts are required either in the case of 'relaxed' categories which are available in adequate quantity. However, in the case of categories which have been 'relaxed' but are still considered 'critical' (i.e. those for which there is still considerable excess demand), 'screening' of indents has to be done for cutting the demands. This presumably is one of the reasons for requiring that all indents be routed through the Iron and Steel Controller's office.

The main reason, however, for routing indents through the Controller's office seems to be that it is considered necessary for distributing the indents as between the various plants and for exercising control over their rolling programmes. In 'planning' the indents, the Iron and Steel Controller is expected to take into account the production capacities of each plant, and indicate the priority (if any) to be accorded to the indents. The producers are then supposed to formulate their rolling programmes on the basis of the orders booked and the priorities attached to them; and to make sure that they do so, they are required to get the final approval of the Iron and Steel Controller for each rolling programme.

Administrative Aspects of Control

We shall first consider briefly the administrative aspects of the routing of indents through the Controller's office. The processing of indents within the Iron and Steel Controller's office, prior to their being 'planned' on the producers, is reported to take anywhere from two to six months. It is only after this that the indents are placed on the order books of the producers and financial arrangements made between them and the customers. At this stage neither the producers nor the customers have any idea as to whom the supplies may be made available. The actual timing of the supplies depends on when the orders are taken up and put on the draft rolling programmes forwarded to the Iron and Steel Controller by the producers, and what changes are made in these programmes by the Controller. There is no arrangement for informing the customers at any stage about the likely date of delivery. Moreover, there are complaints of failure on the part of the Iron and Steel Controller's office to reply to correspondence concerning indents, of indents being returned after considerable time on flimsy grounds, and of indentors having to canvass in various ways to get their indents through.

Some of these deficiencies are traceable to the volume of work that has to be handled by the office of the Iron and Steel Controller and to bad organization and administrative procedures. The office receives no less than 50,000 indents a year, each of which has to be scrutinized and checked, and against which an equal number of 'planning notes' have to be issued. The organization of the office and the administrative procedures followed are not adequate either to handle this volume of work or to prevent abuses and irregularities.

We reproduce, in this connection, some of the observations made in a report by the Organization and Methods Division of the Cabinet Secretariat on the basis of a work study of the office of the Iron and Steel Controller undertaken about two years ago:

> 'There is considerable time-lag in complying with the requests of indentors for re-planning/amendments/cancellation. This occurs mostly on account of the following reasons:
>
> (*a*) Old and current records are lying mixed up in the sections in an unsystematic manner.
> (*b*) Indents are placed in folders without any particular order.
> (*c*) Incoming *dak* is received through the Central R. and I. Section. Some papers are diarized in the Section according to the discretion of the diarist/section in charge while the remaining papers are passed on undiarized to the dealing persons.
>
> 'At present, indents are being planned having regard to the sections which are being manufactured by certain Producers/Re-rollers but without reference to their capacity and/or the existing outstanding orders, although this data is partly available in the Office of the Controller.
>
> 'Apart from the monthly returns received from the producers showing the position of outstanding plannings for which works orders have not been issued or outstanding works orders for which despatches are yet to be made, there is no independent record with the Iron and Steel Controller to show the position of outstandings with the producers. There is no record to show the break-up of such outstandings according to (*a*) categories of steel, and (*b*) priority and non-priority indentors. Even the elementary information regarding the extent of priorities already allotted during a particular period is not forthcoming in these circumstances.
>
> 'At present, in the absence of information regarding category-wise and priority-wise outstanding with producers, the organization is not able to exercise any effective control over the quarterly rolling programmes of the various producers which come to them for approval.'

We have been told that improvements in organization and procedure have been made on the basis of this report. It is, however, our impression that despite these improvements several of the deficiencies still persist. For instance, we have been told by the Iron and Steel Controller that, though the arrangements for dealing with incoming mail are now much better than before, all the incoming mail is still not being systematically diarized and routed. We have also not been able to get from the Controller's office data regarding outstandings of priority indents category-wise.

It is our view that, though many of the administrative procedures can perhaps be further improved without much difficulty, the lapses in the office of the Iron and Steel Controller are, in considerable part, due to its unaccountability to either the producers or the general run of indentors, and the scope for malpractice and corruption which the control system in its present form offers. The methods and channels of malpractice are now apparently so well established that the extent to which the organization can be made to function better seems to us limited in relation to the tasks which this office is expected to perform.

Regulation of Demand

We need, therefore, to examine closely the different functions of the Iron and Steel Controller and see to what extent the present procedures, which involve routing all indents through this office, are really necessary for achieving the objectives. We shall consider first the two main ways in which demand is expected to be regulated by the Iron and Steel Controller, namely 'screening' of indents in the case of the 'critical' categories and administration of priorities.

It is clear that, even under the existing arrangements, the problem of 'screening' has arisen only because control was relaxed over certain categories before the supply was really adequate to meet the demand. In fact, if such premature relaxation had been avoided, the cutting of demand (to the extent necessary) in the case of all categories for which there was excess demand would have continued to be done by the respective sponsoring authorities through the quota system, and there would have been no need for the Iron and Steel Controller's office to involve itself in any kind of screening of indents for this purpose. It is not clear to us why control on certain categories was 'relaxed' when there was no prospect of supply being adequate to meet the demand, and when it only meant replacing the quota system of rationing by a more unsatisfactory system.

As regards priorities, the Iron and Steel Controller gives different ratings of priority according to the nature of each case, Thus some indents receive 'over-riding' priority and some others 'top priority'; the categories of priority have further proliferated and we understand that there is now even a category of 'red hot priority'! The majority of indentors claiming priority are, however, given just ordinary priority. These priority ratings are based partly on an identification of what have been called the 'core projects' in the Five Year Plans and Defence requirements, and partly on a variety of *ad hoc* considerations.

As already pointed out, the Iron and Steel Controller's office does not have with it data relating to outstanding orders with the producers classified according to priority and non-priority indents. 'Planning' of new orders on the producers is, therefore, done without any precise idea of *priority* orders still outstanding. For the same reason, there is no systematic checking as to whether the priorities are in fact being respected by the producers.

Since several priority ratings are given by the Iron and Steel Controller, there are within the broad category of outstanding priority indents several queues with different ratings. The general instruction given to producers is that a certain proportion of indents in each category of priority should be taken up when framing each rolling programme, some from even among those which have not been allotted any priority at all. When demand is considerably in excess of the available supply (and this is true not only of sections in the 'unrelaxed' categories but also of several in the 'relaxed' categories), and the cuts made on the demand side are not adequate to prevent accumulation of outstanding orders, the accordance of priority does not, therefore, really carry with it any assurance as to the period within which the supply asked for will become available. For all these reasons, the allotment of a priority by the Iron and Steel Controller seems to have only limited practical significance unless the indentor is in a position to apply pressure and persuasion at a number of points within the chain of agencies associated with the production and distribution of steel.

In fact, in the context of the heavy outstandings for the scarcer categories of steel, and lack of properly classified data with the Iron and Steel Controller regarding the accumulation of priority indents with each producer, the producers have opportunity to pick and choose the orders that suit them for each rolling programme. We are not sure how far the Iron and Steel Controller is really able to exercise effective supervision over them.

The rolling programmes of the producers are based on technical considerations such as the design and capacity of their plants, availability of rolls etc., and also considerations of profitability and overall output performance. There is no doubt that adjustments are made to accommodate indents which are given 'over-riding priority' by the Iron and Steel Controller, and also any other indents which are similarly kept track of and pushed. The choice of sections by the producers for each rolling programme does not, however, seem to be significantly altered by the indent-wise 'planning' done by the Iron and Steel Controller: we also doubt whether priority ratings are observed in all cases and the indents placed on the order books taken up strictly on 'first come first served' basis within each category of priority.

A priority has, in fact, no meaning unless it is linked with the assurance that the supply will be made available within a specified period of time. The present system gives no such assurance. When demands are met after very long delays, the precise length of which is itself completely uncertain, the final deliveries can seldom serve the purpose for which the demands are initially registered. Such long-delayed deliveries of steel are perhaps the main feeders of the black market. For this reason, anything which helps to reduce the time-lag between the sending in of indents and the final delivery of steel must be regarded as an improvement on the present system.

Control of Production and Prices

We turn now to the system of production planning by the Iron and Steel Controller. One of the main objectives of this system is to ensure that the producers include within their rolling programmes, to the extent necessary and feasible, certain categories and sections of steel which are generally considered 'difficult' to roll. In the absence of the routing of indents through the Controller, it is feared that there might be a tendency for producers to corner (through their sales organizations) orders for categories and sections which are considered by them either 'easier' to roll or otherwise convenient. Under the present system, the producers can get only the indents 'planned' on them by the Iron and Steel Controller and are obliged to roll, at his instance, the 'difficult' categories and sections to the extent considered necessary and feasible by him.

It is important to draw a distinction between *technical* considerations which come in the way of a plant rolling certain categories and sections (such as unsuitability of the installed plant, nonavailability of the required rolls, or inadequacy of storage space) and *economic* considerations which might make it simply unworthwhile. If the obstacles are of a truly technical character, mere issue of directives by the Iron and Steel Controller cannot make any difference. But if the obstacles are economic in character, the reluctance to roll such categories and sections would be greatly reduced provided the additional costs involved are adequately allowed for in the price payable to the producers. We would like to emphasize that seemingly 'technical' considerations, such as the high proportion of projects in the rolling of certain kinds of rails, are sometimes not really technical obstacles to their rolling but of a kind that could be corrected by an appropriate pricing policy.

It is our view that thr pricing policies followed hitherto in regard to steel have not taken adequate account of the need for the prices of different categories and sections to reflect their relative costs. As a result, prices have exerted pressures of a distorting character on the pattern of steel production.

The retention prices payable to producers for different categories of steel have been based until now on the recommendations of the Tariff Commission. The recommendations of the Commission, which are confined to the prices of the base sections in each category, have been governed, however, by a variety of considerations. Until its Report of April 1962, the main objective of the pricing policy recommended by the Commission was to make it possible for the two private sector plants (T.I.S.C.O. and I.I.S.C.O.) to earn profits large enough to finance part of the expenditure on their approved expansion schemes, after earning a specified rate of return on their gross block capital. With this in view, the Commission worked out (at the then existing labour costs and prices for the various intermediate goods required for steel production) an *overall average price* per ton of steel which had to be guaranteed to each of these plants. For categories which were produced by *both* the plants (described as 'common' categories), prices were then fixed with reference to the works costs and overheads of the plant with the comparatively higher level of costs (namely, the I.I.S.C.O.). But, for others (i.e. the 'non-common' categories), prices were fixed merely with a view to ensuring that the plant producing them (namely, the T.I.S.C.O.) would not get for the 'common' and 'non-common' categories put together a weighted average price per ton of steel higher than was required for the objective intitially set out. Naturally, the prices recommended for the 'non-common' categories bore no direct relation to their respective costs of production.

The Commission was aware that a structure of relative prices determined in this manner would tend to distort the pattern of production, in so far as the producers would have a bias against rolling products whose costs were less adequately covered than of others. But, as will be obvious from the following extract from the Commission's *Report* of 1956, such tendencies, it was thought, could be corrected by persuasion and by the direct control over rolling programmes exercised by the Iron and Steel Controller:

'It is recognized that if the pattern of production were determined by purely commercial considerations, a structure of prices based on a uniform average price might create the possibility of certain undesirable shifts in production between the common and the non-common categories. . . . With the co-operation of the producers and, where necesary, by using the power vested in Government to regulate production, it should be possible to avoid any undesirable shifts in production' (pp. 22–3).

This method of fixation of prices for the different categories of steel was modified by the Commission in 1962, in the light of a directive from the Government that what was required was not 'equality of the weighted average price of *each company*' but 'equality of the prices of *common categories*' produced by them. The inclusion of a developmental element in price was also considered no longer necessary. The prices that have been recommended by the Commission in its latest Report for each category are based, therefore, on an assessment of the works costs and on an allowance for overheads.

When prices are fixed on an assessment of costs, there is always a tendency to inflate costs, and not to allow adequately for cost reductions that may in fact be feasible. This will be true both in the case of works costs and certain items of overheads. We are not in a position to judge whether, and to what extent, this factor has been taken account of in the estimates used for fixing retention prices of steel. It is, however, our view that, whatever the inflation under other heads, the allowance made in these estimates for one of the important items under overheads, namely provision for replacement of plant, has been inadequate.

Thus the need to link the value of plant and equipment to their replacement costs does not appear to be fully recognized. According to the estimates of the Commission, the value of the gross block per ton of rated capacity of saleable steel will not fall below Rs. 1,900 in the case of the new Hindustan Steel (public sector) plants even after their next stage of expansion; yet, for the purpose of fixing the retention price of steel, it has chosen to take the value of gross block at Rs. 1,300 per ton of saleable steel. The latter figure is based on the estimated gross block of the T.I.S.C.O. though, as the Commission has itself pointed out, 'about 25 to 30 per cent of the block of T.I.S.C.O. represents old plant and machinery installed before 1954–5 and only the balance of 70 to 75 per cent is comparable to that of the new plant and machinery of H.S.L.'.[2] This procedure keeps the provision for depreciation lower than is required on replacement cost basis, though it is possible that the over-estimation of other elements in the retention price makes up for the deficiency wholly or in part.

The treatment of overheads in the present method of pricing of steel affects, in particular, the relative prices of different categories. In distributing them between the different categories of steel, allowance is not made adequately for the fact that the output of mills measured in tonnage tends to vary with the categories of steel that are actually rolled. (The same has been true of fixation of 'extras' for different sections within the same categories, although this has not been done by the Tariff Commission but by the Iron and Steel Controller).[3] For technical reasons, the rolling time per ton is greater for certain categories and sections than for others. Estimates of rated capacity are based on an assumed product-mix, and distribution of overheads on the basis of such estimates of rated capacity creates, therefore, a bias against moving away from the assumed product-mix if the total output (in *tonnage*) is likely to fall as a result below the rated capacity. This can become a very important factor when a shift is desired in the direction of the lighter sections. It can also affect the attitude of producers when they are asked to produce more tested steel in so far as it takes more time to do so or leads in other ways to a smaller volume of saleable output.

In this connection, we would like to point out that the tendency to judge the performance of individual steel plants in terms of the actual tonnage rolled and the percentage it forms of the rated capacity is also an important factor in persuading the managements to turn out a product-mix that has no necessary correspondence to the pattern of demand. This danger has become particularly serious in the case of the public sector plants which show great anxiety to achieve and, if possible, exceed their rated capacity. Another factor which works in the same direction is the linking of bonus payments to workers with the tonnage rolled.

Thus, partly due to the unsatisfactory basis of fixation of retention prices, and partly on account of the tendency to judge the perfor-

[2] The gross block of T.I.S.C.O. amounted to about Rs. 370 per ton in 1938–9 and about Rs. 590 per ton in 1948–9.

[3] We learn that the question of revision of 'extras' is now under consideration by the Extras Committee appointed by the Iron and Steel Controller. While the revision of 'extras' by this Committee may correct the present under-estimation of overheads to some extent, the net overheads allowed for particular sections might still be inadequate if the present practice of deducting the extra receipts *in toto* for arriving at the prices for the 'base' sections is continued.

mance of steel plants with reference to the tonnage rolled rather than in terms of *value* of the steel produced), there are built in resistances to the adjustment of the output pattern to the pattern of demand even when there are no technical obstacles to such adjustments. Unless the sources of these resistances are removed, the ability of any administrative agency to make the producers roll the product-mix that is required by the consumers is likely to be subject to serious limitations in practice.

Technical Considerations

One important reason, other than price, why producers prefer not to roll certain sections is simply that they often do not have enough orders for what they consider an economic rolling tonnage. Estimates of economic rolling tonnage depend on the technical characteristics of the mills. Orders to roll smaller tonnages result in lower production and higher costs. In countries where there is excess capacity and producers have to compete in a buyers' market, there may be willingness to settle for rollings of smaller tonnage in order to satisfy the customer. In a country like India, however, where capacity is inadequate to meet the growing demand for steel, the objective must be to secure the fullest possible utilization of plant capacity. Where the resistance from producers to rolling certain sections is on account of the anxiety to make full utilization of capacity for rolling sections for which there is unsatisfied demand, it would not, in our view, be correct to force them to do otherwise unless there are special considerations.

One of the important factors which comes in the way of fuller utilization of plant capacity is the wide range of sections and sizes offered by producers to the consumers of steel. The total number of sections and sizes for which the producers are now committed to accept orders is about 3,000; and the consumers naturally proceed on the assumption that the producers will roll to any these specifications. The dispersal of demand over such a large number of sections and sizes is responsible to a great extent for the smallness of the orders for many of them, and for the difficulties faced by the producers in making up economic rolling tonnages. Rolling to complicated specifications results also in considerable loss of time in the mills and in foregoing a larger output that could otherwise be rolled with the same capacity. The more closely the steel supplied conforms to the various requirements of consumers, the less will no doubt be the wastages at the consuming end; but we should take note of what is lost on the production side in making supplies conform to a wide variety of specifications. If it is known in advance that ordinarily only a limited number of sections and sizes will in fact be rolled, the designs drawn up by engineers for the consumers of steel will take this into account and avoid, as far as possible, the sections and sizes which are not likely to be readily available. The failure to rationalize sections and sizes, together with inadequate plant specialization, has in our opinion come in the way of a fuller utilization of available capacity.

The production of sections and sizes for which the demand is not large enough to provide economic rolling tonnage at sufficiently frequent intervals for the main producers could, in principle, be left to re-rollers whose plant and equipment are more suited to smaller rollings. In fact, this is one of the ways in which the re-rollers in the country could be usefully fitted into the newly developing structure of the industry. However, most of the re-rollers are not yet equipped to produce such sections and sizes, and continue to roll precisely those sections and sizes which the main producers seem to be in a position to roll at least as efficiently. The present price structure does not give adequate incentive to re-rollers to install the necessary equipment for rolling the more 'difficult' sections and sizes which it would be relatively uneconomic for the faster mills to roll.

To sum up, it seems to us that the present system of production planning has not succeeded either in ensuring the fullest possible utilization of available capacity or in making the rolling programmes of producers conform to the pattern of demand to the full extent feasible. There has been inadequate recognition of the role a suitable price policy could play in realizing those objectives.

Regulation of Distribution

We turn now the arrangements for the distribution of steel and, more particularly, the present system of distribution through stockists approved by the Iron and Steel Controller.

Under the present system of distribution, a consumer can obtain steel either directly from the main producers at what are called 'Column 1 prices', or from the 'controlled' stockists (who are wholesalers) at 'Column II prices', or from the 'registered' stockists (who are retailers) at 'Column III prices'; in the last resort, he can also have recourse to the black market at what are often referred to as the 'Column IV prices. The 'Column IV prices' depend on market conditions, and sometimes they are even below Column II and Column III prices for certain categories.

Because the sale price of the producers is lower than that of stockists, consumers have now a direct incentive to get the supplies directly from the plants. There is, however, the restriction that, in the case of direct orders placed on the main producers, the minimum tonnage of each section asked for, of certain categories, should be at least ten tons and the total quantity of the order at least a wagon load. This restriction keeps out consumers who require small quantities, and makes it necessary even for the larger consumers to rely on stockists when the demand for any particular section is of a small magnitude.

However, in the case of the larger indentors, the hope of getting at least some supplies directly from the main producers at Column I prices leads many of them to send in indents directly to the Iron and Steel Controller while they also try to secure what they can from the stockists. This results to some extent in double ordering, subsequent reduction or cancellation of orders, and resale of some of the Column I supplies (if and when they are received by the consumers).

Due to the heavy pressure of demand, it has not been necessary for most of the stockists until recently to hold large stocks for long periods. They have functioned more as commission agents passing on the available supplies to the consumers (or other traders) soon after they arrive. As a result, a high proportion of even the 'controlled stockists (who are supposed to be, in principle, wholesalers who can store and handle amounts of steel) have not taken the trouble of developing adequate warehousing facilities. The element of patronage in the appointment of stockists – particularly in the case of 'registered stockists' sponsored by the State Governments – has also led to the recognition of a number of traders who have neither the financial resources nor the other qualifications necessary for being efficient distributive agencies. In an industry such as steel, in which standardized bulk production by high-speed mills is a necessary condition for the efficient use of installed capacity, and the time interval between rolling different sections may be considerable, stockists have really a very important function to perform; but they can perform this function only to the extent that they have adequate storage capacity and are also willing to install equipment for loading and unloading, sharing etc.

The 'controlled' and 'registered' stockists complain that their relative margin has shrunk over time with the rise in the price of steel, since their absolute statutory margins per ton of steel handled have remained unchanged for a long time. This complaint has a basis only to the extent that the prices realized by the stockists have in fact conformed to the statutorily fixed prices.

The distinction drawn between the 'controlled' and 'registered' stockists has only limited significance, since both categories of stockists (as well as consumers) can obtain steel from the main producers at Column I prices. Further, there is no means of ensuring that the actual prices realised by stockists conform to the statutorily fixed prices. It is our impression that, through various channels established by the trade, the prices actually charged from the final users by a large number of stockists are, in the case of scarcer categories and sections, nearer to those prevailing in the black market. Only the book entries may conform to the requirements of the control system. Since it is the small consumers who are more dependent on private stockists for their supplies, the incidence of these free market prices falls more heavily on them than on the larger consumers who get their supplies directly from the producers. We have found that, generally, most of the small consumers are able to get only about one-quarter or less of their supplies at the controlled prices, while many of the larger consumers manage to get as much as two-thirds to three-fourths at these prices and rely only marginally on the free market. It seems fairly clear that the small consumer of steel does not benefit from the present system to the extent generally believed.

Table 1 below shows the relative share of Government, stockists and others in the total despatches of finished steel in recent years.

Table 1

SHARE OF DIFFERENT SECTORS IN DESPATCHES OF FINISHED STEEL – 1957–8

(In percentages)

	Public Sector	*Stockists*	*Others*	*Total*
1957–58	47·7	6·2	46·1	100·0
1958–59	46·6	12·8	40·6	100·0
1959–60	36·5	25·6	37·9	100·0
1960–61	31·9	38·7	29·4	100·0
1961–62	31·2	38·2	30·6	100·0
1962–63	46·6	40·9	12·5	100·0

It may be mentioned that part of the despatches to stockists is on account of Government orders; only the remaining is, therefore, available for meeting private demand.

The growth of the share of stockists in the total despatches indicates the increasing extent to which, with larger availability of steel, private consumers depend on them for their supplies even under the present control system.

The number of traders associated with the distribution of steel at the moment is, however, much larger than the number of legally-recognized 'registered' and 'controlled' stockists. The recent increases in the output of steel plants have necessitated larger holdings of stocks than before but most of the recognized stockists do not seem to have the required holding capacity. A large number of other 'unrecognized' stockists have thus sprung up to make good the deficiency, and the recognized stockists pass on to them a substantial portion of the supplies which they receive. A very complicated network of distributive agencies has thus developed which has no correspondence to the officially-recognized network. A recent order issued by the Iron and Steel Controller to endorse the legal prohibition of unrecognized dealers has not made, and in our judgment *cannot* make, any significant difference to this state of affairs. Further the unrecognized traders harbour grievances against the existence of a closed group of recognized stockists, many of whom receive their fixed margins as privilege rents for just passing on steel (without much storage or risk) to the unregistered traders or 'consumers'. Injustice to new entrants is inherent in any system of distribution with a fixed list of recognized traders.

Stockists complain of large and irregular despatches of supplies to particular centres by the main producers and the difficulties they have in taking delivery of them and storing them. While some rationalization of the rolling and despatching programmes of producers may be possible, the phenomen of bulk despatches is closely linked up with the modern technology of steel production and the need to make fullest possible utilization of plant capacity It is, therefore, our view that the distributive system must be adapted to the requirements of bulk production by fast mills, and not the other way about. With the existing bottlenecks in rail transport (and these are likely to persist for some time to come), bulk despatches to distributive centres, in rake loads rather than wagon loads, may also be necessary to ensure quick movement. From this point of view, it seems to us much more important to build up additional storage capacity in the distributing centres than in the steel plants themselves.

2. AN OUTLINE OF THE PROPOSED STEEL CONTROL SYSTEM

In this Section we shall outline the system of steel control that we would recommend in place of the existing system in the light of our evaluation of the latter in the last Section. The proposed system is designed to avoid introducing excessive rigidity while creating sufficient safeguards to withstand pressures; and, at the same time, to serve well-defined purposes in each of the four main aspects of control:

(*a*) regulation of consumption:
(*b*) regulation of production;
(*c*) regulation of the distribution network; and
(*d*) regulation of the price structure.

In the absence of control, the market does allocate the scarce supply between consumers in a certain way. Even when control exists, the market often reallocates what is allocated administratively in the first rounds but market allocation may be unsatisfactory in some respects. For developing a rational control system it is, therefore, necessary first to identify the specific features of market allocations that need correction on the basis of social considerations, and then to frame administrative mechanisms which do have the effect of altering the allocation in the desired way.

The four important social objectives which unregulated market allocation may not fulfil are: (*a*) the availability, on a priority basis, of steel for 'essential' capital projects and for current production requirements of 'essential' units; (*b*) the availability of intermediate products, e.g. pig iron and billets, to processors other than the producers of these products (who are likely to prefer processing the whole or most of the available supply in their own plants); (*c*) the availability of a 'fair share' of the supply to the 'small' man; and (*d*) a 'fair' regional distribution of scarce supplies. Control in some form is necessary to secure these objectives, particularly under conditions of scarcity.

Administration of Priorities

It follows from our analysis that the first step must be the determination of 'essential' consumption. The dangers to be guarded against are: (*a*) the tendency to dilute the concept of 'priority' over a period, so that a large number of really non-priority demands get 'priority' labels of one kind or another; (*b*) inflation of priority demands; (*c*) failure to relate priorities to time schedules of delivery of supplies; and (*d*) abuses of discretionary power by plant executives or steel control officers in response to *ad hoc* pulls and pressures exercised at all levels.

All steel demands should, in our view, be divided into three, and only three classes: (A) overriding priority demands; (B) priority demands and (C) non-priority demands. 'A' class demands should consist only of defence needs. 'B' class demands should cover the demands of basic industries, e.g. coal, steel, oil, heavy machinery and heavy electrical equipment, fertilizers, agricultural equipment and machinery, ship-building and road transport equipment; and of vital social overheads, e.g. transport and communications (including ports, shipping, railways, posts and telecommunications), irrigation and power. All other demands should be treated as 'C' class demands.

Priority should be fixed according to the end use of the supplies demanded, and not according to the agency or unit which makes the demand. All demands of even the Ministry of Defence need not automatically qualify for priority rating; this is even more true of the demands of other Ministries such as of Agriculture and Railways. For any system of priorities to work effectively, conditions of eligibility for *priority* allocation must be made extremely strict. When less essential uses are given priority status, the label of priority becomes useless.

Once the demand of a project or of a production unit is accorded priority, *all* the categories and sections required should get the same priority grading. If some categories and sections are delivered on a priority basis, but not others, the purpose of assigning priority may be nullified.

We recommend the following administrative machinery to scrutinize demands for priority rating and determine bulk allocations for different groups of priority demands.

The Ministry of Steel should set up a standing 'Steel Priority Committee' in the Ministry. Just before the beginning of every half-year period, the Defence Ministry and Ministries responsible for the basic industries and vital overhead projects mentioned above, should present to this Committee their aggregate demand for each category of steel for the following period, indicating the major components of the demand and the end-uses for which they are required. After examining all the demands received and discussing them with the Ministries concerned, the Steel Priority Committee should determine the bulk allocations of different categories of steel to be made available on a priority basis to each group of priority users in the six-monthly period. If the priority allocations of steel are rigorously determined, we expect that a reasonable proportion of the supply of most categories will be left for non-priority indentors.

The priority allocations made by the Steel Priority Committee should then go to the Joint Plant Committee (see paragraph below) as a directive governing the planning of indents by the latter. The Joint Plant Committee should receive the individual indents from priority users and 'plan' them on the producers in accordance with the directive; these indents should be accompanied by documents proving that supplies are indented against the bulk allocations made by the Steel Priority Committee.

The task of following each priority indent up to the point of final delivery (to ensure that the promised time schedule is adhered to) should be one of the main functions of the Iron and Steel Controller in the future. Once the priority demands are defined and met through this administrative machinery, the task of allocating the remaining supply among consumers could be left to the channels of distribution indicated in the later sections of this report.

Organization and Functions of the Joint Plant Committee

The processing of each and every indent by the office of the Iron and Steel Controller is, in our judgment, unnecessary for securing the objectives of control. Indents should go directly to a Joint Steel Plant Committee consisting of the General Manager of each plant (or his nominee) and the Iron and Steel Controller (or his nominee) as Chairman. The Committee should meet as frequently as necessary, but at least once a week, and take such decisions as are required regarding the indents received in the intervening period. In any quarter, the Committee should first include, in the rolling programme of the two following quarters, the priority indents received in accordance with the directives of the Steel Priority Committee. Such of the other indents which cannot be included in full or in part in the rolling programmes of these two quarters should be rejected and decisions to this effect communicated to the indentors forthwith.

The Joint Plant Committee should establish the principles and general conventions for allocation of indents between plants. These should take into account the need for specialization among plants, the importance of ensuring economic rolling tonnages, the technical requirements of 'balanced' rolling programmes, the need to reduce as far as possible the time-lag between the receipt of indents and the despatch of supplies, and the importance of avoiding unnecessarily long leads in transport. In particular, the Joint Plant Committee should specify, from time to time, the products (including sections and sizes) in which each plant is to specialize; in the case of categories and sections which are to be rolled by more than one plant; the Committee may fix the broad proportions in which indents for them may be distributed between the plants. The Joint Plant Committee should regularly receive from the plants detailed data regarding works orders, despatches made and the outstanding orders for different categories and sections. In the light of these data, the Committee should determine the quarterly rolling programmes of the producers. In doing so, we expect that the Committee will be advised by the engineers associated with actual production in each plant.

The Joint Plant Committee should have a Statistical Unit attached to it, which should be responsible for maintaining and supplying data showing the number of indents received every week, the categories and quantities demanded, the proportion accounted for by priority indents, the indents 'planned' during the week, the quantities delivered against priority and non-priority indents, outstandings at the end of the week, the regional distribution of the non-priority indents and of the despatch of supplies, etc. Judging from the present flow of indents to the Iron and Steel Controller's office, the number of indents reaching the Joint Plant Committee seems unlikely to exceed, on the average, 150–200 per day for some time to come. With mechanical processing and tabulation, the volume of statistical work involved is therefore not likely to present any serious difficulty once the basic procedures and formats are established. The important thing to recognize is that planning of production and distribution on the scale required, if it is to be efficient, must be statistically controlled.

The office of the Joint Plant Committee should also include, at the higher executive level, a representative from the sales organization of each of the main steel plants.

The allocation of indents by the Joint Steel Plant Committee is likely to have several advantages over the present system of 'planning' by the Iron and Steel Controller. The Committee will have a more realistic and up-to-date knowledge of outstanding orders technical peculiarities of the plants, and the quantities of various products likely to be effectively produced and despatched during a given period. With each plant represented on the Committee, and the responsibility for planning the rolling programme fixed on this Committee, it is likely to be much more concerned than the Iron and Steel Controller's office with not making and accumulating promises which are unlikely to be fulfilled within a reasonable period of time. Direct indenting on the Joint Plant Committee will also eliminate the present delays involved in the processing of indents in the Iron and Steel Controller's office.

The role of the Iron and Steel Controller in the Committee should be twofold: (*a*) to help resolve any serious differences that may arise between plant representatives on the Committee, and (*b*) to see that demands accorded priorities 'A' and 'B' are, in fact, given priority in the rolling programmes carried out by the plants.

Indents on producers other than the main plants need not be processed through the Joint Steel Plant Committee. The role of re-rollers will have to be conceived in terms of giving flexibility to the production system by meeting special requirements of regions, and of sections for which there are only small orders. For this purpose, it is our view that the re-rollers should be free to book the orders directly from the consumers.

Arrangements relating to Indents

We consider that, as a rule, the main producers should receive only 'large' indents. Reasonable minimum sizes for orders for different categories should be determined on the basis of (*a*) the tonnage which it is technically possible to roll at a stretch before the rolls require redressing, (*b*) the storage facilities available in the plants, and (*c*) arrangements which, under given transport conditions, will facilitate the quickest movement of supplies from the producing plant to the distributing centre. Orders of small size may be entertained, but there should be a system of levying additional charges as the scale of the order becomes smaller in order to discourage such orders as far as possible. As high speed mills are installed, more plant specialization becomes feasible, and the need for rationalizing wagon use increases, it will be increasingly important that the orders are generally large enough to be economic to roll and despatch.

Simultaneously, the facilities for storage and distribution of steel should be improved so that small individual demands can be met adequately and promptly even though the main producers may execute only large orders (see the section below on distributive agencies).

In order to discourage over indenting of scarce categories, the financial arrangements accompanying the acceptance of orders *for these categories* should be made stricter. It should be made obligatory for indentors to deposit with the producers, when their orders are accepted, a specific percentage of the value of the orders; these deposits should carry interest at the market rate. Letters of credit, and 'financing' through brokers who merely stand guarantee, should not be regarded as a substitute for advance payment against orders in these cases. The proportion of advance payment required to total value of the order should be adjusted from time to time by the Joint Plant Committee in accordance with the relative scarcity of the categories and sections concerned. As a *quid pro quo*, the Joint Plant Committee should ensure that plants promise and adhere to firm delivery dates to indentors. It should also be obligatory for plants to allow adequate rebates when there are delays beyond the promised dates of delivery.

In this connection, we may mention that some Government departments placing orders on steel fabricators advance to them 90 per cent of the total cost of the materials required for executing the orders as soon as these materials are acquired. The arrangement encourages the fabricators concerned to indent for larger amounts of steel than they really require during a given period. We suggest, therefore, that this arrangement be reviewed to ensure that only quantities actually required during any given period are indented for and held.

There is also a very strong case for *reduction* in the number of sections which the plants are called upon to roll. Immediate action should be taken by the Ministry of Steel, in consultation with fabricators, design engineers, traders and consumers to standardize the sections to be rolled by the big plants. The wide range covered by the new I.S.I. specifications and the numerous customary specifications, while they may be desirable from the consumers' point of view and from the point of view of physically economizing steel in some sense, seem to us to be based on very scant considerations of the economies of large-scale rolling. The sections for which total demand is rather small may, as far as possible, be left for supply by re-rollers or from imports.

We may mention here that, following the publication of our preliminary report last February, an engineering association consisting of some important fabricators of steel in India has investigated into the scope for rationalization in the sections now used for the fabrication of their products. It has come to the conclusion that the number of sections required by these fabricators (which producers are presumably expected to roll) could be reduced from 553 to 129 without creating any difficulties. After examining the practical effects of applying the reduced range of sections to a number of existing projects the Association has also found that, except in the case of one project, the increase in the weight of steel consumed would be negligible. This investigation, it should be emphasized, did not presuppose any general changes in design; if the overall designs are modified, weight increases resulting from rationalization are expected to be even smaller.

Standardization and reduction of the number of sections which the big plants will roll should be accompanied by provision of small-scale mechanical facilities (for shearing, cutting, drilling, etc.) near the centres of consumption for adjusting standard sections and sizes to the specifications required by individual consumers. This, in fact, must be regarded as one of the important functions of the larger stockists in the main centres.

Distributive Agencies

We turn now to the problem of distribution. Our review of the present system (see Section 1) has led us to two basic conclusions. Firstly, there is no effective way of checking the resale of supplies from the producers after they are received by the first recipients. Therefore control can and should be really exercised only over first deliveries from the producers. Secondly, the only distinction between different first recipients that can be effectively administered are: (*a*) between those who get a priority rating and those who do not, and (*b*) between those who place 'large' orders, and those who place 'small' orders.

It is our view that anyone should be free to place indents directly on the producers and to receive supplies at the producers' price. Sale and resale transactions after first deliveries should not be sought to be controlled except, of course, in the case of priority deliveries, for which a condition of allotment should be that there will be no re-sale.

Once the financial arrangements accompanying orders are made stricter, and there is no control over the prices at which re-sales are made by indentors (whether traders or consumers), there is no rationale left for maintaining the distinction between 'controlled' and 'registered' stockists or between 'recognized' and 'unrecognized' traders. Anyone should be free to be a trader in steel.

But, with the introduction of freer trading in non-priority steel, we consider it necessary that the Government should hold a small proportion of the non-priority supplies as stocks of its own to meet special needs. We recommend that stockyards under Government control should be opened in selected centres dispersed throughout the country. Some of these may be stockyards of the main plants; others may be established and operated directly by Government or Government agencies; still others may be private stockyards requisitioned or commissioned by the Government. Government depots stocking and supplying steel to small industries or agriculturists may also be recognized as stockyards.

The functions of these stockyards will be to (*a*) stock and supply to consumers (particulary 'priority' users) uncommon and matching sections which may not be readily available from the producers or from the open market; (*b*) ensure as far as possible that the small-scale industries receive a certain minimum amount of their requirements at regular intervals; and (*c*) make available supplies of steel in regions where, either due to transport difficulties or inadequacy of resources among private traders or other reasons, there is a tendency for acute shortages to develop.

Bulk allocations of different categories of steel required by the stockyards should be fixed by the Steel Priority Committee for each six-monthly period. Against these allocations, the Joint Plant Committee should be directed to accord to the indents from stockyards the same priority as for the 'B' category demands. Though this constitutes a deviation from the end-use principle, which we have said should be the governing factor in regard to the priorities, this special treatment for stockyards' indents may be justified as a means of safeguarding to some extent the interests of disadvantageously-placed regions and small purchasers.

If the objectives mentioned above are to be fulfilled by the stockyards, they should be required to sell the steel at fixed prices. These prices should be equal, in the case of each category and section, to the first sale price of producers *plus* a specified margin to cover operating expenses. In order to reduce the risk of a few buyers taking up all the supplies of scarce categories offered through stockyards, the maximum amount that can be purchased at any one time should also be fixed for each category (even though it still leaves open to some extent the possibility of the amounts so purchased being cornered by some buyers). If necessary, an agency may be established by the Central Government to supervise and co-ordinate the operations of these stockyards.

Price Policy

We have also some recommendations to make regarding price policy. There are four different aspects of the present steel price policy which require consideration:

(*a*) the general level of the price of steel allowed to producers;
(*b*) the relationship between the prices for different steel products allowed to producers;
(*c*) the relationship between prices charged at different stages of marketing; and
(*d*) the relationship between prices paid by different sets of consumers and consumers in different regions.

(*a*) *and* (*b*): We have argued in Section 1 that the present retention prices do not provide adequately for the replacement of plant at current (or prospective) replacement costs. It is our view that the gross block should not be underestimated simply out of the fear that the general level of steel prices will have to be raised or that the valuation at replacement cost might enable the older plants in private ownership to accumulate larger surpluses If they accumulate larger surpluses as a result of higher retention prices, but do not deploy them for modernization and expansion, other measures can be taken; it would be wrong to allow the fear of misuse of profits to be made the basis of a price policy which provides inadequately for replacement and expansion. Moreover, if producers' prices are fixed on the basis of anything less than current replacement costs, the public sector plants which are being set up and expanded will be placed in a position of disadvantage and will not be able to earn even the rate of profit that can be earned by the private sector plants set up earlier at lower capital cost.

It seems to us that the fuller provision which needs to be made for plant replacement at current or prospective costs can, and should be, done without a uniform upgrading of the prices of all categories of steel. The additional provision should be made as far as possible through adjustment in the relative price structure of steel which, as it stands, does not reflect true relative costs. There need not be, therefore, a sizeable increase in the *average* price for steel allowed to producers but only increases in the prices of the scarcer categories and more difficult sections. A shift of this kind in the relative price structure is required in the prevailing circumstances.

It is also our view that there should be more flexibility in the fixation of the relative prices of different categories than is allowed by the present system of fixing these prices on the basis of the recommendations of the Tariff Commission. The recommendations of the Commission are based on records of costs already incurred, and the prices finally fixed on the basis of its recommendations take effect retrospectively, If relative prices are to perform their function of directing the use of existing production capacity to the lines where shortages exist, and away from those in which surpluses develop, it should be possible to change these prices more frequently and through less elaborate procedures. For this reason, we suggest that the fixation of the first sale prices of all the main producers should be left to the Joint Plant Committee. These prices should be subject to the approval of the Government. Fixation of prices by the Joint Plant Committee will eliminate *inter alia* the anomaly of 'base' section prices and 'extras' being determined by different agencies, and simplify the whole procedure of fixation of prices.

The Joint Plant Committee should adjust prices from time to time according to demand conditions. A revision of the relative price structure should, in fact, be undertaken immediately, keeping in mind the considerations indicated above. The fact that cost data, in terms of the optimal product-mix for each mill, are not yet available for the new plants is no reason for postponing such price fixation since there will be always new plants coming into production. Prices based on rough approximations are good enough.

Under the new system, it will be necessary to introduce a safeguard against the accrual to the steel producers of much larger surpluses than may on broader social considerations be thought to be warranted.[4] We suggest that ordinarily, when free market prices are such as to justify an increase in first sale prices by the Joint Plant Committee, but the latter are already high enough to more than cover producers' costs and requirements of replacement and expansion, action may be taken by the Government to adjust the sale price realized by producers through imposition of excise duties or other fiscal excise devices. The Government may also issue directives to the Joint Plant Committee in regard to price fixation when necessary.

With the revision of the price structure, the method of fixation of bonuses to workers should also be changed in the plants where they are now related to tonnage rolled; the profits, or the value of output of each plant provide a more rational basis.

(c) and (d): As indicated earlier, there is no point in trying to control prices beyond the first stage in the delivery line. A free market in steel in respect of sales subsequent to the first sale by the main producers should be, therefore, legally recognized.

Free market prices would reflect from time to time the degree of scarcity or abundance, in the market of different categories of steel and have the normal effect of adjusting *non-priority* demands to the available *non-priority* supplies.

The difference between producers' prices and the free market prices will accrue to the intermediaries. If this margin becomes excessively large, the Government could, and should, use (as indicated earlier) the device of excise duties to mop up part of the difference between the producers' and free market prices.

As a general principle, the assignment of priority to particular consumers should not carry with it the implication that they will get any kind of price preference. The price charged in each case will be governed by the same considerations as for others. However, for those users of steel who, it is felt, should be given a price advantage as well, there should be a system of drawbacks allowed by the Government in respect of steel directly purchased from the producers or from Government stockyards. The consumers who are to be given the privilege should be carefully determined and on very strict considerations; the drawbacks should also be allowed only when the

[4] We assume that the prices proposed by the Joint Plant Committee will naturally be such as will include a reasonable rate of return on capital to producers.

actual use of the steel for the purpose asked for has been duly certified by an appropriate agency of the Government. Even subsidized steel should not be sold at prices which are below costs of production; drawbacks should be permitted only in regard to the *excess* of the sale prices charged to consumers over actual costs.

It is possible that sometimes the free market prices of some categories of steel may rule below the producers' prices. In such circumstances, priority consumers may want to purchase from the free market and there is nothing in the proposed system preventing priority consumers from doing so.

One of the important questions relevant to the fixation of sale prices is that of freight equalization. When freight charges are equalized, there is no incentive to minimize the leads in transport or avoid unnecessary cross-haulages. In consequence, a certain amount of avoidable burden is imposed on the transport system. Further, while freight equalization undoubtedly benefits the more distant consumers, it deprives those situated close to the producers of their locational advantage. It is difficult to decide, without further investigation, whether or not this effect on the closer, but relatively less developed, areas is more than offset by the benefits derived through diversion of supplies to the more remote areas. This is a complex problem, requiring a comparison of transport and other costs and the spatial distribution of demands under alternative patterns of industrial location.

We are of the view that the benefits associated with freight equalization can be secured in other ways – for instance, through a system of telescopic freight rates, or through subsidies to selected industries newly-established in less developed areas. But since we have not been able to examine the economic and administrative implications of such alternatives, we have refrained from suggesting a change from the present practice. Pending a more thorough examination of the whole question of regional development in the light of transport and other costs, the existing system of freight equalization might therefore continue.[5] The Joint Plant Committee might, therefore, include in the first sale prices freight element to be realized on all despatches of steel and operate a clearing arrangement whereby every plant receives the excess of freight paid over freight realized and pays out the excess of freight realized over freight paid.

[5] If the Joint Plant Committee 'plans' indents on producers in such a way as to avoid long leads in transport and subsequent adjustments in the region-wise allocation of non-priority supplies, it will help to some extent in reducing the undesirable effects of freight equalization.

The Transition

The transition from the present to the proposed system will require, apart from legal and administrative changes, a solution of the problem presented by the mass of indents and orders outstanding when the new system comes into effect. We propose the following procedure for it.

All indentors should be required to send to the Joint Plant Committee fresh indents (with priority entitlements where necessary) covering their requirements for the six-month period January–June 1964, on the assumption that outstanding indents and orders may not be supplied. The Joint Plant Committee will process them in the usual way. Outstanding orders covering the quantities planned by the Committee against the fresh indents will remain valid for the period under the new arrangements. All other outstanding indents and orders will remain suspended. Despatches against these may be made in the event that the quantity of particular sections planned by the Joint Plant Committee against new requests is not adequate for inclusion in the six-month rolling programme.

Index

additionality and exports 199–206
agricultural growth rates 37, 96
agricultural output 18, 46–59, 123; and commodity aid 174–9; and foodgrains, *see* foodgrains; and foreign aid 172–3; and limitations on economic development 96–102; and unemployment 115
'agricultural strategy, new' 24 & *n.*, 36, 50
agriculture: 'capitalist' 41; and education 153–7; neglect of institutional reforms in 81; technological transformation in 81
Aid India Club (India Consortium) 164, 174, 180, 182

backward areas and Plans 36
Bailey, F.G. 58
balance of payments: constraints 59 *n.*, 67, 112; and food imports 60, 107–11 (*see also under* foodgrains); and import requirements 196; 1950 on 107–12; 1956 on 21–2 & *n.*; viable 27 & *n.*
Bank nationalization 42 *n.*
banking 106
Beteille, A. 58
Bhagwati, J. 68, 81, 237, 257–8
birth control: and aid doners 141–2; cost-benefit analyses of 132, 135; lack of knowledge of 128; and Plans 136–41; and return to expenditure 131, 134–6
birth 'prevention', cost of 133, 135–6
birth rate 95–6, 114; decline in developed countries 126; reduction in, and economic effects 128–36
Blaug, M. 14, 145, 147–50
burden of dependency 130

capital formation, high import-content of 93, 107–12
capital goods industries: fuller utilization of 172; growth of 106–7; and plans for economic progress 116
Cassen, R. 14, 125
Centrally Planned Economies 66
Chakravarty, S. 81
Chaudhri, D.P. 153
Chaudhuri, P. 17
'clearance from indigenous angle' 66 & *n.*, 75, 77
Cohen, B. 15, 109–10
Consortium, *see* Aid India Club
consumer goods, imports of 72 & *n.*
Cooley loans 67 *n.*
co-operative farming 59
cotton manufacturers, export of 108–9

Dandekar, V.M. 58
Dantwala, M.L. 56
death rate: fall of 125; and population control 125–7
debt servicing obligations 22, 63, 66, 161–4, 196, 212
defence expenditure 67
demographic transition, theory of 126
dependency ratio and birth rate 130
depression, effects on industry 70
Desai, P. 68, 237
devaluation of rupee (1966) 60–1, 68, 75
Directorate General of Technical Development (D.G.T.D.) 239, 242–4, 247–8, 252
distribution, need for government control over 53
dividend remittances and foreign investment 224–9

economic planning, objectives in 25–8
education: drop-outs in 156–7; expenditure on 144; impact of, on agricultural productivity 153–7; over-expansion of higher 158–9; primary 156–8; and productivity 145–6; returns from investment in 145–50; and unemployment 149–50
electricity supply 105
employment: creation 44, 57, 83–4, 93; and Plans 27–8, 36; transfer and reabsorption 114; *see also* unemployment
engineering education 150–1
engineering industries, unemployment in 45, 150–1, 158
engineers 104–5
Enke, S. 132, 134
Epstein, S. 58
export(s) 62; commodity-composition of, and industry 71; expansion and foreign aid 171–2; promotion 121–3; slow growth of 107–11; to socialist countries of Eastern Europe 197–212; of subsidiaries 234–6; *See also* jute; tea

fair-price shops 56
family labour in agriculture 43 & *n.*
family planning 136–41; *see also* birth control
feasibility studies and foreign aid 187–8
fertilizer plant, Sindri 79
fertilizers 55, 56 *n.*, 100, 184
Five-Year Plans, *see under* Plans
fixed capital formation 102–5
food: aid from America 173–9; distribution 57; procurement policies 57–8; sector, inflation in 92, 112
foodgrains: importation of 48, 60, 98 (*see also under* balance of payments); production 27–8, 47–50, 96
foreign aid 60–9; and birth control 141–2; commodity-tying of 66–7, 175 (*see also under* food); costs and benefits of 166–73; country-tying of

66, 80, 181; and external debt servicing 161–4; food from America 173–9; and industrial development 74; licensing 74–7; project-aid, *see under* project; slow utilization of 165, 184–6; from socialist countries of Eastern Europe 196–212
foreign currency loans 229–31
foreign exchange: allocation of 20–1; constraint 59–69; crisis (1956–7) 21, 60; crisis (1957–8) 169; and industrial licensing 242, 255; and public sector enterprises 79; and shortfall of Plans 73
foreign investment and industry 213–14, 218–31

Gough, K. 58
Government, basic strategy in economic policy 80–1
'green revolution' 41, 55, 98–101; and cereals imports 111
'growth objective' 26
growth rate: and Plans 33; in service sector 29 *n.*

handloom industry 44
Hanson, A.H. 29
Harberger, A.C. 14, 145, 147
Hazari, R.K. 42, 243, 249, 255–6
Hill, R. 14, 160
Hindusthan Machine Tools 79

import(s): of capital equipment 102–5; controls on 51, 63, 72, 169; credit-financed 196; of food 173–9; and foreign aid 169–71; from socialist states of Eastern Europe 208–11; of subsidiaries 233–4
import-substitution 71–2, 122–4, 170, 234
income: distribution 39; distribution and licensing system 76; national, *see under* national; *per capita* and Plans 29–38; *per capita* and population growth/control 132–5; redistribution 26, 83
Indian Telephone Industries 79
industrial licensing 74–7, 237–58; economic efficiency of 240–52; and locational policy 252–4; and monopoly power 254–8; three categories in 249
industrial sector: growth since 1951 69–80; project planning in 73–4
industrialization programme: high cost of 74, 81; and import-dependence 71; and unemployment 44, 114
industry: foreign investment in, through subsidiaries 213 *ff.*; value of production of subsidiaries 232–6
infant mortality 127
inflation and Third Plan 29
international trade and structure of production 119–21
investment: and Five-Year Plans 35–8; goods, and plans for economic progress 117; goods industries, and savings 118; level 29–38; in producer goods industries 83; rate, planned 26; ratio of, to national income 112–13, 117–18; social, and birth rate 131
Iron and Steel Controller 260–3; and screening of indents 263–5
irrigation 50, 53 & *n.*, 54, 99
I.U.D. programme (intra-uterine device) 137–40

Johnson, President 174
Joint Steel Plant Committee (proposed) 276–8, 285
jute manufacturers, export of 108–9, 121, 203

Kidron, M. 14
'Kipping Loans' 165

labour force and reduction of birth rate 136
Ladejinsky, W. 58
land nationalization 57
land reform 41 & *n.*, 53, 58–9
Layard, P.R.G. 145
letter of commitment procedure 181
Lewis, J. 13
licensing, *see under* industrial, *and* foreign aid
life expectation 39
Lipton, M. 56, 135

machine building industries and plans for economic progress 116–17
Mahalanobis Strategy 27 *n.*, 116
malaria and child mortality 128 *n.*
Malenbaum, W. 13
Malnutrition 60
Mann, J.S. 178
manufacturing sector: employment in 45; growth of 36; increase of power, 1951–8 41–2
marriage age and birth rate 126–8, 138, 141
Mason, E.S. 56
maternity and child benefits 141
Mathur, P.N. 73
Mathur Study Team 243–4, 247–8
medicine, unemployment in 151–2
Millikan, M. 56
mineral resources 23
Minhas, B.S. 52
Mining, Manufacturing and Transport 21
mining production 70
Monopolies Inquiry Commission (1965) 255
monsoon failures 95

Nalla Gounden, A.M. 145, 147
Narain, D. 14
national income: composition of 105–7; and economic progress 95; and import dependence 71; planned rise in 26; and Plans 29–38
Nehru, Pandit 19 *n.*, 26 *n.*, 41 *n.*

'one factor analysis' 17

partial financing technique in foreign aid 193–4
Patel, I.G. 14, 116
Patel, S.J. 15
petroleum-chemical complexes 70
'phasing' of investment decisions 23 *n.*
Planning Commission 19 *n.*
Plans, Five-Year: and agricultural outlay 53–4; and foreign aid 160–1, 171; and investment 35–8; and population control 125
First 26, 29
agricultural programmes in 26 *n.*
Second 20, 26 *n.*
and employment 27, 43
and heavy industry strategy 53
and industrial production 67–70, 81
Third 26
and employment 27–8
Fourth, 1969–74 26 *n.*, 95, 113
first draft of 112, 132 & *n.*, 136, 169
and performance of economy 32
and sources of increased agricultural production 98
and target for agricultural production 101
population: control 26 *n.*, 125–43; density 22 & *n.*; growth/increase 32, 114; growth and income increase 95; growth and problem of poverty 34 & *n.*, 42, 96; growth rate 18, 38, 125; rural-urban distribution of 126
poverty: and foodgrains distribution 58; and growth objectives 84, 113–14; and Plans 38–9
price mechanism 24 *n.*
price policy in agriculture 55–8
private sector, use of resources in 82
producer goods industries: investment in 82; and plans for economic progress 116–17
project-aid 64–5, 77, 104, 165, 180–1, 185; disbursement procedures 190–3
project reports and foreign aid 188–9
public sector: countervailing power of 27; growth of 20–1; industrial investment in 77–8
Punjab, rapid growth of 38

Raj, K.N. 24, 56, 81
Raj Krishna 59
Rao, Hanumantha 52, 59
Reddaway, Professor 114
regional variations: in agricultural production 47, 52; in growth performance 36–8
reimbursement procedure 181
rent-ceilings 41, 58
resource allocation and pricing mechanism 82
risk-insurance schemes in agriculture 55
Robinson, A. 13–14, 92

rural-urban disparities in standards of living 41
rural works programmes 44–5

savings: domestic, and Plans 35–6; marginal levels of 112–14; ratio of, to national income 117–19; and reduced birth rate 131–2
Sen, A.K. 14, 144
service sector, employment in 43 & *n.*
Singer-Prebisch thesis 52
Singh, M. 15
steel: consumption, priority in 274–6; control system 259–73; distribution 260, 270–3, 280–1; and economic rolling tonnage 269–70; indenting system, proposed 278–9; pricing policies 266–9, 281–4; production 123; production planning 265–90; sector, losses in 79
sterilization 139
Streeten, P. 14, 160
Swaminathan Committees (1964, 1966) 247–8

Tanzer, M. 14
taxation: effect of, on childbearing 141; and Fourth Plan 112 & *n.*, 114
tea, export of 108–9, 121, 200, 203
technical collaboration arrangements 214–16
tenancy rights 58–9
tenurial reforms 19, 24 *n.*
textile sector 36 *n.*;
textile sector 36 *n.*; growth rate 70–1; export of 121
Thamarajakshi, R. 56
trade and payment agreements 196–8
trade gap: and aid requirements 169; 1968–9 110–11
transport 106
tubewells 100

unemployment 40; and birth rate 130; 'disguised' 152, 159; and economic policies 42–6; educated 144, 149, 151, 158; in medicine 151–3; rural 44, 115; urban 114
United Kingdom and foreign equity capital 219
United States and project aid 22, 66–7
urban bias in planning 52–3
urbanization and birth rate 126
U.S.S.R. and aid 183

Vaidyanathan, A. 52

wage-goods, supply of 59 *n.*
wealth, redistribution of 26–7
welfare as consumption per head 130
welfare objectives and growth of the economy 84
women in labour force 130
Woodhall, M. 145

zaminders, abolition of 58